THER SOMETHING ABOUT EDGEFIELD

Shining a Light on the Black Community through History, Genealogy & Genetic DNA

EDNA GAIL BUSH *and* NATONNE ELAINE KEMP

Rocky Pond
PRESS

Rocky Pond
PRESS

Dedicated in Loving Memory of
Phyllis R. Kemp

FIG. 1. PHYLLIS AND HER DAUGHTER, NATONNE, AT THE EDGEFIELD COUNTY ARCHIVES

With the express permission of
Tricia Price Glenn, photographer

CONTENTS

⊶••••⊷

ILLUSTRATIONS

●•••◄

TABLES

•••••

ACKNOWLEDGMENTS

•••••

Three women blazed the trail of researching individuals of African descendant in Edgefield District, South Carolina (subsequently Edgefield County). We are eternally grateful to the late Gloria Ramsey Lucas for her groundbreaking compilation, *Slave Records of Edgefield County, South Carolina*. The other two pillars, Sameera Thurmond and Alane Roundtree, have kindly blessed this publication by penning the foreword and introduction.

This book project started in January of 2014 with three co-authors. By December of 2016, however, Donya Williams elected to pursue a different path. Although Donya did not complete the race with us, we are grateful for her enthusiasm, determination, and dedication, which helped make this dream a reality. Thank you so much, Donya!

Every author needs stalwart supporters, individuals who believe in her venture. We were fortunate to have two key ones with roots in Edgefield: Edna Gail Bush's cousin, Sheila Hightower-Allen, and Brian Sheffey, blogger extraordinaire (*Genealogy Adventures*).

We wish to thank Kevin G. Lowther, author of *The African American Odyssey of John Kizell: The Life and Times of a South Carolina Slave Who Returned to Fight the Slave Trade in His African Homeland*, and his wife, Patricia Lowther, for their reviews, critiques, and suggestions. Tricia Price Glenn, the *former* Edgefield

County Archivist, and Tonya A. Guy, Director of the Tompkins Library (home of the Old Edgefield District Genealogical Society) and *current* Edgefield County Archivist, were invaluable in assisting us with our research as well as sharing their knowledge of Edgefield's history and records.

The authors are especially indebted to Stephanie Kemp, our principal copy editor (who is of no known relation to Natonne Elaine Kemp). The authors knew the best copy editor for their project was someone not only highly qualified to edit their manuscript by correcting errors in grammar, punctuation, and style, but also familiar with genealogy, who has personally studied and traced her own ancestors. A copy editor conversant with genealogy would better understand the information the authors relayed and would ensure that the authors presented information in the clearest, most engaging manner possible. Stephanie Kemp met and exceeded our expectations.

Our dreams of publishing this book would not have been realized without the services of additional, talented individuals. A book about history and genealogy is incomplete without an index. We are so grateful to Lydia A. Jones, Add An Index, for assembling our index with genealogists and family historians in mind, by including parenthetical phrases such as parental information, spousal information, dates, and locations. Information designer/architect Colleen Sheehan designed the interior of our book, enhancing our stories through her creative visual presentations, graphic artist Lauren Harms, designed our dynamic book cover, and permissions editor Veronica Oliva provided guidance on matters of copyright, permissions, and privacy.

Individually, *Edna Gail Bush* wishes to acknowledge:

First and foremost, I thank God for making this book possible. It was written in love, honor, and memory of my parents,

Abner and Victoria Medlock Bush, Great Aunt Willie Mae Davis, and Cousin Little Joe Palmore, whose memories and oral histories all served as the basis for starting my research journey. I thank my sister, Brenda W. Bush-Bell, very close friends Evelyn Lomax-Moore and Mary Baker Brown, and cousins Ernest J. Grant, Ph.D. and John Elliot Simpkins, who acted as proofreaders and sounding boards. Thank you for your patience and critiques. Thanks to my brothers, Abner Calvin Bush and Victor L. Bush, for being willing to have their DNA tested and to my cousin, Denise Brown-Sampson, for sharing her grandmother's documents of the 1896 court case that whetted my curiosity for more information. Thanks to my newly-found cousin, Elizabeth Contreras, who shared the background of our kinship through the Stevens and Burton lines. Final thanks to Robert Nathaniel Pinckney, who has been a stead-fast supporter and encourager from the beginning, and who is an Edgefield descendant whose maternal great-grandfather baptized my father at Shaw's Creek Baptist Church. I am so grateful.

Finally, *Natonne Elaine Kemp* wishes to acknowledge:

I wish to honor the faceless, nameless, forgotten individuals of African descent who, stripped of their language, their heritage, their faith, and their *own* names, endured under the yoke of slavery in Edgefield and carved some dignity of existence for themselves and their children. To my Chinn cousins, Viloria Arttaway and Sameera Thurmond, the first cousins I met on my father's maternal line in August and September of 2001, thank you for the welcoming embrace, sharing your histories, and encouraging me on my journey of discovery. While researching my paternal ancestors online in 2001, I met Alane Roundtree who became my genealogical angel. She answered my questions, searched for records, and shared her knowledge about genealogical resources. In finalizing this manuscript, Alane was a bedrock of support and assistance by employing her editorial skills and historical knowledge of Edgefield. Thanks to my brother, Nathan Kemp, Jr., the true writer of the family, who critiqued my chapters with precision, and to my sister, Nakesha Kemp-Hirst, for her support. Thanks also to my son, Nolan, who brings joy to my life. I am most appreciative of my paternal aunt, Evangeline Kemp Marshall, for sharing what she knew of her parents' Edgefield roots. I honor my late father, Nathan Kemp, Sr., his sister, the late Vivian Kemp Burgess, and all other Kemp and DeVore descendants with this book. Finally, I acknowledge my mother, the late Phyllis R. Kemp, who died 1 January 2016, sadly before the publication of this book. Edgefield was not her ancestral home, but she joined me nonetheless on four long road trips in three years to Edgefield, South Carolina. Working as a team, we located many records on my paternal ancestors. Thank you, Mom, as always, for your love and support. Your quest to discover your maternal roots inspired me to uncover my paternal ones. I miss you so much.

PREFACE

●•••◄

In writing this book Gail and I sought to adhere to the citation standards of the genealogical community as reflected in Elizabeth Shown Mills' *Evidence Explained: Citing History Sources from Artifacts to Cyberspace, 2ND Edition*. We applied the "Genealogical Proof Standard," summarized by the Board for Certification of Genealogists, to our research. Further, we followed several guidelines of the *National Genealogical Society* including the "Guidelines for Sound Genealogical Research," "Guidelines for Sharing Information with Others," and "Guidelines for Use of Computer Technology in Genealogical Research."

In accordance with the practice of the genealogical community, dates are listed in what is often described as the European or military style, 2 May 1868, instead of the American style, May 2, 1868. The latter format is used only when quoting a source listing the date in the American style.

Gail and I quote from a variety of sources including historical newspapers, government records, church records, and legal proceedings. We quote *precisely* from these original sources. If we modify the original text, we use brackets to indicate an alteration.

Finally, the descriptor for individuals of African descent varies in our chapters—colored, negro, black, mulatto—in accordance with usage by the historical source. Further, the word "negro" is often spelled with a lower case "n" instead of a capital "N." No offense is intended; we present the word as listed by the original source.

Natonne Elaine Kemp
Washington, D.C.

FOREWORD

◆•••◆

My introduction to Edgefield County came in the early 1980s when I embarked on researching my genealogy, which originated (so I thought) in Edgefield. I visited both the county library and the Old Edgefield District Genealogical Society and found nothing regarding African Americans. I was actually shocked to learn that I could find nothing about *any* African Americans, let alone my family, as if there were no Blacks and had never been any Blacks in the county. I couldn't understand how written records of any kind could be developed for historical holdings without including detail about African Americans. For a brief period, there were more slaves than whites, so there were many tales of working and personal relationships. The most salient rationale for the absence of written records is that relations between slaveholders and those in bondage were contentious and abusive in the most extreme and horrific ways. It is the nature of human beings to want to be remembered in the most caring, compassionate, kindhearted, and well-meaning way. Most often, typical slaveholders cannot be so defined. There were exceptions, but we, as by-products of those held in bondage, were prone, no doubt, to hear about the more shocking stories. The horrors enacted by slaveholders reverberated in the slaves' descendants' memories. We cannot forget them because, as today's society reflects, too many of the past's beliefs, perceptions, and standards still hold our society in bondage today.

Like me, authors Bush and Kemp wanted to know who their African American forefathers were and where, if possible, their roots could be traced to on the African continent. There were times when the genesis of a family began with a white male and a Black female slave, so a researcher is compelled to determine who that progenitor was, based on calculations of who was living where and under what ownership. From this juncture, many deductions could be made in the absence of known facts. The quest was as exciting as climbing Mount Everest! There were the impediments that threw them off course only to lead them to discover facts of which they hadn't heard or dreamed. These detours led them to discover unknown familial relations right in Edgefield County with whom they would form a bond. Like so many in the discipline of genealogy, they became consumed and took on a system of research that might very well require the rest of their lives. This was a passion to which both would commit themselves and never look back.

I am delighted that these two women, one to whom I am related, asked me if I would provide a foreword to their book. This book is a composite of personal outlines of families and the turbulent times that surrounded them in "Bloody Edgefield." It is imperative, when reading stories about the lives of slaves and former slaves, to understand the events that drove them to take such varying paths in life. Here, there are stories that I found riveting because any African American could say their stories were almost identical. The authors went to great lengths to write the fascinating stories of land purchased and land lost and, in some cases, painstakingly reported familial rivalry. This book is professionally presented—the authors go to great lengths to present details and facts that support their analyses. They pose questions for the reader to momentarily ponder, then provide their analytical results. The authors are clear and concise about how they reached these conclusions. They are professional in every way, right down to their recording of citations. They have included one narrative that focuses on providing insight as to why a white man would sell property to a Black man despite social custom forbidding it. I was especially anxious to read this, as I personally had not given any thought to it. It was a learning moment for me.

Kemp and Bush have laid the foundation of research upon which others in their families can and may wish to build. They have reduced the emotional vacuum that our African American brothers and sisters have felt but were unable to articulate. A little of the soul of the Bush and Kemp progeny have been healed, allowing them to move both on and up!

Sameera V. Thurmond
Augusta, Georgia

1871 MAP OF EDGEFIELD

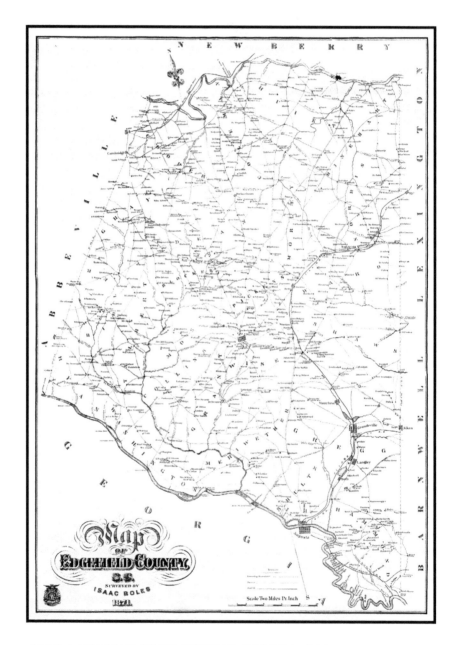

MAP 1 1871 MAP OF EDGEFIELD COUNTY, SOUTH CAROLINA

By Isaac Boles; courtesy of the Tompkins Library, Edgefield, South Carolina

INTRODUCTION

●●●●◆

Deacon Daniel Webster Moody was three months shy of celebrating his 91st birthday when I took some time to visit with him in the spring of 2009. The telephone conversation began with a memory refresher.

"It's Sarah Roundtree's brother's wife," I said. I told him I was calling that day to ask for a special favor. I asked him if we could take a little trip.

"Where to?" he replied.

"Well, wherever and however far you want to go. I was hoping we could take a trip down memory lane."

As one of the elders of The Runs Baptist Church, I asked Deacon Moody if he could share his knowledge of the early history of the church and in particular his memories of my husband's grandfather, Rev. George Bryant, who preached at The Runs for nearly forty years. The Runs was founded in the early years after emancipation in 'Old' Ellenton, South Carolina. Over the course of our conversation Deacon Moody treated me to a moving rendition of an old spiritual. As I listened to him sing and stomp his foot in cadence with the hymn, I was briefly transported to a different place and time. Then a realization swept over me. As a child growing up, some of the voices Deacon Moody heard singing his beloved hymns were the voices of former slaves. The echoes of their voices were in his. After he finished humming the last refrain he lamented, "They don't sing hymns like that anymore." After a short pause he offered,

"You know, I remember my Great Granddaddy."

"Sir?"

"Yes ma'am, I sure do. Riley. James Riley was his name."

"You remember your Great Grandfather, James Riley?"

"Yes, ma'am."

I was taken aback. Could that be right? James Riley had been a respected leader in the black community and an eyewitness to the Ellenton Massacre which occurred in Aiken County in September 1876. Mr. Riley was born about 1835 in Barnwell District, South Carolina and died at the age of ninety-five in 1930. I quickly did the math. Deacon Moody was born in 1918, making him twelve years old when his Great-Grandfather died. My goodness.

"He was losing his eyesight," Deacon Moody recounted. "I was about ten, and Granddaddy said, 'Come with me. There's something I want you to see.'

"We took the wagon and he drove me all over and out by the pond he told me to pay attention! 'See, boy, look over 'ere! That's where all hell broke loose! Men died in that pond'. He took me all over there. Yes, he did. He showed me an old broken down cabin and told me people had been shot and killed there. It's all gone now. He wanted me to remember. He was going blind and he wanted me to see and remember what happened there."

I was momentarily speechless. I told Deacon Moody I had read the testimony given by James Riley, and the other witnesses. They had traveled from Ellenton to Columbia, South Carolina in late November 1876 in the protective custody of United States Marshals to testify before a Senate subcommittee on Privileges and Elections which was appointed to gather evidence on the Ellenton Massacre and the denial of the Freedmen's elective franchise during the election of 1876. Some of the witnesses waited a month or longer in the capital city to give their testimony. The South Carolina subcommittee, consisting of three United States Senators, left Washington, D.C. on 13 December 1876 and proceeded to Columbia, where they remained until the completion of their investigation on 12 January 1877. James Riley gave his testimony on 19 December 1876. The sworn accounts describe in often chilling detail the terroristic acts committed upon the black citizens of Ellenton by Confederates who vowed openly, "To have the election if we have to wade in blood up to our waists."

"I had no idea you heard first-hand accounts of those events, Deacon Moody. You may be the only person in the world who can make that claim."

There was a long pause and then he said, "They shot 'em down like dogs."

"Yes, sir. They murdered them. They were hell-bent on keeping the Freedmen from voting and from having an equal place at the table. James Riley was asked during the hearing, 'What had the white people against you?' and he answered, 'Just because we wanted to vote for our rights. It seems impossible that men wanted to kill us for our voting rights, but it was for nothing else'."

In that moment I recalled something from the testimony of Jerry Thornton Moore. Mr. Moore identified himself as a former slave of Mark Etheridge of Edgefield, but stated his residence was in Beech Island, South Carolina. During his examination he described the character of one of the leaders involved in the massacre by stating he was the "kind of man who drawed a brick and hid his hand." I asked Deacon Moody if he had ever heard of that phrase.

"No," he chuckled, "but sounds like someone who can't be trusted."

"Well," I said, "some folks are still 'drawing bricks and hiding their hands' when it comes to telling the truth about what happened during that period of time in our history." Before I hung up, I offered to send him a copy of the transcript of his Great Grandfather's testimony.

"Well, don't wait too long," he mused. "I'll be 91 years-old in June. I'm going to try and make it as long as Granddaddy did. Yes, sir. We'll see."

African Ancestored family history research has gone through a remarkable metamorphosis in the last two decades. But for two modern day miracles the book you are holding in your hands could not have come to fruition and it's unlikely I ever would have had the pleasure of knowing Natonne Elaine Kemp and Edna Gail Bush. The marriage of their intelligent and dedicated research, coupled with the empowerment of the internet and the mainstream incorporation of DNA science into the field of genealogy, has made this important contribution to our knowledge of Edgefield County African Ancestored history possible.

Natonne Elaine Kemp first introduced me to her ancestors via the internet in 2001 and it was through them that I came to know her. At the time I was three years deep into my research of the Silver Bluff Slave Community, which comprised a village of individuals held captive by James Henry Hammond on his plantations in Barnwell and Edgefield Counties, South Carolina. Every connection I made with a fellow researcher who had an interest in enslaved family history in that region was something to be celebrated. Because our shared purpose included research in Edgefield County I automatically felt a kinship with Natonne and I certainly understood and respected her mission. It was evident from our earliest correspondence that she possessed a deep and determined sense of responsibility to 'get it right' and a steadfast commitment to reclaim the stories of her Blair and Chinn ancestors.

Gail Bush reached out to me regarding her research of her great grandmother, Emma Reed Medlock in 2007. The Freedman's Bureau bank record bearing the name of her ancestor, Smith Reed, remains one of the more memorable documents I have seen in more than thirty-five years of family history research. In the space of just a few precious lines, Mr. Reed left a footprint in time and in the process a lasting impression which still serves as a reminder to me of the incomparable worth such documents have to those fortunate enough to discover them. Gail embraced the gift her ancestor left behind and then spent the next ten years amplifying the blessings by pursuing and documenting the truth about the lives of her Edgefield forefathers and mothers.

There are no guarantees, but advancements in how we conduct genealogical research are providing researchers with unparalleled opportunities to recover the lost and stolen identities of enslaved ancestors. At the time I began corresponding with the authors, the internet was just beginning to expand and provide researchers with the ability to connect, discover, and share their interest in genealogy and family history in unprecedented ways. An online community dedicated to African Ancestored family history research was growing exponentially and we were reaching out to one another in cyberspace roundtables to share wisdom, support, and guidance. Recovery and documentation of the Ancestors' life stories were the goals. Pioneering message boards like *The AfriGeneas Slave Research*

Forum became the new meeting house where "newbies" and academic scholars alike could congregate, offer encouragement, exchange ideas and gather valuable information. Brick walls were common walls and the determination and strategies to scale them or go through them was a constant topic of conversation. It was within this online environment that research paths crossed, colleagues were found, and friendships were forged.

To those of us who began the uphill journey to resurrect the stories of those who lived in bondage during this country's African Holocaust, and spent years honing our research skills in libraries and spreading notes and family group sheets across dining room tables, the advantages of internet technology and DNA research are clear. The days of impatiently waiting for the delivery of microfilm and other research materials via interlibrary loan and carefully copying every needed page before the due date arrived to return it, have given way to almost instantaneous access to an ever-growing collection of digitized records which have opened a virtual floodgate of discovery from the comfort of our homes. Obscure books and materials that once languished in far-flung archives and were even purposely hidden from view can now occupy space on a virtual library shelf on our computer. Likewise, the marvel of genetic science is now uncovering and confirming undeniable truths. These research innovations are not without their pitfalls, and the need to patronize our libraries and archives are still essential to good research practices and the mining of knowledge, but these transformative advancements have helped reduce some of the time-consuming tasks that researchers routinely faced in the past and have made access to a variety of resources more widely available and in the case of genetic DNA research, increasingly more affordable. As a result, the research playing field has been leveled in some significant ways for the African

Ancestored researcher. The challenges are still legion, but it's an exciting time to be engaged in this journey.

When my husband and I had the good fortune to meet Alex Haley at a book signing event in December of 1988, the television film, *Roots: The Gift,* had just premiered. The film was the second sequel to Mr. Haley's award-winning mini-series *Roots* which had inspired so many to begin their own research with the dream of recovering their lost heritage. What could not be imagined from that vantage point, nearly three decades ago, was how much more obtainable and within reach that dream would become within the span of a generation. In Mr. Haley's film we learned the meaning of 'The Gift' was freedom, but freedom was not slavery's only casualty. I have come to believe that among the greatest of the great sins of slavery was the systematic and deliberate attempts to extinguish from historical memory the true identities of an entire people and the relentless efforts to eliminate their ability to tell their own stories.

The wisdom of the ancestors tells us, "*Until lions become their own historians, every story will glorify the hunter.*" Natonne once shared with me her firm belief that "the ancestors want us to uncover and declare what they endured." By uncovering and telling the stories their ancestors could not tell themselves, the authors have respectfully elevated them to a place they could not occupy when they were alive and in the process they have set them free.

Alane Roundtree
Eagan, Minnesota

PATERNAL LINE

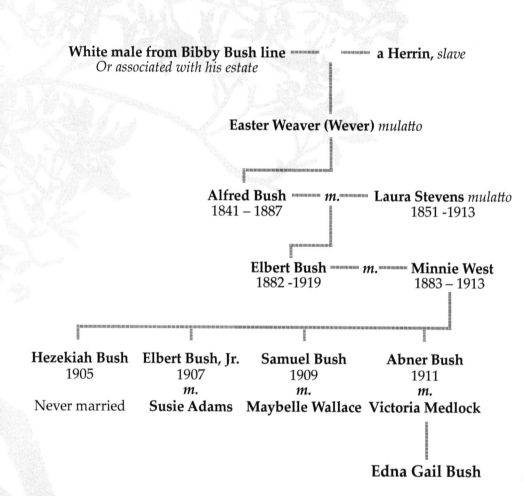

White male from Bibby Bush line ····· ····· **a Herrin,** *slave*
Or associated with his estate

Easter Weaver (Wever) *mulatto*

Alfred Bush ····· *m.* ····· **Laura Stevens** *mulatto*
1841 – 1887   1851 -1913

Elbert Bush ····· *m.* ····· **Minnie West**
1882 -1919   1883 – 1913

Hezekiah Bush	**Elbert Bush, Jr.**	**Samuel Bush**	**Abner Bush**
1905	1907	1909	1911
	m.	*m.*	*m.*
Never married	**Susie Adams**	**Maybelle Wallace**	**Victoria Medlock**

Edna Gail Bush

FIG. 2. EDNA GAIL'S PATERNAL FAMILY TREE

CHAPTER 1
ALFRED BUSH, FROM SLAVERY
TO LAND OWNERSHIP
Edna Gail Bush

►•••◄

*We all descend from the past, and no individual exists
free from his or her patrimony.*

Fox Butterfield, *All God's Children*[1]

As a child, I was always curious about those who lived
before me. This curiosity was fueled by the fact that none
of my grandparents were alive when I was born. Thus, the only
knowledge I had of them was through the precious, fading, and
fragmented memories of my parents. More often than not, the
memories shared led to questions my parents could not answer.
Fortunately, I received some answers while attending our annual
family reunions, which began in 1968 in New York. State chapters were organized, and subsequent reunions were held in
New Jersey, Pennsylvania, Virginia, North Carolina, Florida,
the home state of South Carolina, and Washington, D.C. The
early reunions included the Bush, Little, Hightower, Jennings,
and Oliphant families, all related by blood and marriage. It
was during these early reunions that I first heard about my
great-grandfather Alfred Bush being a land-owner. As I gathered information over the years, I realized the unique place

my ancestors held in Edgefield County, South Carolina. I was determined to get to the truth.

The truth of my ancestors' existence often seemed like a deep memory, as if I could hear my Edgefield ancestors whispering a flurry of words or feel them prodding me to get a move on in the telling of their stories. There are so many of them often visiting me in my dreams, smiling and nodding when they see that I'm working on one of their stories. They love my curiosity and will often gift me with an ancestral memory to pursue. They are not happy that only half of the history of Edgefield has been told, the part that did not include them as productive, hardworking individuals, striving to raise their families and contribute to their communities. They tell me, "Open your spirit, daughter. You are one of the chosen to tell the truth of our lives."

In researching that other half of Edgefield history, I discovered that during the exhilarating, turbulent, and often terrifying years of the Reconstruction Era, blacks in Edgefield County sought to locate family members that they had been separated from during slavery and to establish livelihoods, preferably away from former plantation owners. Meanwhile, many whites were destroying black homes and churches, trying to control and restrict black workers and keep them dependent. During this volatile time, the Freedmen's Bureau received numerous reports of murders of black men, leaving many black women as widows.[2]

When the *Washington, D.C. Chronicle* reported the burning of black homes in Edgefield County, the *Edgefield Advertiser* responded by writing, "As to the burning of negro's dwelling . . . it is well known that negroes don't have dwellings. Nineteen out of twenty live in outhouses belonging to white people."[3] With every passing decade after the Civil War ended, restrictions on blacks worsened. For example, while my great-grandfather Alfred was able to vote in 1868, by 1904 my grandfather Elbert could not. The stripping of rights began after the Hamburg Riot (see my co-author's chapter for details) and the election of Wade Hampton in 1876. A participant in the riot, and future governor and senator of South Carolina, Edgefield native Benjamin Ryan Tillman stated, "We have done our level best [to prevent blacks from voting, and] we have scratched our heads to find out how we could eliminate the last one of them. We stuffed ballot boxes. We shot them. We are not ashamed of it."[4] Having discovered this volatile environment, I wondered how one of my paternal great-grandfathers was able to acquire land during a time that certainly seemed to work against black people. Apparently, as in most situations in life, there are exceptions to the rule. My great-grandfather, Alfred Bush, was one of these exceptions.

MY PATERNAL ANCESTORS

I descend from Alfred and Laura Bush through their youngest son, Elbert Bush. My father, Abner Bush, was the youngest son of my paternal grandparents, Elbert and Minnie West Bush. In addition to four grandparents, each of us has eight great-grandparents, 16 great-great-grandparents, 32 third great-grandparents, and so forth. I was determined to find and name as many of them as I could, especially my most distant known paternal male ancestor, the man who established the family surname.

Alfred, born about 1841, and Laura, born about 1850, were enslaved, so I started my search by trying to find them in the 1870 US Federal Census. This was not as easy a task as I thought it would be. I believed they were a couple because, according to family oral history, Laura was given to Alfred by her white slaveholder father to get her away from his wife. She was in her early teens.

In the early 1990s, at the National Archives, a research committee consisting of my sister and about four Bush cousins, found the 1880 US Federal Census, which listed Alfred and Laura with their large family and included Alfred's mother, Easter Weaver, age 88. About six years after receiving this information, I found Alfred and Laura in 1870, not as Bush, but with the name Wever. Besides Alfred and Laura, the family included Adam (6), Eldred (3), Lizzie (1), and Mary ("Margaret," 3 months). Living in Edgefield County's Turkey Creek Township (later Pickens Township), Alfred was identified as a "farm laborer."

I initially came across another couple with a similar name, but they were a different Alfred and Laura. This couple was known as Alfred and Laura Weaver, and they lived in Horn's Creek Township. They were about the same age as Alfred and Laura Wever, but they didn't have children with names I recognized as family. After finding the Wevers, I had to find out why they had initially chosen that surname. Had it not been for Gloria Ramsey Lucas's book, *Slave Records of Edgefield County*, I don't think I would have been able to piece together the puzzle of my great-grandparents. In her book, my ancestors were listed among family groups I recognized.

PATERNAL LINE SLAVEHOLDER

On 24 May 1841 a wealthy slaveholder, 72-year-old Jonathan Wever, died.[5] Among the many enslaved persons listed in his estate were Easter and three unnamed children. I have found that when children are grouped with their mothers, they are usually infants or very young. She and her young children were sold to Lawrence Wever for $1,125.[6] I believe my great-grandfather Alfred was one of the three unnamed children, since he was born about 1841. Four "negro boys" were also listed in Jonathan Wever's estate to be sold: Jerry for $895, Eldred for $570, Abner for $404, and Elbert for $380. Eldred, Abner, and Elbert were sold to R. Wright Adams, and Jerry, who was noted to be "not sound," was sold to O. Towles. By the time of the 1870 US Federal Census, most of these young men had chosen the surname Bush. When I first saw the given names—Jerry, Eldred, Abner, and Elbert—I recognized them as names that frequently repeat in my father's paternal line.

When I initially began researching my ancestors, I was surprised to see that they were not actually freed until the fall of 1865. Only after Lee's surrender would the South concede. However, Edgefield County remained in rebellion for as long as it could after the war. White residents were actively buying, selling, and giving as gifts, black people throughout 1865. I was surprised to find my Bush ancestors were among those still being treated as slaves. From 31 March 1865 to 13 November 1865, Abner and his wife, Eliza, their children, Abner's brother Elbert, Elbert's wife, Martha, their children, and my great-grandparents Alfred and Laura, were either sold or given as gifts by R. Wright Adams within his family and to others.[7]

President Lincoln's warning, via the 22 September 1862 Preliminary Emancipation Proclamation gave the Confederacy until 1 January 1863 to return to the Union or forfeit its slaves. The Proclamation stated that the liberty of those formerly enslaved, would be recognized and maintained by "the executive government of the United States. . . ."[8] Edgefield County would not free them in 1863. Only the enslaved along the coast of South Carolina, where there were federal troops, were freed in 1863. Many of those newly freed in 1863 joined the Union army to battle for the freedom of all enslaved.

Despite the declaration of freedom in Edgefield County in 1865, new restrictive forces rose in the South to control the freedom and movement of blacks. For a brief time, the Black Codes were enacted.

EDGEFIELD'S UGLY HISTORY

The Black Codes were a compilation of laws, statutes, and rules issued by southern states immediately after the Civil War to regain control over the freedmen and maintain white supremacy. The editor of a newspaper in Edgefield announced that if Congress failed to allow the proposed Black Codes "compelling the negro to labor,"[9] the only option was to keep the freedmen from becoming landowners. The editor called for a "tax of one to five thousand dollars upon every white man who sells, rents, gives, loans, or in any way conveys, to a negro, any tract, parcel or acreage of land."[10] Fortunately, Congress quickly responded by passing the Civil Rights Act of 1866, which made it illegal to discriminate against the freedmen by assigning them an inferior legal or economic status. On 9 July 1868, the states ratified the 14TH Amendment, which guaranteed "equal protection of the laws" to residents of every state. Despite this, a freedman testified to the Freedmen's Bureau, that it was "dangerous for a black man to live in the Edgefield District, SC,"[11] because white men were murdering the freedmen.

THE SEARCH AND DISCOVERY

Spurred on by the bits and pieces of family history I had overheard at family reunions, my curiosity was piqued. I wanted to thoroughly understand the times in which my ancestors lived and died. The oral history given by my father's first cousins suggesting that my great-grandfather owned 300 acres of land just did not seem to fit in this atmosphere of extreme racial hatred. I began researching in earnest after I retired by travelling to Edgefield County, visiting the Tompkins Library, joining the two local genealogical societies (the Old Edgefield District Genealogical Society (OEDGS) and the Old Edgefield District African-American Genealogical Society (OEDAAGS), and attending workshops and researching at the South Carolina Department of Archives and History (SCDAH) in Columbia, South Carolina. I have also purchased many books about South Carolina that contained information about Edgefield County, particularly the periods encompassing slavery, Reconstruction, and the early 20th century.

In 2008, I acquired the estate papers of my great-grandfather Alfred and his brother Elbert from the SCDAH. While reviewing the papers, a puzzling fact emerged—fewer than 22 years after being freed from slavery, black men in my family owned property in Edgefield. How did they acquire the property? This discovery led me to search for related documentation that might answer that question.

At another family reunion in 2009, a cousin (whose grandmother was a first cousin of my father) shared documents her late grandmother had acquired. These documents included a 1935 map of Edgefield County that lists the name of Morris Bush, my father's uncle, as a property owner. According to the map, Morris's immediate neighbors included John Oliphant, Robert Brown, F. A. Weaver, Marion Weaver, and E. McKinney. These are all recognizable family names. I have found that family members usually lived close to each other for community and support, especially after slavery ended. Another document shared was a copy of a few of the 1896 court papers concerning a lawsuit among family members to divide the property. Further research into the lawsuit was needed, because it was the basis for the beginning of the loss of their property. There were several documents referencing the family land that caused me to wonder who guided my great-grandmother Laura in legal matters and why. So, along with the estate papers and other related information I had found, I started to piece together the story of how my great-grandfather was able to own land in one of the most racially divided and violent counties in South Carolina.

Alfred Bush died intestate or without a will sometime between 18 and 22 December 1887 at the age of 46. These dates were recorded in a Bible belonging to his son Morris as well as in his estate papers and in those of the 1896 family lawsuit. How Alfred died is unknown, since death certificates were not required at that time. There was no family lore about his death. At the time of Alfred's death, his wife Laura was pregnant with their youngest child. Mary Jane was ultimately born in the winter of 1888. At the time of his death, Alfred possessed personal property of about $200 and land totaling 256.5 acres.[12] I wondered how he, a former slave emancipated in 1865, was able to own that much land.

It was not until September of 2012 that I was finally able to verify how my great- grandfather acquired the land. According to documents from the Edgefield Archives, he purchased the land with cash. With the help of Edgefield Archivist Tricia Price Glenn, I obtained two copies of the deed and one copy of a document called the "Title to Real Estate for Alfred Bush." When I first saw Alfred's name in a record book that listed all land transactions of Edgefield County, I was overcome with emotion, but it was not until I saw the actual documents that I allowed the tears to flow. I was overwhelmed to have finally found documentation to support the family lore. I discovered that on 15 January 1874, Michael W. Clark and Jackson Holmes each signed deeds to property to my great-grandfather. M. W. Clark sold 39.25 acres to Alfred for $314.00, and Jackson

Holmes sold him 9.25 acres for $92.50. Then, in December 1883, Henry T. Wright sold Alfred 208 acres for a huge sum.

I read the description of the transaction over and over again: "...he paid to me in hand $1,456.50."[13] I was beyond amazed! I thought of a phrase my mother used to say when confounded: "Well, fan me with a brick and a razor stick!"

How did Alfred accumulate so much money? According to MeasuringWorth.com, the amount he paid was the equivalent to $346,000.00 in today's money. During that time, living in Edgefield County was comparable to experiencing a second Civil War for the freedmen, yet my great-grandfather somehow managed to acquire the money to purchase 258.5 acres of land with cash. I also now had proof that not all of the white men had agreed to block freedmen from acquiring land. So who were these white men who sold the property to Alfred, and why did they go against the "gentlemen's agreement" to refuse to sell land to blacks?

I decided to look at local newspapers to try and find answers. I could not find digital images for the years I was researching when I searched the *Edgefield Chronicle*. In the absence of local black newspapers, I read available copies of the *Edgefield Advertiser* for 1873 and 1874.

I noticed several properties were listed for sale. Executor sales of land for the estates of Nathan Bodie, Joseph Talbot, Guthridge Cheatham, and F. W. Pickens were advertised. Apparently these men needed cash and were eager to sell land. As for the underlying reasons for that eagerness, I discovered that during the years 1873 to 1879 a national economic depression occurred. Many banks had failed, and the landowners likely found it necessary to liquidate some property. This fact only compounded the mystery of how my great-grandfather was able to have so much money. I still could not find concrete evidence of any relationships to the men who sold land to my great-grandfather, but I held onto the possibility that these men did, in fact, have at least a friendly relationship with Alfred. Maybe they pretended to be friendly, having heard that he had money. One of the sellers later gave testimony that some of his land was of poor quality. Was that the land he sold to my great-grandfather? I learned that of those who sold him property, Clark and Holmes were Confederate veterans, and Wright was a wealthy lawyer and former slaveholder. Beyond that, who exactly were these white men who acted against the norm in their interactions with a black man?

THE SELLERS

Michael Watson Clark was born in 1846. During the Civil War, Private Michael W. Clark served with Company A, 19TH Regiment South Carolina Volunteers.[14] By 1870, he had married a woman named Marina, and they were living in the township of Spring Grove (later Ward Township). At age 24, he owned real estate valued at $600 and personal property valued at $400.[15] In 1880, Clark was still living in Ward Township with his second wife, Mollie. In March of 1888, he served as one of the appraisers for Alfred's estate along with Milledge Williams and John Bush. By 1890, Clark had married his third wife, Mattie Cogburn. During the Bush family lawsuit in 1897, he gave sworn testimony about the value of the land. Still living in Ward Township in 1900, he and his wife were neighbors of my great-grandmother Laura and five of her children. Our two families had clearly maintained a long association since 1873. Laura apparently trusted Michael Clark to some degree, since he was involved in the personal affairs concerning her late husband's estate.

Jackson Holmes, a member of the large Holmes family of Edgefield County, was born in 1827. In 1850, at age 23, he was unmarried and lived next door to relatives Gabriel Holmes and Lewis W. Holmes. He also owned seven slaves.[16] He was a Confederate veteran who had served in the same regiment as Michael W. Clark. At the time of the 1870 US Census, Holmes reported that he owned real estate valued at $6,500 and personal property valued at $1,200.[17] Like Clark, Holmes was living in Spring Grove with his wife, Martha (34), and a W. C. Posey (8), and Grant Bell (35), a black farm laborer. I noticed a curious thing on the 1880 U. S. Federal Census. Holmes' wife was described as "Mu" for mulatto, even though in 1870 she was identified as white.[18] By the time of the 1900 U.S Federal Census, the Holmes family had moved to Xenia Township in Greene County, Ohio, and Martha Holmes was identified as black.[19] Holmes may have had some empathy towards my great-grandfather because of his wife's race. Jackson Holmes and Michael Clark both attended and served at Philippi Church, and there appears to be a definite relationship between the Clark and Holmes families. The land both of these men sold to my great-grandfather was in Ward Township.

Born in 1819, the third seller, Henry T. Wright, was a lawyer, teacher, slaveholder, and landowner. From 1851 to 1855, he served as the Ordinary (Probate Judge) of Edgefield. Known as H. T. Wright, he was a member of Harmony Church for over 30 years and a founding member of Johnston Methodist Church in 1875.[20] Wright owned a lot of land in and around Johnston, although he never lived in Johnston. At the time of the 1860 U. S. Federal Census, he lived in Edgefield Village, which is about eight miles from Johnston. Then, in 1870, he and his wife, Frances Kenney Wright, moved to Turkey Creek Township. My great-grandparents were also living in Turkey Creek Township in 1870. At this time, Wright owned real estate valued at $12,000 and personal property valued at $10,000.

The land that H. T. Wright sold my great-grandfather was in Turkey Creek Township (later Pickens Township). By 1880, H. T. Wright and his wife still lived in Pickens Township, as did my great-grandparents. Henry T. Wright died in December of 1888.

I found this information on these men interesting, complicated, and strange. They were upstanding men in the local community. Why would they disregard the accepted rules by selling land to a black man? To this day, I don't know the true reason for the real estate transactions. I was leaning closer to the belief that my great-grandfather, or his wife, may have been somehow related to Clark, Holmes, and/or Wright, but I needed to find evidence. These men were not alone in selling land to freedmen. Between 1868 and 1879, 14,000 black families owned small farms in South Carolina through the South Carolina Land Commission program. The majority of these land transactions occurred on the coast, however. In Edgefield, only two percent of freedmen owned land. The land available to blacks was often of poor quality due to over-farming and soil erosion. In addition, land prices were usually inflated due to money scarcity for many years after the war.[21] All of these facts only compound the mystery as to how my ancestor might have acquired the wealth to purchase land.

ALFRED AND LAURA'S CHILDREN

Alfred and Laura had a large family: five sons and seven daughters. They were: Adam (1864-1931), Eldred "Elliot" (1867-1950), Elizabeth " Lizzie" (1869-1893), Margaret (1870-1907), Della (1872-1945), Calvin (1873-1946), Morris (1875-1945), Clara (1876-1904), Cornelia (1878-before 1896), Julia (1880-1902), my grandfather Elbert (1882-1919), and Mary Jane (1888-1904).

Neither Alfred nor Laura could read or write, but most of their children could to some degree. I've seen the signatures of Eldred, Calvin, Della, Morris, Clara, Julia, and my grandfather Elbert on various legal documents. In addition to establishing a pattern of landownership, Alfred and Laura ensured their children were literate and placed a value on education.

After 1880, the eldest child, Adam, was not listed in any subsequent census with the family. Research has uncovered a black man named Adam Bush who lived in the Edgefield Poor House between 1920 and 1931. I believe this Adam was Alfred and Laura's first born son born in 1864. He might have been challenged mentally, physically, or in both ways. Many of those committed to the Poor House were not able to take care of themselves. None of the documentation concerning the lawsuits mentioned Adam.

Sadly, the family treated him as if he didn't exist. Whatever his disability was, I believe there may have been a genetic connection down through the generations. I have a nephew with a dual diagnosis of mental illness and developmental disabilities. At a family reunion several years ago, I also met a Simkins cousin and a Bush descendant who behaved in the same way as my nephew. Maybe this is how my Great Uncle Adam was. Adam died at the Poor House in 1931. According his death certificate, the cause of death was "paralysis."[22]

In the years after Alfred's death, it appears that Laura fought to protect the family land and leaned on her second oldest son, Eldred, to help her. As her children married and started families, however, the pressures of providing for them became the main focus. Within a few months after her husband's death, Laura sought the counsel of Attorney Arthur S. Tompkins.

BEGINNING OF THE LEGAL BATTLES

Ex Parte

Alfred Bush Estate

Whereas Alfred Bush departed this life on or about the 22nd of December 1887 intestate, leaving a personalty of about $200, and real estate. Laura Bush your petitioner is his widow. Wherefore she has said that she be appointed as the Administrator of the Estate of Alfred Bush, deceased.

6 February 1888

A.S. Tompkins, Attorney

her mark
Laura X Bush[23]

Her attorney followed through by putting a notice in the *Edgefield Chronicle* on 8 February 1888:

CITATION. State of South Carolina Edgefield County.

Whereas Laura Bush has made suit to me to grant her Letters of Administration of the estate and effects of Alfred Bush, late of said County, deceased. These are therefore, to cite and admonish all and singular, the kindred and Creditors of the said Alfred Bush, deceased, that they be and appear before me in the Court of Probate for the said County, to be held at the Edgefield Court House on the 23rd day of February 1888 at 11 o'clock in the forenoon to show cause, if any they have, why the said Administration should not be granted. Given under my hand and the seal of the Court, this 6th day of February 1888. Published on the 8th day of February 1888 in the Edgefield Chronicle.

J. D. Allen, Probate Judge

After the appraisers valued Alfred's personal property, Laura had her son Eldred write the following note to her lawyer, A. S. Tompkins. It is presented here exactly as written in the court documents, with the exception of my additions in parentheses:

12 March 1888

Mr Author Tomkins,

Laura Bush say that she can not have no sail[sic] for the reason she say that the settlement says that we (don't have) any thing that they want but our mules and we are blest[sic] to keep them the appraisers says that they aint no youce[sic] to have no sail[sic] for they praise every thing for as mutch[sic] it is worth and by that there aint no youce[sic] to have no sail [sic] for the majority say they don't want what we have got."[24]

Despite the above, the sale of the personal property amounted to $284.40 in the end. Michael W. Clark, Milledge Williams (a cousin) and John Bush (another cousin) served as the appraisers.

Beginning in November of 1896, in an effort to keep the land from being divided, Laura went to the Court of Common Pleas in Edgefield. Court records show that she was joined by her adult children—Eldred, Margaret, Calvin, and Morris—as the Plaintiffs. The Defendant was her daughter Della Bush Hammond and the rights of the minor children as represented by the *guardian ad litem*, M. P. Wells. Laura's attorney was Arthur S. Tompkins, and Della was represented by the Sheppard Brothers. These lawyers came from influential families in Edgefield. John C. Sheppard and his brother Orlando established the Sheppard Brothers Law Firm in 1875. John also served as Governor of South Carolina in 1886 for five months.[25]

When Alfred Bush died in 1887, his real estate was free of both mortgage and lien. In 1892, shortly after her marriage to a 50-year-old widower named Jonas H. Hammond and with seven children in her care, Della asked her mother Laura for her share of the "rents and profits" from her father's land. Court papers revealed that Laura refused to give her money but did offer her a "bedstead and a young heifer."[26] This was not satisfactory to Della. She and her husband had moved off of the family land to live in Shaw Township in Aiken County and had a rapidly growing family. Their daughter Jennie was born in 1893, followed by Carrie Belle in 1895, Nannie Mae in 1897, and Charles in 1899. These younger children joined Hammond's five minor children from his first marriage.[27]

This family division in the lawsuit could not have been a good thing for the younger Bush children, and it had to have been devastating for my great-grandmother. My grandfather Elbert was 15 years old at the time. I can't imagine what impression this family battle made on him. I wonder if he was aware of the court testimonies of his mother, his sister Della, and his brother-in-law Jonas Hammond.

Reading the sworn testimonies of the parties and witnesses was fascinating to me. The actual words of my ancestors revealed their mindsets and pieces of family history. For example, Jonas H. Hammond stated that his "wife [had] not received any portion of the rents or any portion of the land since she married [him]." Commenting about his mother-in-law, he said, "Laura Bush has been working the home place, about 25 or 30 acres every year." Della verified in her testimony that she was 24-years old and had lived on the "place" until she married in 1892. After her brother-in-law Squire Jackson died, she asked her mother to allow her and her family to live on the place he had been working but her mother refused the request. Della testified that her mother promised to give her the rents from it, but never did.[28]

It would appear from my great-grandmother Laura's testimony that she favored Eldred. She stated that she would rent the land that Squire Jackson Sr. had lived on to anybody, but she had decided to let Eldred have it without paying rent. She made it clear in her testimony that he did pay taxes on the property every year he lived there. She stated that since the place was "in bad condition" she allowed Eldred to improve it. When he first moved on the property, only eight acres were cultivated, but he was working 20 acres as of 1897. According to Laura, Eldred had also built a barn, corn cribs, and a buggy in addition to boring a well.[29]

Michael W. Clark, one of the original owners of the property, was also a witness giving testimony. He stated that the land where Laura and her younger children lived (Ward Township) was "poor and badly managed." This was shocking considering that he had sold the land to my great-grandfather in 1873 and was now stating under sworn testimony that the family could not make a living and pay either a 450-pound bale of cotton rent or any other rent from it. Other witnesses were Mat Simkins and H. G. Williams, but there were no statements from Eldred or from his siblings Calvin, Margaret, or Morris Bush, who were all 21 years and older.[30]

The partition was issued on 8 July 1897, based on the report of the Commissioners. They recommended that tracts 1, 3, and 4 be sold because "there is so many children it is not expedient to divide this land among them." There was the plan to ensure that the property did not go to the next generation. Michael W. Clark, Silas Yonce, and W. Grim were the commissioners. Clearly my ancestors should not have trusted Michael W. Clark. The Decree also stated that Laura Bush was entitled to one third of the real estate as the widow. She received Tract 2 in Pickens Township, which consisted of 56 acres, and the "poor" 50 acres in Ward Township. Tracts 1, 3, and 4 were ordered to be sold on the first Monday in November 1897. Each child was entitled to one tenth of the sale proceeds. The late Elizabeth Bush Jackson's two sons were to share her tenth.[31]

It was further ordered that Eldred Bush was to pay his sister Della Hammond the sum of $25 as rents and profits due her by him. If he failed to pay her, the Master (appointed by the Court of Common Pleas to oversee judgment) was required to take that amount from his part of the proceeds of the sale plus interest.

At the sale, Tract 1 was purchased by Mark Yonce, the son of Commissioner Silas Yonce, for $295. The 50 acres of Tract 3 were bought by Della Hammond, and the 48 acres of Tract 4 were purchased by Eldred Bush for $285. It seems clear that Laura and her grown children made an effort to keep the land in the family, but now it was no longer solely heir property. Only the property in Laura's name would give the other children a chance to inherit land. This was the beginning of the loss of the heirs' property. The acreage had been reduced from 258.5 acres to 200.5 acres.[32]

The Family Land in the Twentieth Century

By 1900, most of the family was living on their land in either Pickens or Ward Townships.

**TABLE 1. DISTRIBUTION OF BUSH LAND
PER THE 1900-1910 US CENSUSES**

	FAMILIES	TOWNSHIP	OWNED	RENTED
1900	Eldred & Mamie Bush	Pickens	X dwelling 174	
	John & Henrietta Bush	Pickens	X dwelling 175	
	Laura Bush	Ward	X dwelling 94	
	Jonas/John H. Hammond & Della Bush Hammond	Shaw		X dwelling 24

FAMILIES	TOWNSHIP	OWNED	RENTED
1910 Smith Harrison & Della Bush Harrison	Pickens	X dwelling 144	
Eldred & Mamie Bush	Pickens	X dwelling 148	
John & Henrietta Bush	Pickens	X dwelling 149	
Elbert & Minnie Bush	Pickens		X dwelling 155
Laura Bush, Morris & Annie Bush	Pickens	X dwelling 158	
Rev. F. A. & Alice Weaver	Pickens	X dwelling 159	
Ellen Bush Williams	Pickens	X dwelling 166	
Toney Williams	Pickens		X dwelling 170

During Great Aunt Della's marriage to Hammond, she never lived among the family. Their marriage may have been affected by tensions from the Bush in-laws, and it was not blessed to be a long one. I learned from my father's first cousins of the unfortunate incident of Della's husband being shot and killed while at church. On 8 March 1903, at the Mount Pleasant Baptist Church near Johnston, Jonas (Joe H. Hammond) was killed by James Henderson. Several others were wounded in the incident. By this time, Jonas and Della had five children. The murder was covered in the *Edgefield Advertiser* in the 11 March 1903 issue under the headline "Church Row and Homicide." Della must have married again within a few years of Hammond being killed, because by 1908, she had had her tenth child, Elizabeth ("Doll"), by her second husband, Smith Harrison.

In Pickens Township in 1910, some family seemed to be holding their own, yet it appears that no family was living on the property in Ward Township during this time. The fact that

Laura had moved to the property in Pickens supports the idea that something significant had occurred.

TABLE 2. DISTRIBUTION OF BUSH LAND PER THE 1920 THROUGH 1940 US CENSUSES

	FAMILIES	TOWNSHIP	OWNED	RENTED	UNKNOWN
1920	John & Henrietta Bush	Pickens		X dwelling 131	
	Ellen Williams	Pickens	X dwelling 136		
	Calvin Bush	Pickens			X dwelling 139
	Eldred & Mamie Bush	Pickens		X dwelling 140 (1)	
	Toby & Leila Bush Eidson	Pickens		X dwelling 140 (2)	
	Morris & Annie Bush Rev. F.A. & Alice Weaver	Pickens Pickens	X dwelling 269		X dwelling 261

	FAMILIES	TOWNSHIP	OWNED	RENTED	UNKNOWN
1930	Eldred & Mamie Bush	Pickens		X dwelling 163	
	Calvin Bush	Pickens			?
	Morris & Annie Bush Rev. F. A. & Alice Weaver	Pickens Pickens	X dwelling 138 X dwelling 120		

FAMILIES	TOWNSHIP	OWNED	RENTED	UNKNOWN
1940 Eldred & Mamie Bush	Pickens			?
Calvin Bush	Pickens			?
Morris & Annie Bush	Pickens	X Bland Baptist Church Road – property value $800		

In 1910, there was another lawsuit and the revelation to the public of many creditors. After the first lawsuit, the family was barely holding on to the 200.5 acres. Despite this acreage, the family was cash poor. On 13 December 1905, Eldred and Calvin Bush borrowed $200 from Matt C. Parker, due in one year.[33] Then, on 10 April 1907, Eldred borrowed $225 from Jefferson C. Lewis. The following year in March and December, Eldred and Calvin borrowed a total of $650 from John D. Eidson. Other creditors included Sam Wolfe as well as Ramsey and Jones. Ramsey and Jones, Parker, and Lewis were either farmers or merchants in Edgefield County; John D. Eidson, by 1910, was the president of the Edgefield Bank.

On top of all this debt, on 20 January 1910 Eldred made a promise to repay in one year $900 secured by his 48 acres, Calvin's 50 acres, and Laura's land in Ward Township.[34] The Ward property was subsequently lost to foreclosure. Regarding Calvin's acreage, family lore states that Della had sold her land to her brother sometime around 1910. This new mortgage was given by the Equitable Home Company of Aiken. The mortgage was recorded in the Court of Common Pleas on 24 January 1910 in Book 82, page 101. After one year, this loan became past due. However, from October 1910 to October 1911, Eldred made small payments totaling $70 that were credited to the account. Calvin also made small payments towards the loans. The testimonies of the defendants, attorneys and some of the creditors were most revealing, however.

Court Testimonies, Round 2

According to Eldred's brief testimony, he stated that, "he did not know exactly" how much he owed J. D. Eidson, but the amount due Eidson was owed partly by his mother Laura and brother Calvin.[35]

Attorney Arthur S. Tompkins, one of the lawyers for the Equitable Home Company, verified that he knew the defendant, Eldred Bush. This is the same A. S. Tompkins who represented my great-grandmother Laura and her family as plaintiffs in 1896. Tompkins stated that Eldred did not receive any of the loans directly, as Tompkins had paid it out to the various prior creditors of Eldred Bush.[36]

M.P. Wells, the lawyer who served as the *guardian ad litem* for the minor Bush children in the 1896 lawsuit[37] and who was now the attorney representing creditor M. C. Parker, stated he had the mortgage and note made by Eldred, Laura, and Calvin Bush dated 13 December 1905 for $200. On a trip to Columbia, South Carolina, however, the mortgage was lost. Wells claimed that after a diligent search, the documentation could not be found. However, a record of the transaction was still recorded in Book 76, page 327 on 23 December 1905 in Edgefield County in the office of the Mesne Conveyance. Calvin Bush admitted in sworn testimony that he owed the Equitable Home Company $350. He had paid $10 on 16 September

1911 and \$43 on 9 November 1911. He also paid Sam Wolfe a total of \$44 between October 1910 and February 1912.[38]

John D. Eidson claimed to have had "a great deal of dealings with Eldred Bush, Calvin Bush and Laura Bush, and had taken several mortgages from these negroes at various times as will appear by record, and that they have failed to pay him something on some of the mortgages." He stated that Eldred and Calvin Bush owed him \$650 with interest at 8% and attorney fees at 10% in total.[39]

THE MASTER'S REPORT

The meeting to receive the Master's Report on 26 October 1912 was attended by Edgefield County legal heavyweights Croft and Croft as well as A. S. Tompkins for the Equitable Home Company, M. P. Wells for creditor M. C. Parker, and Thurmond and Nicholson for creditor Sam Wolfe. Calvin and Morris Bush attended without counsel, as did J. D. Eidson. Eldred and Laura were not present, however. Perhaps the expected outcome was too hard for Laura to hear, but she also may have been sick—she died seven months later in May of 1913. The Master decreed the secured property, about 148 acres, would be sold to satisfy the outstanding mortgages and liens.

The Equitable Home Company was the first to be paid out of the proceeds of the sale. The rest was paid out in the following order: M. C. Parker, then J. D. Eidson, followed by Sam Wolfe.[40] Calvin Bush's land was sold to J. D. Eidson on 2 December 1912 for the sum of \$640. Eidson was the highest bidder.[41] There was no record of who purchased Eldred's and Laura's land in the court documents I received from the Edgefield Archives.

Laura, six of her daughters, and my grandfather Elbert had all died by 1920. Della and some of her family moved north to New Jersey. The family's land ownership had significantly changed. Ownership of the land on which Calvin Bush lived was identified as "un" (ownership unknown). Next door, Eldred and his family lived on rented land. Morris and his family also lived on property noted as "un." John Bush was also a renter. Meanwhile, Ellen Bush Williams (now 62) still owned dwelling 136 and Frank Weaver owned dwelling 138. Leila Bush Eidson, a daughter of Eldred, rented dwelling 140 with her husband, Toby. By 1940, Morris was the only child of Alfred and Laura to still own and occupy land, but I could not find evidence of whether any of it was part of his parents' original property.[42]

What happened to this family that caused some of them to heavily mortgage the property to the extent that it was lost to foreclosure? The lawsuits that had occurred severely fractured the family's solidarity, and some members subsequently cut ties. Many years later, hard feelings remained. With the exception of my father, none of his brothers were close to any of their over thirty cousins. They knew some of the truth that some of the land should have come to them. In reality, there was nothing for them in Edgefield County so they left for Columbia, Washington, D.C. and New York. Caesar and Squire Jackson Jr. seem to have disappeared. More than likely, they ran away from the uncles who probably used them as free labor after their grandmother died in 1913. I could not find them in any census after 1910.

The court drama over my great-grandfather Alfred's land left me feeling frustrated and sad by the fact that the first-born son Adam's rights were ignored and that the heir rights of Caesar and Squire Jackson Jr. (sons of Lizzie Bush Jackson, my father's aunt), my father, and his brothers were stolen from them. I began to think about the family lore my father told me concerning his uncles and his memories of the night his father died in 1919.

My Father's Memories

One of my father's most prominent memories was the night his father died. He remembered his brother Hezekiah coming into the bedroom he shared with his brothers Elbert and Sam, saying, "Elbert, wake up! Pa's dead! We're gonna have a good time now!"

Uncle Hezekiah may have been expecting a big inheritance, but he was mistaken. He soon realized that he was not going to receive anything, and I believe it caused a bitter root to grow in him. At the age of 14, he ran away to keep out of the reach of his uncles who initially used him to work.

My father remembered his Uncle Eldred "Elliot" as a fashionable dresser who liked to wear a white suit with a white silk shirt and hat and ride a white horse in and around Edgefield. I am sure that did not go over well during the Jim Crow period in rural Edgefield County. My father remembered hearing that white men had tricked Eldred and taken the land he had in his possession. This was probably the root cause of all the suspicious legal maneuvers in the Court of Common Pleas, along with the exorbitant interest and fees. Men seemed quick to loan money secured by the property. My father's older brothers, Hezekiah, Elbert Jr., and Sam, probably knew more of the truth of how their inheritance was stolen. Uncle Hezekiah, whom I met once, never married or owned property, and he never went back to Edgefield County South Carolina after he moved to Columbia, South Carolina.

My father remembered his twin stepbrothers William and John Powell taking him into the woods after my grandfather Elbert died to hide him from his uncles, Eldred, Morris and Calvin. According to family lore, the uncles came for my father's older brothers to use them as workers on rented land. One of my paternal first cousins told me of her father (Elbert Jr.) having bad memories of being used as an indentured servant by one of the uncles. My uncles had many unpleasant memories of family and living in South Carolina. None of my father's uncles wanted him because he was often sick and too weak to work due to nutritional deficiencies. As such, my father remained with his stepmother, Annie Powell Bush, when she moved to Shaw Township to live in the household of her brother.

In 1920, Annie Powell Bush lived with her brothers and sisters, her sons (John and William Powell), and my father and his brothers. My father's oldest brother Hezekiah, who was 14 years old, had run away from his stepmother and boarded with the Ollie Coleman family in Ward Township. This census evidence also refuted family oral history. My father and his brothers never lived with their uncles. No one had legal guardianship of my father or his brothers. They remained with their stepmother through her third marriage to Archie Thurmond, then left South Carolina when they were over 18. Like his father, Alfred, my grandfather died intestate. His widow was entitled to one third of any heir property, and the rest should have been protected for his four sons. About 50 acres remained of the family land in 1913. Exactly who controlled it remains a mystery, but it was probably lost to foreclosure.

My father had mostly fond or amusing memories of his Uncle Calvin. He often told us that his uncle was known as a "root doctor" in and around Edgefield. He had bottles filled with mysterious potions and many books in his cabin. Calvin had a favorite chair that he loved to sit in. My father remembered his uncle saying, that "if it wasn't for that chair, I could get some work done!" He also had the habit of using so much bear fat in his hair to slick it down that his hair turned red. When my father was preparing to leave South Carolina, his uncle gave him a good luck talisman of a little pouch filled with herbs to wear around his neck. It had such a bad odor that he had to get rid of it. Uncle Calvin died in 1946. My father said that by the time they found his uncle, rats had started to feed on him.

I remember my father mentioning how awful the behavior of Benjamin Ryan Tillman and Strom Thurmond was towards the black folks in Edgefield County. Tillman died in 1918 when my father was seven years old, so he could not have had much direct knowledge about him. I believe he was repeating the comments he heard his father and other adults make. The impressions made a lasting memory.

WHAT THE Y-DNA REVEALED

Alfred Bush was my most distant known paternal male ancestor. His mother was identified in the 1880 U. S. Federal Census as Easter Weaver, but the only clue to his father's identity that I had was through the Y-DNA tests taken by my brothers. The results were a shock. Y-DNA passes from father to son almost unaltered for a long period of time. According to Family Tree DNA, the results showed ancestral origins of my direct paternal line as being from only European countries. There were exact matches in England and Henrico County, Virginia, and close matches in France, Ireland, Italy, Sweden, Portugal, Wales, and the United States. No African countries were listed among the matches! One of my brothers and I thought there had to be a mistake. When I followed up on the results, the DNA administrator assured me the results were accurate. The fact is, for many African Americans, a European progenitor serves as the original head of the paternal line.

On 11 February 2013, Dr. Henry Louis Gates of the website The Root published an article titled "How Black is Black America?" that supports this statement. According to this article, 35 percent of "all African American men descend from a white male ancestor who fathered a mulatto child sometime during slavery." DNA doesn't lie. The facts show that my brothers' DNA test results were an exact match with white males who descend from Richard New, who was born in England in 1620.

I have found New males living in Edgefield County in the Johnston area. I am grateful to two white New descendants who have given me very detailed genealogies of the New family. A male in the line of William New who was born in 1775 in North Carolina and died in Edgefield County is the probable contributor of the DNA that started my paternal line. It is not clear whether William's parents came from Georgia or from Virginia. It is known that the Great Wagon Road was travelled by a throng of settlers from Pennsylvania and Virginia into the Carolinas. William New's DNA connects him to ancestors from Virginia.

It was amazing to study the DNA results of the white New males on FamilyTree DNA and see how my brothers' DNA matched exactly with direct descendants of Richard New of Gloustershire and Bristol, England. To name a few, this included: William New, born in 1759 in Virginia, who was an exact match with 37 markers; Samuel New, born in 1802 in Virginia, was an exact match with 12 markers; Jacob New, who was born in about 1760 in Virginia and died in Newton County, Georgia, and was an exact match with 12 genetic markers. There were many other matches, and paternity from this line during slavery cannot be denied. But the mystery remains as to why my great-grandfather Alfred changed his surname from Wever in 1870 to Bush in 1880. I do believe that my great-grandfather Alfred and the Bush boys enslaved by Jonathan Wever knew their blood connection.

Then there is the question of Laura's ancestry. DNA evidence supports the oral history of one of her granddaughters, Annabelle Bush Nipper, a daughter of Eldred "Elliot" Bush. Annabelle told me during the 1983 family reunion that Laura was a slaveholder's daughter. In an effort to cover up the fact that he had a mulatto child by a slave, the slaveholder gave her in marriage to Alfred when she was 14 years old. DNA proves that one of my 2nd great-grandfathers was Elisha Stevens Jr. Laura was one of at least six known children that he had with an unknown slave. I am grateful to an Ancestry.com match who analyzed our match and determined that she and I are fourth cousins two times removed. Our common ancestor was Elisha Stevens Sr., Elisha Jr.'s father. DNA helped me to find the previously unknown maiden name of my paternal great-grandmother, Laura Stevens Bush. A study of the 1870 U. S. Federal Census gave evidence that Laura had her first child, Adam, when she was about 14 years old.

In addition, during an interview in 1995 with Elizabeth Harrison Hill (Cousin Doll), the youngest daughter of Della, I learned that her mother often told her that they were descended from Jewish and Cherokee people.[43] My DNA also shows Native American and European Jewish ancestry. Maybe one of these hidden ancestors was the source of the funds that helped Alfred purchase his land with cash. Cousin Doll was also amazed to learn of the number of siblings her mother had. She told me that her mother never talked about having any sisters and only mentioned the names of two brothers: Calvin and my grandfather Elbert.

THE LEGACY

Alfred and Laura Bush had 31 grandchildren whose lives spanned 112 years from the birth of the eldest, Caesar, in 1892 to the death of one of the youngest, my father, Abner, in 2004. They left a legacy of descendants with a strong faith in God, many of whom established businesses, earned advanced degrees, and became property owners.

This ancestral journey of discovery and truth has brought me face to face with the realization that I come from some fascinating and unique ancestors. In their youth, Alfred and Laura sowed deep roots of faith and a desire to have their own property during the bonds of slavery, and within their lifetimes, they reaped a reward in property ownership that defied the odds. When I take a giant step back, the bigger picture becomes clearer—what is often impossible with man is possible with God. What He has planned, no man can take away as His Word is honored. I have seen that God will often use the simple or weak to confound the wise and strong. It seems that God will sometimes move people away from their beginnings, in order to work out His perfect will for their lives.

From the 1920s through the 1940s, my father, two of his brothers, two of his stepbrothers, two stepsisters, and many of his first cousins, left Edgefield County for New York. During those years, South Carolina lost about ten percent of its black citizens, the biggest decrease ever recorded in the state.[44] Fueled by extreme poverty, the Depression, racism, and violence, my father's generation joined the Great Migration and went north. They left to realize their dreams for a better life, to establish businesses, obtain jobs with better salaries, and most became property owners in their own right. This legacy also reminds me of my grandfather's Bible.

In April 2000, my father and I were shocked to hear of the sudden passing of my cousin Linda Jean Powell, my father's niece and goddaughter. After the funeral services, her sister Barbara asked me to help empty Jean's apartment. Like me, Jean loved to read and had many books. As I organized her collection, I came across a very old Bible with fragile pages. Knowing that family history was often recorded in Bibles, I carefully opened the cover. What I saw shocked me to my core. Before me was written, in a masculine hand: "Elbert Bush, Annie Bush, 1919." I showed it to Barbara, and, for a few minutes, we just stared at it.

Barbara then said, "Please give this to Uncle. Tell him I sent it."

I couldn't wait to get home.

When I told my father that Barbara had sent his father's Bible, he immediately sat up in his bed and extended his arms towards me, eagerly reaching for it. The last time my father and that Bible had been under the same roof was 81 years earlier, in Johnston, South Carolina, when he was seven years old. It was the only tangible thing he had ever possessed of his father's. It was a true inheritance—God's Word in a timeworn, fragile Bible returned to a rightful heir. From that day forward, I saw my father reading from his father's Bible instead of his own. He told me that he wanted to be buried with it. I really didn't want to let it go, but it wasn't my choice to make. His wish was honored.

It has become clear to me that the most important legacy passed through my paternal line is the example of my father's life and his great faith. It is not as important what is left to your children as what is left in them. If parents plant godly values, everything will work out all right. According to my father, his father was a minister and a strict disciplinarian. He planted godly values in his sons that took hold in most of them. Although my father and his brothers were robbed of their inheritance from their grandfather's estate, God had a far greater inheritance for them. My father was an outstanding father, who presided, protected, and provided for his family. I've reflected often on the many positive and fruitful outcomes of his life, and I'm trying to follow his example.

His accomplishments may not seem like much to most people, but to those who knew and loved him, they shine like brilliant stars. By faith, he left Edgefield County, South Carolina, with his few belongings in one battered suitcase, heading north. He attended night school in Washington, D.C,. to improve the very basic and inadequate education he received in the little one-room schoolhouse at Mount Pleasant Church in Johnston. His Powell stepbrothers encouraged him to come to New York, and that is where he was able to find a church in which he actively served for over 60 years. My father married at the age of 30, started a family at 37 bought our family home in Great Neck, New York at 43. He raised and provided for his family and put all four of his children through college. At 59, my father became a grandfather, and at 83, a great-grandfather. At 91, he was the last surviving grandchild of Alfred and Laura Bush, and the only one to live into the new century. The one who was too sick to work had been brought a mighty long way. The weakest had become the strongest and the last of his generation. My father was the first Bush male descended from Alfred to live with strength past 80 years.

"So teach us to number our days, that we may get us a heart of wisdom."[45]

My father lived a total of 33,978 days. His last ten years amounted to 3,650 days. It was during that time that some unbelievable events occurred at home that served as a constant reminder to me of God's steadfast love and protection.

There was a large rock imbedded in the dirt on the bank of our front yard. I planned to create a small flowerbed, and I wanted that rock moved to the area under the living room windows. One day, when my nephew Anthony came to cut the grass, I asked him to move the rock when he was finished with the lawn. He made several attempts to lift it, but finally told me that he couldn't move it. At the time, my father was out front raking leaves and cutting grass. He had quietly observed Anthony's attempt but said nothing. Several days later, when I had returned home from work, I was stunned to see that the rock had been moved and was perfectly placed in the spot I desired for the flowerbed. I asked my father who had moved the rock, and he told me that he had. I was amazed and then concerned that he might have hurt himself. He assured me, however, that he was fine. I just couldn't understand how my 86-year-old father was able to move that heavy rock when his strapping 14-year-old grandson couldn't budge it from the ground. Even as a "super" senior, my father still sought to provide for me in any way he could. How much more will our heavenly Father do for each of us! My father's life continued to glorify a living God who empowered an 86-year-old man to move a very heavy rock.

When my father told us his life story, he said that he and our mother looked for a nice place to raise a family. More importantly, he had already established the foundation: "Therefore, whoever hears these saying of mine, and does them, I will liken to a wise man who built his house on the rock; and the rain descended, the floods came, and the winds blew and beat on that house and it did not fall, for it was founded on the rock."[46]

I have wonderful memories of hearing many of my father's testimonies. One of my favorites began with these words: "I want my family and my Church family to know that I thank

God for all His Mercy. I've had my ups and downs, my Red Seas, my good times, and bad. But I thank God for bringing me a mighty long way . . . and for being so good to me." My father was a gently humble, self-effacing man who had strength of character that amazed me. He was an exceptionally loving and excellent father; I am eternally grateful for the spiritual legacy he established in our family.

Some may ask about the message given to me by my great-grandfather. I think he wanted me to know and to pass on to his descendants that he was somebody who, after being enslaved, "stood for a brief moment in the sun"[47] and that he and his wife's lives mattered. I also believe that my Edgefield ancestors are happy to be found and their lives valued and studied, shining a bright light on some of the good and bad interactions in Edgefield County, South Carolina. They lived during a time of great transition, yet their experiences of those times were never an ongoing positive dialogue in any of the local newspapers. By sheer numbers, they had a powerful voice that was placed on mute. The absence of their history in their voices gives a lopsided view of the social history of the county.

My journey of discovery has identified all eight of my great-grandparents, seven of the 16 great-great-grandparents, six of the 32 third great-grandparents, and, recently, one of my maternal fourth great-grandmothers. The journey continues.

To the many descendants of Alfred and Laura Bush, and all descendants of people who were once enslaved, I leave you with these words from Sankofa: "Return and get it. We must return and claim our past in order to move towards our future. It is in understanding who we were that will free us to embrace who we are now."[48]

FIG. 3.
ELLIOT BUSH (TOP PHOTO); PARENTS VICTORIA MEDLOCK BUSH
AND ABNER BUSH (BOTTOM PHOTO). SIGNATURES OF PATERNAL
ANCESTORS: ELLIOT BUSH, CALVIN BUSH, LAURA BUSH, JULIE BUSH,
CLARA BUSH, JONAS HAMMOND, AND ELBERT BUSH.
*Photos with the express permission of the author; signatures from
documents obtained from the Edgefield Archives*

FIG. 4. REVEREND ELBERT BUSH, SR.
Photo with the express permission of the author

MATERIAL LINE

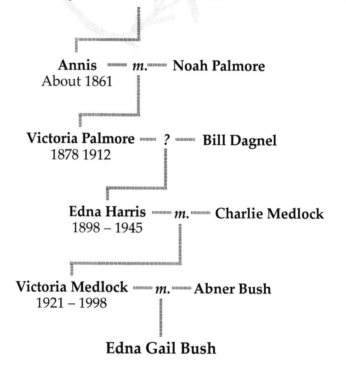

Nelly
About 1799 in Madagascar – about 1880's USA

Edna (Nancy) Burton
About 1820's – about early 1900's (later surnames – Hamilton, Hammond)

Annis   *m.*   **Noah Palmore**
About 1861

Victoria Palmore   *?*   **Bill Dagnel**
1878 1912

Edna Harris   *m.*   **Charlie Medlock**
1898 – 1945

Victoria Medlock   *m.*   **Abner Bush**
1921 – 1998

Edna Gail Bush

FIG. 5. EDNA GAIL'S MATERNAL FAMILY TREE

CHAPTER 2
IN SEARCH OF MY DIRECT MATERNAL ANCESTORS
Edna Gail Bush

►••••◄

*I knew my family had more truth to tell, and so I traveled
down a whispering well to know myself through them.*

"After All." By Dar Williams. *The Green World* (2000)[49]

Direct maternal ancestors have always fascinated me.
These are the ancestors that passed their DNA to me;
generations of mothers and daughters, we connect in a special
bond. I've long wanted to know their names—all of them—
as far back as I could go. Due to the shadow of slavery, the
documentation of that bond has often been difficult to verify
beyond a certain point.

In many of the slave narratives I've read, the enslaved
revealed little about their origins to their children. It seems
that many felt it was better for their children not to know the
truth. Usually, this truth was the fact that the slaveholder was
also their father or that the women in the family were used
for the pleasure of the slaveholder, his sons, or an overseer. In
my own maternal line, the women were used as breeders for
the monetary benefit of the slaveholders. I don't think these

early mothers wanted to leave such a wounding truth in the minds of their enslaved children, or even their freed grandchildren, that would cause a bitter root to grow.

The television program *Ancestors* on BYUtv revealed that only ten percent of all people's family histories are written. This leaves ninety percent of family histories living only in the memories of our parents and grandparents. Once they are gone, the family histories are lost. My mother did not know much about her direct maternal line, and I never knew my maternal grandmother (also my namesake), who died four years before I was born. However, I was fortunate to receive my own precious ten percent of my maternal family history from my grandmother's sister, Great Aunt Willie Mae, and her maternal first cousin, Little Joe Palmore.

PALMORE COUSINS

Beginning around 1900, my grandmother Edna, her sister Willie Mae, and cousins Virnette and Little Joe Palmore, always lived with or near each other in Graniteville, South Carolina, in Aiken County. These first cousins maintained a close relationship all their lives. They were, respectively, the children of two siblings: my great-grandmother Victoria, (1878-1922) and her brother Joseph Palmore, Sr.

My maternal great-grandmother, Victoria—the oldest child of Noah and Annis Coleman Palmore—had a short and somewhat tragic life. Family lore states that there was strong evidence to believe she was raped when she was about 15 years old. A much older married man named Bill Dagnel was the actual father of her first daughter, Edna. At the time of the 1910 US Federal Census, Edna was identified with the surname Stewart, since that was the surname of her maternal grandmother, Annis, in whose household she lived. After my great-grandmother gave birth to her second child, Willie Mae, by Yancy Harris, eventually both daughters carried Harris as their surname. Then, when Victoria developed a relationship with Frank Croft that resulted in two more children, Lorraine and Frank Jr., these latter two carried their father's surname.

FIG. 6. VICTORIA PALMORE HARRIS CROFT
Photo with the express permission of the author

Victoria contracted tuberculosis sometime during her relationship with Yancy Harris; both died from the disease. Victoria died in 1922, and Yancy followed many years later in 1935. Victoria's two youngest children, Lorraine and Frank Jr., also succumbed to the disease. My mother remembered her own mother telling her that, shortly before Victoria died, she had told Edna not to worry about Lorraine and Frank because she would soon be back for them. Both died within a month of their mother.

GREAT UNCLE JOSEPH PALMORE

I remember Great Uncle Joe Palmore. He was born in Edgefield County in 1879 and died in Graniteville, South Carolina, in 1970. It was the year my niece, Nyja, was born; one leaves, and a new one is born.

I remember being in awe of Great Uncle Joe. He seemed ancient, and he was blessed with a long life—a trait, I later learned, was characteristic in the maternal line. I also remember watching him as he studied us, the children of his grandniece and grandnephew. While observing us, his words were few. But somehow, I knew he was pleased with us: how we looked and talked and our good manners.

Great Uncle Joe served as patriarch of our maternal line for a long time, watching over his sister's children and grandchildren in addition to his own. By trade, he was a brick mason. He had built and owned a house in Graniteville, on a hill not far from where my grandmother and Great Aunt Willie Mae lived.

Great Uncle Joe's father, Noah Palmore (my 2nd great grandfather), and his grandfather, Griffin Palmore (my 3RD great grandfather), were among the very few known fathers in my direct maternal family. I was fortunate to find in the history of the Mount Canaan Baptist Church that Griffin Palmore and his wife, Eliza, were among the seventeen founding members of the church. It was established by the Reverend Alexander Bettis in 1869.[50] Those seventeen early members had withdrawn their memberships from the First Baptist Church of Edgefield Village, a church they had been forced to attend alongside their slaveholders.

IGNITING THE SPARK

Although Cousin Little Joe had a remarkable memory for family history, I don't think he knew about our family's history with the Mount Canaan Church. I believe if he had known, he would have proudly mentioned it. My mother, her brother, nor Great Aunt Willie Mae ever mentioned a connection to Mount Canaan. They proudly shared their memories of the Bethlehem Missionary Baptist and Valley Fair churches, but never Mount Canaan. During a visit to South Carolina, I discovered Mount Canaan Cemetery was the final resting place for many of my great-grandmother's (Victoria Palmore) first cousins.

Cousin Little Joe was generous with the history he did know. I was impressed by the way he weaved a story from the passed-down memories he possessed about an ancestor. Cousin Little Joe gave me the names of some of the siblings of his grandmother, Annis Coleman Palmore. He mentioned Isabella (nicknamed "Aunt Beanie"), her brother Miles, and her sister Maria Jeanette. This information helped me to connect the relationships many years later when I received additional information.

During the summer of 1979, I remember standing on the front porch of Great Aunt Willie Mae's home in Graniteville with my mother and great aunt. Cousin Little Joe responded to a question I had asked him by saying, "You know, Gail, you are the third and last Edna." I was surprised, because I thought I was the second, named for my grandmother Edna Harris Medlock.

He then uttered the words that further surprised my mother and me: "The first Edna was part Indian and white mixed and lived to be 106 years and was so light, she was buried in a white cemetery."

That was the spark that fueled my desire to find documentation of the first Edna's existence. Cousin Little Joe's words have haunted me over the years, prompting me to search for some evidence of the life of the first Edna, my direct 3RD great-grandmother. It was not until the spring of 2013, after hiring the services of a certified genealogist, that I was able to finally uncover documentation that not only verified the existence of the first Edna, but also that of her mother.

The Burton Slaveholders

After many years of looking for the first Edna, the certified genealogist put me on the right path. She found her, and other relatives, in the 1839 estate of Allen Y. Burton (1794-1840).[51] Now that I had the slaveholder's name, I wanted to see what additional information I could find in Gloria Lucas's book, *Slave Records of Edgefield County, S.C.* As usual, her book did not disappoint me. On 2 January 1821, Richard Johnson, Allen Y. Burton's maternal grandfather, sold "Nelly, Maria, Isaac and Edney" to Sampson Butler Sr. for $1,050. On 30 January 1822, however, Mary Burton, administrator of her father's estate, transferred ownership of Nell, Maria, Isaac, and Edna, to herself. This time, however, no monetary value was given.

This group was identified as consisting of a "negro woman and children." Here was evidence of my 4TH great-grandmother, Nelly, along with the older siblings of my 3RD great-grand-mother, the first Edna. Born during the presidency of James Monroe, Edna's approximate birth year was 1820.

But how did Mary Johnson Burton obtain ownership of Nelly and her children from Sampson Butler, Sr.? It appears that Butler had been in poor health; he died on 9 January 1822. Whatever financial arrangements he had made with Richard Johnson to purchase my ancestors, he did not fulfill them. So, Nelly and her children were returned to the estate of Richard Johnson and then to his daughter, Mary Johnson Burton.

Sometime between June 1839, when Allen Y. Burton wrote his will, and May 1840, when his estate was probated, Nelly gave birth to a child identified as Emeline in the Burton estate. Edna (also called Edney) had two identified children—Sam and Caroline. Maria's children were Andrew and Fanny. Edna's brother Isaac had fathered a son, Alfred, by Kitty; the boy, Alfred, was also listed as property in Burton's estate.

When Burton died in his forty-sixth year, he did not have a wife or any legal issue. Based on the family lore of the first Edna's appearance, it is possible that some, if not all, of Nelly's older children were his. This hypothesis is supported by the fact that I have both white and black Burton DNA matches. Burton's entire estate was to be kept intact for the welfare and benefit of his parents, Richard (1759-1840) and Mary (1761-1839) and his siblings, Martha "Patsy" and Richard J. Burton and their children. Burton's estate also included 900 acres in Edgefield County, very close to former Governor F. W. Pickens' property, on both sides of the waters of Log Creek. However, a major part of the estate consisted of people, including my ancestors, all 21 related to me by blood or bond. This is how slaves were recorded—as chattels.

The death of a plantation owner often resulted in the devastating separation of enslaved family members. Burton directed his executor to immediately sell three specified enslaved men to pay for his debts and burial. These men were Tom (valued at $450 and sold for $380 to Jasper Gibbs), Solomon (valued at $700 and sold for $580 to William Carson), and Jerry (valued at $900 and sold for $805 to an unidentified buyer). The remainder of the estate was to "be kept together under the control of his executor for the purpose of maintaining, out of the rents, profits and proceeds thereof, during their natural lives," his father, mother, brother and sister, and their children.[52] Unfortunately for the enslaved, slavery was a business.

Despite the directive, the estate actually sold four enslaved adult males during 1840. In addition to Tom, Solomon and Jerry, a man named Simon was sold on 6 July 1840. He was purchased for $730 by the Trustee N. L. Griffin.[53] Based on the sale prices, it can be determined that Tom was probably the oldest of the four men. The youngest man, Jerry, was valued highest. Nelly's oldest son, Isaac, who was in his twenties, was missing from the inventory in 1840. He may have been sold, but there was no record of the transaction.

The only remaining adult male from the Burton estate was Gabe, valued at $600. Four women, two of whom were my direct ancestors, were grouped with very young children: Nelly and her child, Emeline (valued at $450), Maria and her children, Andrew and Fanny (valued at $1,000), Edna and her children, Sam and Caroline (valued at $1,100), and Kitty and her child, Alfred (valued at $800). During my research I have found that infants or very young children still nursing were grouped with their mothers. As a family group, these four mothers, with very young children, suffered loss through the sales of the fathers of some of their children. Seven additional children were listed singularly and ranged in approximate ages from 5 to 12; they were valued from $200 to $700. Their mothers were more than likely Nelly or Maria, although a few may have been purchased as children.

With not much remaining manpower, how were the Burton enslaved earning enough to provide for the Burton heirs? Available court documentation shows many subsequent years of struggle for the heirs, which must have trickled down to the enslaved in the form of an extremely stressful existence on top of the misery of slavery. Allen Y. Burton's will was recorded at the Edgefield Court House on 20 February 1840, but the executor, Nathan L. Griffin, was not appointed until May 18 of the same year. I believe that Allen's brother, Richard J. Burton, may have managed the estate during this brief period, until the executor was approved by the court. By trade, Burton was a butcher. Some of the enslaved may have been hired out, while others worked on the Burton land. I did not find actual documentation of the hiring out until 1848. Some of the enslaved were used to provide extra income for the family on other farms.

At the time of the 1850 census, Richard J. Burton was listed as the slaveholder on the slave schedule.[54] The enslaved included a 60-year-old female, who was more than likely Nelly. But there was a problem with her age; it appeared to be an error when compared to her age as 60 in the 1870 U. S. Federal Census. Researchers should not put a lot of confidence in early records that included black people. I have found far too many errors that included the wrong names, no names, incorrect ages, confusion about the race of a person or even the sex. For example, my paternal grandfather's sister Julia was identified as Julian, a 16-year-old male, in the 1900 census. Returning to the 1850 record listing Richard J. Burton, there was one 28-year-old female, who I believe was Edna (or Edney). The census record for the general population revealed that the slave-owner, Richard, age 53, had married Lucinda Delaughter, in 1842, and they had four children Richard's 65 year old sister, Martha (nicknamed Patsy), was also living with him.

Burton Heirs vs Estate Trustees

From the early 1850s until the will's resolution in 1858, the Burton heirs were in and out of court fighting for better management of their property and the execution of the Trusts and provisions of the will. The first executor, Nathan L. Griffin, was in failing health; he died in February of 1853. Having performed his role for thirteen years, he was the longest-serving executor for the estate. He was also a very wealthy man who owned over 200 enslaved. After his death, the remaining Burton heirs requested, by petition to the court, that attorney B. C. Bryan be appointed as their Trustee.

In June of 1853, B. C. Bryan was appointed; less than six months later, however, the Burton heirs complained of his administration. They claimed he "failed to give to the Commissioners the said bond so required" by the court, and therefore could not take charge of the estate. Burton heirs Richard J. and Patsy then requested that "their friend" William F. Durisoe be appointed as Trustee to manage the estate.[55]

At a hearing held in April 1854, after the testimony of H. T. Wright and L. W. Youngblood, the presiding Chancellor, Francis Hugh Wardlaw, was satisfied that William F. Durisoe was a "fit and proper person to take the trust of this estate." At this time, 23 enslaved persons were named: Seaborn, George or Drayton, Caesar, Andrew, Sam (about 16), Henry, Pierce, Bill, Alfred (about 15), Nelly (my 4TH great-grandmother; about 54), Edna (my 3RD great-grandmother; about 33), Kitty, Sukey, Eliza, Betsy, Emeline (14), Caroline (14), Angelina, Ellen, Lucy, Marvin, Ariana, and Maria. These 23 enslaved individuals were valued at $16,000.[56] The above named enslaved persons, identified by age, are my direct line ancestors.

Initially, there must have been relative peace between the Burton heirs and Trustee William F. Durisoe. However, sometime between his appointment in 1854 and 1857, both siblings of Allen Y. Burton had died. Richard J. died in the latter part of 1857, and, shortly thereafter, his widow, Lucinda, filed a petition on behalf of her seven children. She claimed that the funds given her, from the labors of the enslaved, were insufficient for the welfare and benefit of her children. She wanted the court to allow a division of the slave property by sale. William F. Durisoe refused to sell and wanted to follow the intent of the will to keep the enslaved property together.

However, I found evidence that the Burton heirs were possibly dividing and selling acreage from the original 900 acres. On 27 July 1859, an ad in the Edgefield Advertiser stated:

> One tract of land containing 135 acres, more or less, on waters of Log Creek and bounded by lands of the estate of R. J. Burton, deceased, A. J. Smyly, and land of the Poor House. This is a first rate Tract of Land, about 80 acres which are cleared.
> L. S. Johnson.

With a bit of the real estate sold, Lucinda Burton also fought to sell my ancestors to provide her with more money. Several sworn witnesses gave testimony on both sides of the argument.[57]

THE WITNESSES

Mark Etheredge, a slaveholder of 17 in 1850, stated that he lived about half a mile from where Richard Burton lived. He reported that he had hired a portion of the Negroes and had been doing so since the beginning of 1848. In what capacity did my ancestors work? I believed the younger ones more than likely toiled in the fields. Etheredge testified that he hired them for five years and paid $400 to the estate. If, on occasion, he hired for a sixth year, he paid $775 to the estate. At the time, he believed it was a fair price. Etheredge mentioned that cotton was paying five-and-a-half to seven cents per pound at the time. He also stated that he "had the privilege" of clearing 100 acres and had the use of the place, except for the mill. But he also wanted it known that the land "in cultivation was old and poor." He observed that the Negroes were "tolerably well divided as to men and women," but there were a good many children because the "women are breeders."[58] Here was documented proof that my direct maternal ancestors were used as breeders! This was upsetting to realize, though not entirely surprising from the knowledge I had.

When the importation of slaves was declared illegal on 1 January 1808, the demand for free labor in the southern states steadily increased. Breeding occurred in the slave states to meet the demand for more free labor. Sadly, slave breeding included coerced sexual relations between male and female slaves. There were also forced sexual relations between the slaves and the slaveholders—or any white male and enslaved girls and women—in order to produce more slave children, since the child's status followed that of the mother. According to Etheredge, six enslaved children were born to the estate in 1856 and 1857. More than likely, Edna's son Miles was one of them. According to the 1870 US Federal Census, he was born about 1857.

Etheredge believed that the estate was not able to support itself. However, during the first and second years when he had rented the property, the income of the place did support Richard J. Burton's family. According to him, the first Trustee, Nathan L. Griffin, informed Etheredge that he had authorized S. F. Goode to allow Richard J. Burton to have goods out of his store and that Goode was to show the account monthly. After two or three months, he ceased to perform this duty, and the account for the Burton heirs increased to a considerable amount without the knowledge of the Trustee. In his opinion, the expenses of the Burton family had increased considerably since the marriage due to their rapidly increasing number of children. He stated that he did not think Mrs. Burton should receive any further support for her children and that $1,000 a year should be more than sufficient. According to Measuring Worth.com, that amount was valued at $29,700 as of 2014, a princely amount in 1858.

John Huiet, a slaveholder about 40 years old in the late 1830s, did not agree with Mark Etheredge that the money received annually from the labor of the slaves was sufficient for the Burton family's welfare. He believed that it was hardly even enough in the early years when the family was small. Huiet also believed that a more realistic amount for the support of the Burton children should be at least $1,210 per year.[59]

James Swearingen, a slaveholder of 15 enslaved persons in 1861, stated that the estate was composed largely of women and children but was rapidly increasing. This statement contradicts Mark Etheredge, because Swearingen didn't report an equal number of adult men and women. Swearingen also stated that when Richard Burton married Lucinda, there was only one adult enslaved male (Gabe). He reported that Mrs. Burton had to make a great effort to support herself and her children by her own labors and had greatly suffered.[60]

Store owner S. F. Goode stated that Nathan L. Griffin had incurred indebtedness to him for the Burton family in the amount of $240. Griffin required him to make a monthly accounting of the expenses for the family and was very particular. His store provided flour, sugar, coffee, bacon, and cheap clothing. Mrs. Burton always picked up the provisions. He believed that there was evidence of a great deal of economy in the expenses for the family considering the small number of slaves hired out for the first five years and the rapidly increasing Burton family. In addition, B. C. Bryan reported that the estate owed a debt to Lodrick "Lod" Hill, a slaveholder of 27 persons, in the amount of $200 at the time of Nathan L. Griffin's death. Bryan stated that he had paid this account and also a debt to Dr. Mims for shoes. According to him, these accounts were over and above what he paid out with funds from the estate. A Mr. Penn stated that Nathan L. Griffin purchased bacon from him in 1852 for the Burton family, and a Mr. Frazier stated that the amount of unpaid accounts to him amounted to $70. An unpaid account to a Mr. Nicholas was $35.[61]

Through the years, the estate had been burdened by mounting debts due to the needs and demands of Richard J. Burton's large family and probably weak management by some of the Trustees of this large estate. Although, in fairness to Trustee Durisoe, he did ask the court to be allowed to sell "one of the negroes for cash" to meet the pressing needs of the Burton family.[62] As a result of the sworn testimony, Chancellor Wardlaw decided in favor of the seven minor children and allowed a complete partition of the Burton estate.[63]

SOLD!

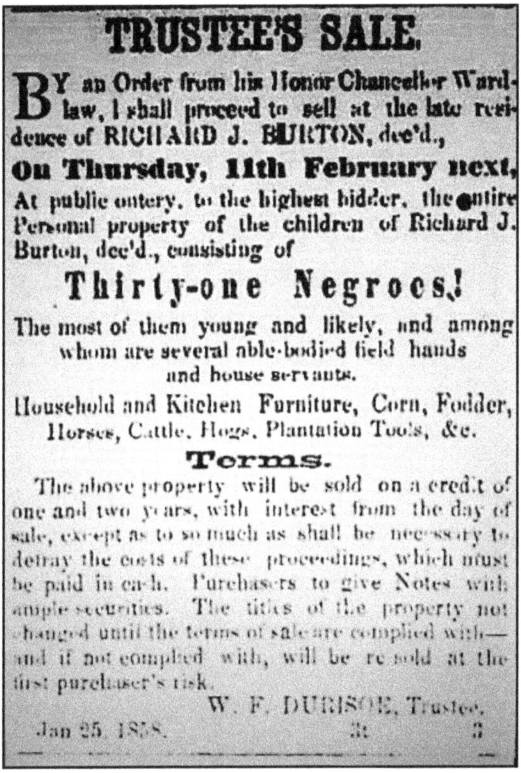

TRUSTEE'S SALE.

BY an Order from his Honor Chancellor Wardlaw, I shall proceed to sell at the late residence of RICHARD J. BURTON, dec'd.,

On Thursday, 11th February next,

At public outcry, to the highest bidder, the entire
Personal property of the children of Richard J.
Burton, dec'd., consisting of

Thirty-one Negroes,

The most of them young and likely, and among
whom are several able-bodied field hands
and house servants.

Household and Kitchen Furniture, Corn, Fodder,
Horses, Cattle, Hogs, Plantation Tools, &c.

Terms.

The above property will be sold on a credit of
one and two years, with interest from the day of
sale, except as to so much as shall be necessary to
defray the costs of these proceedings, which must
be paid in cash. Purchasers to give Notes with
ample securities. The titles of the property not
changed until the terms of sale are complied with—
and if not complied with, will be re-sold at the
first purchaser's risk.

W. F. DURISOE, Trustee.

Jan 25, 1858.

FIG. 7. 1858 TRUSTEE'S SALE NOTICE
Courtesy of the Edgefield Archives

In January of 1858, the *Edgefield Advertiser* published the upcoming sale of the Burton enslaved in a Trustee's Sale to be held on 11 of February. All 31 of my maternal ancestors—from Nelly and Edna to their children and grandchildren—faced the auction block. I tried to find information on who purchased them, but I faced a serious brick wall. I did find a document dated 27 December 1859, from which I learned that Lucinda Burton "bargained and sold...in plain and open market...the following negroes to wit, Nellie, Kit, Sam, Marvin, Eliza and her three children together with the future increase of the females" to G. M. Roper, D. R. Durisoe, and W. F. Durisoe.[64] Nellie was about 59 years old, and she was sold with some of her grandchildren and a daughter, Eliza. Why is there no record of the outcome of the sale on 11 February 1858? It must not have gone well for these eight to have remained in the possession of Lucinda Burton. This transaction was also not documented in Gloria Lucas's book, *Slave Records of Edgefield County*. I believe, therefore, this transaction reflects a private sale. According to the 1860 Slave Schedule, in addition to the above named, Lucinda kept seven others who lived in one cabin. This means on 11 Feb 1858, 16 of my 31 ancestors were sold.

In 1860, when Lucinda Burton managed the estate for her children, the remaining real estate was valued at $19,000 and the personal property at $6000.[65] On the morning of 28 December 1866, she suffered a great personal loss. Her sixteen-year-old son, Richard Jr., accidently shot himself while hunting with his younger brother, Allen.[66] From 1860 to 1870, she also lost a considerable amount of the wealth she had received for her children from the sale of slave property. By 1870, she and her children had moved to the Saluda Division area and possessed real estate valued at $3,000 and personal property of only $450. In 1880, Lucinda, now fifty-eight, lived in the household of her son, George W. Burton, in Pickens Township. George had taken up farming. No values were given for any real estate or personal property. Apparently, the once great wealth of the Burton heirs was gone.[67] By 1900, they had left South Carolina for Texas.

It is a sad fact that the only way I have been able to trace my enslaved ancestors is by looking through records that pertain to property, which may or may not even give the dignity of a name. As I studied the listings of my ancestors across the years, I wanted to get an idea of the number of children my 3RD and

4TH great-grandmothers brought into this world. From 1822 to 1840, documentation supports that Nelly was the mother of Maria, Isaac, Edna, and Emeline. As the eldest of the Burton enslaved, she was the probable mother of Caesar, Prudence, Susan ("Sukey"), Betsey and Elizabeth ("Eliza"), and George ("Drayton"). There may be a few others, but she was the mother of at least ten children. Edna, my 3RD great-grandmother, was the documented mother of Sam, Caroline, Isabella, Maria Jeannette, Ellen, Miles, Annis (my second great-grandmother), and Alexander. There may even be others. Based on the many DNA matches I've received, it seems like my maternal ancestors contributed a great deal to the population of Edgefield County, South Carolina.

I now wondered if the lives of my ancestors improved after slavery ended. Where would I find them after emancipation?

ILLUMINATING THE LIVES OF
MY ANCESTORS AT FREEDOM

In Edgefield County, the enslaved were freed in 1865. Most spent some time trying to locate family members and to obtain compensated work. I was able to find two of the labor contracts for individuals who had been enslaved by the Burtons. Surprisingly, both Nelly's daughter Eliza and Kitty's son Alfred returned to work for the Burtons. Their "contracts" read as follows:

> Edgefield 25 April 1867
>
> Hired the girl Elizer[sic] for one year she is to work for $3.00 per month and feed her which is equal to $36.00 for one year she agreed to this and commenced work the 1st of January.
>
> > George W. Burton
> > Lucinda Burton [68]

Edgefield 25 April 1867

Hired the boy Alfred for one year he has agreed to work with me one year for the sum of one hundred dollars and I feed him which is about $ 8 ½ per month. Alfred promised to work faithful and obey orders this he agreed and commenced work on 1st. January.

George W. Burton

L. Burton[69]

Both contracts were written and signed by the Burtons, but neither Eliza nor Alfred had made their mark on them as was required by the Freedmen's Bureau in Aiken. I wonder why they were willing to work for the Burtons after being enslaved by them. Was it a case of "better the devil you know than the one you don't?" Were they hoping to discover where their family had been sold? There certainly did not seem to be any mutual respect on the Burtons' part. Both Eliza and Alfred were in their early thirties, neither being a child.

After slavery ended, surnames often offered a clue about family connections, but I have found in my family that was not always so. A major difficulty I had in finding my ancestors was the fact that they possessed different surnames. Several of the women had changed their first names. The only unifying surname was Burton, but out of the original 21 enslaved by the Burton estate in 1839, only three chose that surname in 1870.

TABLE 3. SURNAMES USED BY THE BURTON ENSLAVED

1840	1870	1880	1900
Nelly	Timmerman	Hamilton	Deceased
Maria/Mariah	?	?	
Edna/Edney	Coleman	Nancy Hamilton	Nancy Edna Hammond
Kitty	Bacon	Ryan	Died in 1904
Isaac	Bacon	Ryan	Died in 1890s

Caesar/Sezar	Walker	Walker	?
Seaborn	Burton	Burton	?
Susan/Sukey	Cranshaw	Cranshaw	Cranshaw/ Crenshaw
Betsy	Burton	Burton	?
Prudence	?	?	
George or Drayton	?	?	
Andrew	?	?	
Fannie	?	?	
Sam	?	?	
Alfred	Bacon	?	
Emeline	?	?	
Caroline	Christie	Christie	Caroline and infant son died from typhoid in 1880[70]
Gabe	?	?	

A major source of information in family history research is studying the census records, which were generally compiled every ten years. Census data provides listings by households and shows who resided together, their occupations, ages, race (in the USA), and relationships with each other. It was here that I searched for information to determine where my ancestors resided after emancipation.

1870 Census

My 4TH great-grandmother, Nelly, is listed as living in Spring Grove Township in the household of her grandson-in-law Peter Christie and his wife, Caroline (Edna's oldest daughter). Nelly had chosen the surname Timmerman. There was another woman identified as Harriet Timmerman (35), and her two children, General (2) and Eliza (1), *the first in the family to be born free*. The name Eliza was probably in honor of Nelly's daughter Elizabeth, who was also called Eliza or Lizar. Therefore, I'm sure there is a blood relationship between Nelly and Harriet and that the name Harriet may have been chosen to replace the name she had while enslaved. Next door was the household of Caesar Walker (45) and his wife, Jane. I'm sure this is the same Caesar listed in the Burton estate in 1839, making him a probable son of Nelly.

Edna, now about fifty, was the head of a household living in Shaw Creek Township with her younger children Miles (12), Annis (about 9), and Alexander (7). Edna's household also included one of her older daughters, Isabella Glover (22), and her two children, Laura (5) and Elbert (2), *who were both born free*. I know Isabella was not the name she was given at birth; there was no Isabella named in the 1854 listing. Based on this census, her birth year was about 1848. There was a two-year-old female on the 1850 Slave Schedule.

Also, she should have been named in the 1854 listing of the Burton enslaved in the court papers. There was no Isabella listed. In the March 1854 listing of the enslaved, the youngest females were identified as Angelina, Ellen, Lucy, Ariana, and Maria. Isabella, who would later be nicknamed "Aunt Beanie," was about six years old and had started life with another first name.

Living next door to Edna's household was the G. W. Turner family, Edna's employers, where she worked as a domestic servant. Thus, all of my known maternal ancestors were perfectly lined up in my 3RD great-grandmother's household. I knew about Miles and Annis, Edna's grown daughter Isabella, and her granddaughter Laura, but Alexander and Elbert were a surprise. Neither Cousin Little Joe nor my mother ever mentioned them, so I believe they must have died young.

Living next door to the Lucinda Burton household in the Saluda Division township was Isaac Bacon (55, Nellie's oldest son), his wife Kittie (48), and their children Alfred (34), Maria (21), and Moselle (18). Here was evidence that Isaac was the father of Kittie's son Alfred. He had been sold to Thomas G. Bacon in 1840. Isaac must have been in close proximity to remain in contact with his family. Next door to Isaac's household lived one of his younger sisters, Eliza Burton (36 and under contract to work for Lucinda Burton), and her children Jordan, Harriet, Georgie, Anna, and Mary, *the last three born free*. It appears that all of my ancestors strived to maintain family stability.

The answer to a part of the mystery of what happened to about half of the Burton enslaved at the sale on 11 February 1858, was found in Louisiana. Nelly's daughters Susan ("Sukey"), born about 1828, and Betsy, born about 1834, were married and living in Ward 6, Grant Parrish. Whoever purchased them in 1858 had gone west. A big surprise was to see Seborn, born about 1827, and Betsy married, but with no children. They lived near Betsy's brother-in-law and sister, Daniel and Susan Burton Cranshaw, and their eight children. The four adults all stated that they were born in South Carolina. Daniel also possessed real estate valued at $250 and personal property valued at $300. They were beginning to prosper.

1880 CENSUS

In 1880, Nelly and Edna had moved to Silverton Township in Aiken. I wonder what factors caused this move? Was it the increased racial violence in Edgefield? Both the Hamburg and Ellenton massacres had occurred in 1876, among many other killings. Out-migrations by blacks to Africa, and further south and west within the USA, had occurred by this time, as well as moves to other counties. Nelly and Edna (who had changed her first name to Nancy), both now using the surname Hamilton, were living in the household of another one of Edna's daughters, Ellen Lewis and her husband Joseph Lewis. Edna was identified as the mother-in-law to the head of household, Joseph, and Nelly as the grandmother-in-law. Both of their ages were off by at least ten years. Early census takers went door to door to gather information given them by whoever answered the door. Coupled with their own biases, there were many errors. With three young children in 1822, I approximated Nelly's birth year to 1799.

At this time, Ellen Lewis and her husband had four children ranging in ages from four years to eight months. After 1880, I could no longer find a census record for Nelly, leading me to the conclusion that my earliest known maternal ancestor had passed.

Annis Coleman Palmore (19), a daughter of Edna, was living with her husband Noah and two children in the township of Wise in Edgefield County. These children, Victoria Palmore (2), and her brother, Joseph (1), would become the ancestors most remembered by my mother, uncle, and great aunt.

Maria Jeannette Coleman, another daughter of Edna, was about 30 in 1880, and lived in the township of Gregg in Aiken County. She was married to Elbert Coleman. At this time, she and her husband had six children: Joseph, Sallie, Amelia, John, Willie, and George.

Isaac and Kitty had changed their surname to Ryan and moved to Pickens Township in Edgefield County with their daughter Maria and nine-year-old granddaughter, Minnie Ryan. I could not find their son Alfred or daughter Moselle.

Daniel and Susan Cranshaw lived next door to Seborn and Betsey Burton in the Second Ward of Grant Parrish, Louisiana. The Cranshaws had four children still at home. Seborn and Betsey had a niece Mary ("Maria," 17), living with them.

1890 Census

A great unknown for all researchers is a missing decade of census records from the late nineteenth century that were lost due to smoke and fire damage. However, a few conclusions can be made based on who appeared or disappeared in the censuses before and after 1890. During this decade, there were many births including my grandmother Edna and her sister, Willie Mae. Both my 4TH great-grandmother, Nelly, and her oldest son, Isaac, must have died sometime between 1881 and 1890, because I could not find them on any subsequent census records with any of their known descendants.

1900 Census

By 1900, my 3RD great-grandmother, Edna, was using the name of Nancy E. Hammond. She was now living in the household of her grandson-in-law William Vanderhorst, and his wife, Laura, the daughter of Isabella (now 58, and also living in this home). They had moved to Gregg Township (Graniteville) in Aiken County. This is the last time I would see any mention of my 3RD great-grandmother, Nancy Edna. She had had a long life, journeying from slavery to freedom during changing, turbulent times in Edgefield County.

Next door lived Edna's daughter Annis Palmore Barney Stewart, a widow. She stated that she had given birth to four children and had four living. Her sons, Joseph Palmore (21), and Ernest Barney (15), and her daughter, Isabella Barney (13), lived with her. Victoria Palmore, Annis's eldest (and my great-grandmother) lived in another household in Greenville, South Carolina.

Maria Jeannette Coleman and her husband, Elbert, also lived in Gregg Township. She stated that she had given birth to thirteen children and had nine living. Her children included: George, Elijah, Fred O., James, Katie, Morris, and Elbert Jr. Her eldest son, Joseph, lived next door with his wife, Anna, and their children. His wife reported giving birth to ten children, with eight living. The children living with them at this time included Lillian, McKinley, Nellie, and Anna.

Kitty Bacon Ryan, Isaac's widow, lived alone in Pickens Township next door to Thomas G. Bacon's widow, Angeline Bacon.

I could not find either Joseph or Ellen Lewis in this census, but the reasons for that would not be made evident until I searched the next census.

By 1900, neither Daniel and Susan Cranshaw nor Seborn and Betsey Burton could be found. However, the Cranshaws' son Albert (34) was married and had three children: Elijah (7), Edna (5), and Opie, 3. I was delighted to discover another Edna! They were living in Ward 4 of Natchitoches Parish in Louisiana.

STRUGGLING WITH A SURNAME

My 3RD and 4TH great-grandmothers, Edna and Nelly, both went by the surname "Hamsmiton" in 1880, which was an obvious misspelling by the census taker, presumably based on my ancestors' pronunciation. Somewhere along the line, it was corrected to Hamilton. The delayed birth record for one of Edna's grandsons, Charles, by her daughter Ellen Lewis, stated his mother's maiden name as "Hampdenton," another obvious misspelling, maybe intended to be Hampton.

By 1900, Edna had changed her name to Nancy Edna Hammond. Was this the name they were struggling to remember? It is curious that I have DNA matches for all three surnames: Hamilton, Hampton and Hammond.

1910 CENSUS

Isabella "Aunt Beanie" Glover Cheatham was now about 62, and widowed again. She worked as a cook at a boarding school in Aiken and lived alone. Maria Jeannette Coleman (58), lived in Gregg township with her youngest children: Katie (20), Morris (15), and Elbert Jr. (12). She also had her uncle Lewis Burton (71), living with her. In 1870, Lewis had been a domestic servant and lived in the household of Sheriff John McDewitt.

Living in the township of Madison in Aiken County was my 2ND great-grandmother, Annis Palmore Stewart. This household included my grandmother Edna (14), Joseph Jr., Cousin Little Joe, and Annis's son, Joseph Sr.

Victoria Palmore Croft (32), lived in Greenville, South Carolina, with her husband, Frank Croft Sr., and her youngest child, Frank Jr. She stated that she had three children, all living. But she actually had four. Her eldest was my grandmother, Edna, who was living with her own grandmother, Annis. But where were her daughters, Willie Mae and Lorraine? I could not find them in 1910.

Edna's daughter, Ellen Lewis, had about seven children with her husband Joseph. The only children I could find in 1910 were their daughter Ella Lewis Coleman and son Charles Lewis. Ella and her husband, Willie, had married in 1905. By 1910, they had five children and lived in Barnwell, South Carolina. Charles was 23 years old and living with his father, Joseph, and Joseph's second wife, Helen, in Four Mile Township of Barnwell County. They had been married one year. Great Aunt EllenHampton Lewis had died in 1907.

Albert and his wife, Eliza Cranshaw, had moved to Ward 7 in Grant Parrish, Louisiana, and had seven children. Although Albert stated that he couldn't read or write, he owned his home mortgage free. This would be the last time I would find Albert and Eliza Cranshaw in a census.

1920 Census

In Madison Township, in the households numbered in the census as 433, 435, 437, 438, and 439, my ancestors had created their own little community. Katie Coleman Fair and her husband, Julian, lived in 433 with their daughter, Jeannette (7), and son, Arthur (5). Next door at 435, lived Katie's brother Elijah Coleman. Their mother, Maria Jeanette Coleman, now 68, lived in household 437 with a roomer named Julia Davis and Julia's son, Tom. Anna Coleman, the widow of Maria Jeanette's son Joseph, lived in household 438 with her children: McKinley, Nelly, Anna, Irvin, and William.

In household 439, Laura Glover Vanderhorst (55), lived with her mother, Isabella "Aunt Beanie" Glover Cheatham (72), and Uncle Joe Palmore (41). This would be the last census record in which Aunt Beanie appeared. She must have died sometime between 1920 and 1929, because I could not find any record of her in the 1930 census.

Although I could not find a record of her death, an interesting story about her has been passed down. My mother was told by her mother that Aunt Beanie was in the habit of feeding the chickens every morning at seven o'clock sharp. Family members living in the house with her remembered hearing her footsteps and the door creaking open before slamming shut. For two weeks after her death, however, they continued to hear her footsteps each morning at seven o'clock, with the door opening and closing. Then the noises just stopped. Not too far away, in Gregg Township, lived my grandmother's sister, Willie Mae Davis, and her husband, Haston Davis. Miles Hammond (Miles Coleman in 1870) lived a few doors down in the household of his Palmore cousin, Noah Fells.

1930 Census

Winds of change began to blow my maternal ancestors northwards. Cousin Katie Coleman Fair, husband Julian, son Arthur, daughter Jeanette, and mother Maria Jeanette Coleman, moved to Washington, D.C.

Aunt Jeanette's daughter-in-law, Anna Coleman, three of her children (Nellie, William, and Irene Coleman Dudley), and her husband, David Dudley, moved to Asheville, North Carolina.

My grandmother, Edna Medlock, lived in the household of Cousin Laura, along with my mother, Victoria (9), and her brother Charlie (6) in Graniteville. Aunt Willie Mae, Uncle Joe, and Cousin Little Joe also remained in Graniteville. Meanwhile, Ella Lewis Coleman was widowed and still lived with three of her ten children in Barnwell.

The Coleman Connection

In 1870, Edna went by the surname Coleman, as did the four children living in her home. Who her husband was and what became of him is unknown. Edna's daughter Maria Jeanette married Elbert Coleman. Was he a relative? Were she and her sister Isabella full siblings? No, they were not; they had different fathers. Fortunately, several of Maria Jeanette's sons left records that included her maiden name, which was Richardson. Although her son James's 1918 death certificate stated her maiden name as Richards, the death certificates for Maria's sons Joseph and Morris stated it as Richardson. In addition, her son Elbert Jr.'s delayed birth certificate in 1962 also gave his mother's maiden name as Richardson.

Ella Lewis (1885-1950), a granddaughter of Edna, married Willie Coleman in 1905. By 1910, they had five children and lived in Barnwell, South Carolina. Did she marry her first cousin Willie Coleman, son of her Aunt Maria Jeanette? No, Aunt Maria Jeanette's son Willie was born in 1878, whereas Ella's husband Willie was born in 1885 and had always lived in Barnwell. The Coleman surname has long been a popular and prominent one in South Carolina.

1940 Census

By this time, my grandmother Edna was a widow, living with her daughter, Victoria, and her son, Charlie. She owned a house next door to Cousin Laura in Graniteville. Her sister, Aunt Willie Mae, rented a home nearby.

Uncle Joe and his second wife, Emma Hatcher Palmore, owned a brick house in Graniteville that he had built. His son, Cousin Little Joe, was 37 and lived with Cousin Laura in Graniteville. Cousin Katie, her daughter Jeanette, and her son, Arthur, along with his wife, Lucia, their sons, Arthur Jr. and Theodore, lived together in one house in Washington, D.C.

David and Irene Coleman Dudley now had five children: daughter Barbara and sons David Jr., Elbert, Julius, and Jerome. Irene's sister, Nellie Coleman (37), lived with them. Irene and Nellie's mother, Anna Blalock Coleman, had died in August of 1932.

After this point, many of my ancestors seem to disappear with no records of their deaths, while others demonstrate surprising longevity, like my 4TH great-grandmother Nelly.

Edna's great-granddaughter Irene Coleman Dudley lived ninety-three years and had even survived most of her children. I could not find any record of Irene's sister, Nellie Coleman.

Aunt Beanie's only daughter, Cousin Laura Glover Vanderhorst (1865-1958), my first cousin three times removed, never had children. She was the first of her generation in my maternal line to be born free and was the first woman in my direct maternal line to never conceive any children. After a long line of my maternal ancestors, used as breeders, bearing many children, subsequent childbearing in my line slowed to a trickle. During a visit south around 1955, I remember Cousin Laura crying over my sister and me, as she hugged us to her and said, "Lord, Lord you've allowed me to live long enough to see Edna's grandchildren." I feel honored to have met my most distant living maternal ancestor.

Towards the end of Cousin Laura's long life, my great-aunt Willie Mae served as her caregiver. Then, when the time came, my mother and I served as Aunt Willie Mae's caregivers. Both Cousin Laura and Aunt Willie Mae lived long lives, past 90 years, like their foremothers Nelly, Nancy Edna, and Irene Coleman Dudley.

In 1976, Cousin Katie's daughter, Jeanette Fair Jeter (and who was also my godmother) died. My mother and I attended her funeral in Washington, D.C. At the time, her husband gave me a small plant. That plant, which I have divided several times for family and friends, now stands four feet tall. However, the strangest thing occurred around the time my mother died — that plant bloomed for the first and only time. It had beautiful, delicate, and fragrant flowers that looked like lilies of the valley. My mother and Cousin Jeanette were like sisters.

My mother often shared with us things she had experienced in South Carolina. One remarkable yet unsettling occurrence involving her mother has always fascinated me. My grandmother Edna died on 8 December 1945 of congestive heart failure. Three months before her death, her doctor advised her to lose some weight, warning her that otherwise she would not live too much longer. Due to the many sorrows she endured including a father-in-law who was lynched, it was a battle she did not overcome. About thirty days before my grandmother's death, my mother was in South Carolina on a visit and heard a loud boom that seemed to come from the center of the house. She ran to her mother, who was in the kitchen, and asked her what had caused the noise. My grandmother calmly told her, "the mothers will be here for me soon." Within the month, she was gone.

FROM NELLY TO NYJA'S BIRTH: 171 YEARS

It seemed like paranormal activity often surrounded my mother, but it was in the realm of precognitive dreams that my mother was really remarkable. My sister and I also possess this ability to some degree. I've experienced several dreams warning of impending deaths in my family or a deep "knowing" of a transition of those I've been close to: my daughter, mother, and father. The dreams usually come in threes, each giving me a little more information. Beforehand, I know something is getting ready to happen, but I can't exactly say when it will happen. After the death happens, however, my hindsight is so clear, and I can see that everything shown in the dreams has occurred.

My maternal line has shown patterns of resilience. They have endured great loss through deaths: mothers burying children and husbands. The auction block and the great shame of breeding during slavery did not deaden their talents or survival skills. There were women who were fabulous cooks, like Isabella and my grandmother Edna. Cousin Laura was a boarding house owner, most were domestics and laundresses, and many of my female ancestors who were heads of households were able to support themselves and their families. My grandmother Edna taught herself how to play the piano and make her own clothes.

My direct maternal bloodline can now be documented from my 4TH great-grandmother, Nelly, born about 1799, to my niece Nyja, born in 1970. It is also the end of my direct maternal line, since my niece had a son. Although her son inherits his mother's mitochondria DNA, it will not pass to any future daughter he sires.

I've had my DNA tested with three companies: FamilyTree DNA, 23andMe, and AncestryDNA. Was there any truth to the rumors of the first Edna being mixed with European and Native American ancestry? Yes! My initial admixture showed 77% sub-Saharan African, 18% European, and 5% Native American/Asian. I remember Great Aunt Willie Mae telling me how we, my siblings and I, came from beautiful-looking people, and I have seen older maternal relatives who were obviously of mixed races.

In August of 2015, I noticed that the picture of my great-grandmother Victoria was attached to another person's Ancestry.com tree, an "extended" version. When I reviewed the tree, I saw only white people with the exception of one mixed-raced-looking woman. I contacted the tree's manager. On 2 September 2015, he wrote:

> Edna,
>
> My late wife…has family roots on her side in Saluda, S.C. My knowledge is limited based a bit on family lore, but mainly on research…I'm not sure where your line and my wife's cross, but it seems that there is a connection or two

there. I've heard it said that most of Saluda and Newberry Counties are related. Hope this puts you on the trail.

Edgefield County was a vast area that once included a part of Saluda. The path that this Ancestry user has led me to requires further research. The one thing that is undeniable, however, is that my DNA results reflect my Edgefield County heritage. I have a large number of prominent Edgefield County surnames as matches from the three DNA sites. They include: Adams, Bettis, Bing, Black, Blalock, Blocker, Boatwright, Brooks, Burris, Bush, Butler, Cartledge, Coates, Coleman, Cook, Davis, Glover, Hamilton, Hammond, Hampton, Harris, Jackson, Jones, Lewis, Manning, Medlock, Merchant, Nicholson, Norris, Ouzts, Palmore, Powell, Reed, Richardson, Simpkins and Simkins (both Palmore and Bush lines), Smith, Stevens, Timmerman, Walker, Ward, Washington, Watson, Weaver, West, Williams, Wright, and Young.

My most interesting DNA results show matches all over the African continent in every direction and even in Madagascar. I didn't give the Madagascar matches too much thought until I received the following e-mail that opens up another area to research:

> Hi Edna, …When I first saw your match with my mom's at the 5th-6th generational line…I was interested because of the Hammond shared surname and where that Hammond, at one point, sat on your tree…My oldest known maternal ancestor was a Darcas Hammond born about 1780 to allegedly a Charles Hammond…When I first went through your tree… South Carolina threw me for a loop…however, afterwards I had extensive MTDNA testing done, which brought my maternal DNA data within a genealogical time period that I could research. I know that Darcas Hammond was a B4a1a1a2…,which is known as the Polynesian Motiff to Malagasy Motiff. How this B4 line made its way into Colonial America is a subject of a lot of current research.

Madagascar was not part of the mid-Atlantic slave trade… however there were a handful of pirated Malagasy slaves brought to America…I decided to go back to your tree and spend some time looking more closely at your Ged-matches…because your Hammond and South Carolina keeps creeping into association with some other maternal matches of mine. I came across one of your matches which did not surprise me…(it) only confirmed that I have been on the right track in regards to your ancestry and mine…you have a match at the 6th/7th generational line with a CJ… (who) is related to me as one of the 14 B4/Malagasy Motiffs and we share the same Malagasy grandmother ancestor at the 7th generational line, which would be the mother or grandmother of my Darcas Hammond…You actually share matches with pretty much all the B4s…There is a match on your Gedmatch with a Y-G who also matches CJ…when I looked into her research…she was hunting down Burton slaves, believing her ancestry to be wrapped into a slave sell with a Burton family.

TABLE 4. DNA TESTING TERMINOLOGY

MTDNA – mitochondrial DNA, maternally inherited

HAPLOGROUP – a genetic population group of people who share a common ancestor; B4alala2 is an example.

AUTOSOMAL DNA – describes DNA which is inherited from both parents' chromosomes

FULL GENOME SEQUENCING – a laboratory process that reveals the complete DNA make-up of an organism.

GEDMATCH – a free non-profit utility website; DNA testers can upload DNA test results from DNA testing sites to compare with a large existing database of test results.

This e-mail encourages me to continue researching, because the full truth of my maternal ancestors will probably take me beyond Nelly. There is so much to look into, but it seems like I have genealogical angels helping to guide me to the truth. A sad fact is that I, as is the case with many researchers, am still finding relatives because of what happened during slavery!

When I turned 50 years old, I remember thinking that I had reached the age that bridged the former generations to the younger generations. I remember the older relatives—my grandparents and great-grandparents' generations—and have lived to see the great-grandchildren of my parents. There is a responsibility that those in the position of the bridge generation pass on family history to the children and grandchildren. Many in my generation with southern ancestry remember using a one or two-seater outhouse or seeing a chicken or hog killed for immediate or future sustenance. Visiting Graniteville, South Carolina, in the 1950s and 60s, the atmosphere always had the smoky odor of burning wood because many were still connected to the past, living without centralized heat. I believe it is important that the children in each family know something of the people from whom they came. They should know how they connect, know the patterns that often repeat, and even know the bad along with the good—the successes and the poor choices. They need to know the price that was paid and how the way was paved, by many prayers, for them to live in freedom. I have been able to document eight generations from Nelly Burton Timmerman Hamilton to Nancy Edna Burton Coleman Hamilton Hammond, and onwards to Annis Coleman Palmore Barney Stewart, Victoria Palmore Harris Croft, Edna Harris Medlock, Victoria Medlock Bush, and, finally, to me, Edna Gail Bush, my late daughter, Stacey Jeanette Bush-Little, and my sister Brenda and her daughter, Nyja. The year 2016 marked 217 years since the approximate birth of my 4TH great-grandmother Nelly. My Edgefield County, South Carolina, roots run deep and strong. With much awe, gratitude, and love, I bow in honor of the strong, independent women of my direct maternal line. The first Edna was born in March about 1820, Cousin Edna in Louisiana was born in December of 1894, and my grandma Edna in September of 1895. I was born in March of 1949, the closing of a circle. I am the fourth and last Edna.

FIG. 8. MATERNAL ANCESTORS
TOP RIGHT AND LEFT: GREAT AUNT JEANETTE COLEMAN;
BOTTOM LEFT: EDNA MEDLOCK; BOTTOM RIGHT:
UNKNOWN MATERNAL ANCESTOR. [71]

CHAPTER 3
TRACKING THE FOOTPRINTS OF MY
BLAIR ANCESTORS
Natonne Elaine Kemp

●•••●

Attending a funeral—is it ever easy? My particular anxiety can be traced to the first funeral I remember ever attending, my father's, when I was four years old. He died in August 1971. I don't recall much. I remember wearing a dark-colored, short sleeve dress sprinkled with little lambs. A lot of people were gathered at the church, or was it a funeral home? I sat on my mother's lap. At one point she passed me to someone else. I cried uncontrollably. My mother picked me up and carried me to what looked like a bed. There was daddy. He was sleeping. When would he wake up?

Friends and family have told me my father took me everywhere. Sadly, I do not have a single recollection of any moment I spent with my dad. I imagine, on more than one occasion, I sat on his shoulders, perched high on his 6'3'' frame.[72] I was a daddy's girl. As an adult, I have been described as serious, reserved, or quiet. Who I am today is directly related to my childhood experiences. My world was forever altered by my father's sudden passing. In ways I, as a four-year-old child, could not understand or articulate, my heart was shattered into many pieces incapable of being made whole. A void developed that has never been filled.

I wasn't the only child left without a father. My sister was 1 ½ years old and my brother was six months old when our father, Nathan Kemp, died. Thirty-four years later, a period longer than our father walked this earth, his mother and our paternal grandmother, Nellie Blair Kemp, died in August 2005.

During those intervening thirty-four years I spent very little time with my paternal grandmother, despite living in the same city, the District of Columbia. I knew a handful of my father's relatives, some of his siblings, but otherwise was clueless about my paternal relatives. I thought, if I attended my grandmother's funeral, I would be a stranger, an outsider. I could not reminisce about my grandmother's hugs, her scent, her laugh, her cooking or how she nurtured me. I had no fond memories to share. Ultimately, however, I decided to attend my grandmother's funeral. My sister, Nakesha, accompanied me. Bernice Bennett, a family researcher from Silver Spring, Maryland, met us at Mount Pleasant Baptist Church to attend my grandmother's Homecoming Service.

Bernice and I had met a year earlier, in July 2004, at a Red Lobster restaurant in Silver Spring. We were both researching Kemp ancestors from Edgefield County, South Carolina. We both arrived at the restaurant with identical white binders containing our research notes. We bonded quickly. At that time we believed we were descendants of Andrew and Matilda Kemp, Bernice through a son named Richard and I through a son named James. I was so thrilled to connect with a distant cousin.

A month before my grandmother's passing, however, Bernice began questioning me about James Kemp, wondering if my James Kemp was the son of Andrew Kemp or, perhaps instead, the son of George Kemp. I had conducted my research on this Kemp line in November 2001 by visiting the National Archives and Records Administration, before the ease of researching online. I reviewed my research and confirmed Bernice's suspicions (and subsequently wrote about this misidentification in an article titled "Stumbling Without the 1890 Census").[73] My 2ND great-grandfather, James Kemp, was indeed the son of George Kemp, Sr. and not the son of Andrew Kemp. Andrew and George Sr. were enslaved boys in a household together in Edgefield when an inventory was compiled in December 1844 listing assets sold and distributed.[74]

Were Andrew and George brothers, cousins, or perhaps not related at all? The inventory did not identify the relationships among all of the slaves. Since these slaves were property, the only important issue was their monetary value. The individual compiling the inventory did not even list the ages of Andrew and George. Bernice and I cannot state with any certainty whether our enslaved ancestors were related and thus, in turn, whether we are distant blood relatives. The legacy of slavery, therefore, is still felt today. Despite the uncertainty about our connection, Bernice nevertheless paid her respects and supported me by attending my grandmother's funeral.

During the funeral I fixed my gaze on a beautiful family portrait, likely taken in 1924 or 1925, of my great-grandfather, Clifford Blair, with his daughter Nellie, his son Walter, and his second wife Jannie.

**FIG. 9. PORTRAIT OF BLAIR FAMILY
(CLIFFORD, JANNIE, NELLIE AND WALTER)**[75]
With the express permission of the author

Nellie, born in 1914, was probably 10 or 11 years old. In looking at this portrait, my eyes gravitated to Clifford. Although he was seated, he was the same height as my grandmother, who stood next to him. Clifford wore a three-piece suit with his jacket unbuttoned. He had piercing, dark eyes. His facial expression was somewhat stern, as were the expressions of his children. I suspect they were given precise instructions for the pose, and consequentially, my ancestors don't appear relaxed in this photograph. Nevertheless, there were expressions of love. Nellie and Walter, standing on either side of their father, each had a hand draped over Clifford's hands.

I first laid eyes on this beautiful family portrait a few days before my grandmother's funeral. At a gathering at Aunt Dot's house (where I met many paternal relatives for the first time), someone brought out this portrait. However, I was aware of its existence before I ever saw it. Three and a half years before my grandmother's passing, in January 2002, I spoke with my grandmother's brother, Uncle Archie, to learn more about my Blair ancestors.

When I called Uncle Archie, he agreed to meet me on Friday, 25 January. However, that morning, Uncle Archie called and told me he had an appointment later that day and thus could not meet me. I was disappointed but feigned my understanding. Uncle Archie paused; I sensed he did not want to speak further. Just before I spoke to end the conversation, Uncle Archie broke the silence by revealing he is not a Blair. He is not the son of Clifford Blair. What? I did not expect this!

Now I understood why Uncle Archie seemed hesitant to speak with me. I felt the void of my father's absence as I grew up. Yet I could pull out the photo album, turn the pages and see photos of my dad, my mom, and me, or just of my dad, or of me and my dad. But I cannot imagine growing up believing a specific individual is your father and later being told by your mother that another man is your father. Your whole world is thrown upside down. You are no longer who you thought you were. Perhaps Uncle Archie figured it out himself since he was born in July 1927, more than a year after Clifford Blair died in

January 1926. However he learned the truth, I unknowingly reopened a wound, pouring salt on it. I listened intently as Uncle Archie revealed his true paternity to me.

He then encouraged me to ask my questions. I asked him to tell me as much as he knew about Clifford Blair. He told me Clifford died in Washington, D.C. He also revealed Clifford worked for the railroad and specifically recalled being told Clifford worked at Union Station as a baggage porter. Uncle Archie further recalled Clifford worked for the railroad in South Carolina, then moved to Richmond, Virginia, and ultimately that job brought Clifford and his family to Washington, D.C.

Because Uncle Archie answered my initial inquires, I peppered him with additional ones. What was Clifford's faith and what church did he attend? He believed Clifford was a Baptist, although he did not know which church Clifford attended in the District of Columbia. He remarked Clifford may have been a member of Shady Grove Baptist Church when he lived in South Carolina. His denomination was not a surprise since it was the same faith as my father's family. Although I attended a Baptist church when I was very young, my mother converted to Catholicism and I am a practicing Roman Catholic.

I continued to ask more questions. Where did the Blair family reside in the District of Columbia? Uncle Archie responded they lived in the unit block of E Street. I asked him to describe any distinguishing physical traits of Clifford. He remarked Clifford was over six feet tall. The phrase 'six feet tall' reverberated in my head. Then I recalled my mother telling me my dad was over six feet tall, 6'3".[76] I wondered if my father's height was a Blair trait.

After this momentary distraction I resumed my conversation with Uncle Archie. Because I had heard stories about my grandmother's possible Native American roots, I asked

Uncle Archie if Clifford had any Native American heritage. He replied he believed Clifford descended from Native Americans because he had high cheek bones.

Because Uncle Archie never met Clifford but seemed to know a lot about his physical attributes, I asked if he possessed any photographs of Clifford. Uncle Archie disclosed that, for many years, his mother, Jannie Blair, had kept an oversized family portrait of the Blair family hanging in their home. Besides his mother, the portrait included Clifford with Nellie standing to his right and Walter standing to his left. I was excited to learn of the existence of this portrait. I asked Uncle Archie if I could obtain a copy. He told me he gave the portrait to either Dot or Vivian, two of my father's sisters. I made a mental note to follow up with my aunts. Despite my subsequent inquiries, however, the family portrait remained hidden until shortly before my grandmother's funeral.

At my grandmother's funeral, besides the family portrait of Clifford, Jannie, Nellie, and Walter, a second photograph was on display. I shared this photograph with my father's family, for the second time, days before the funeral. It was a photograph of my grandmother's mother, Sarah Ann Chinn Blair. How did I come into possession of my great-grandmother's photograph?

In July 2001 I began posting messages on Ancestry.com's message boards for various branches of my paternal ancestors. Under the Chinn-Family History & Genealogy Message Board on 11 July 2001, I posted the following message:

> My gg-grandparents, Carter Preston Chinn and Kitty T[] ompkins Chinn, lived and died in Parksville, SC.

> They had several children: Anne, Abraham, Daniel, Edward, John, Joseph and Sarah.

Carter and Kitty were active members of Mt. Lebanon Baptist Church in Parksville. Carter died in 1934 and Kitty in 1958.[77]

On 27 August 2001, I received the following response from another message board participant identified as "msyee581":

Carter Preston Chinn was the son of Preston and Ausley Chinn. I'm sure you've already heard from Sameera Thurmond, who is a descendant of Preston and Ausley. I am also descended from them. I would love to hear from you so we can share information.[78]

I replied that same day:

I didn't have any information about Carter Preston Chinn's parents.

Would love to share information with you.[79]

I was not familiar with Sameera Thurmond, but I learned "msyee581" is Viloria Arttaway[80] of Philadelphia, Pennsylvania. She told me she is a descendant of Preston Chinn through a daughter named Harriet Chinn Thurmond. Viloria and I shared what we knew about our respective ancestors. During one of our conversations in 2002, Viloria mentioned having photographs of several of her ancestors. One of those photographs included a daughter of Carter Chinn. This daughter was identified only as "Babe," because her first name had been forgotten over time. Viloria wondered if this "Babe" might be Sarah Ann Chinn. I told her I would ask one of my aunts.

I turned to Aunt Evangeline, one of my father's sisters. She assisted me in the mid-1990s by sharing as much information about my father's family as she learned from what her mother Nellie could recall. My interest in tracing my paternal ancestors had been sparked by my mother's trip to Abbeville, South Carolina, to trace her maternal roots. I first learned from

Aunt Evangeline that my great-grandfather, Clifford Blair, worked for the railroad. She told me the Blair family lived in the District of Columbia, but, strangely, never mentioned Clifford Blair dying in the District of Columbia. That nugget of information from Uncle Archie was completely unexpected. I learned the importance of speaking with multiple individuals in researching my ancestors.

When I called Aunt Evangeline in 2002, she was living with her mother (my grandmother). I understood from her that my grandmother had some medical issues. There were times when she was lucid and times when she was not. I explained to Aunt Evangeline how a Chinn cousin I met online has a photograph of one of Carter Preston Chinn's daughters. I asked if she knew whether Sarah Ann Chinn was ever known as "Babe." A few days later, Aunt Evangeline returned my call. During a lucid moment my grandmother confirmed her mother was known as "Babe." I thanked Aunt Evangeline and subsequently informed Viloria.

Several days later, I received in the mail a photograph of a man and woman sitting side-by-side, arms touching one another's, dressed formally. The man wore a three-piece suit, and the woman wore a light-colored blouse with a bow and a black skirt. The back of the photograph was labeled "Nebuchadnezzar Thurmond[,] son of Harriet Chinn Thurmond & Babe (First Name Unknown) Chinn[,] Daughter of Carter Chinn." This is the photograph I shared with my father's family and which was on display at my grandmother's funeral. Through these photographs, I felt my grandmother was finally reunited with her parents.

**FIG. 10. PHOTO OF NEBUCHADNEZZAR
THURMOND AND SARAH ANN CHINN**[81]
With the express consent of Viloria Arttaway

Almost 80 years elapsed before this reunion. My grandmother, born 1 January 1914, had lost her mother, sister, and father by the age of 12. First, Sarah Ann Chinn Blair died in approximately December 1916, a couple of months after giving birth to my grandmother's younger sister, Elouise. This date is approximate because, despite South Carolina mandating death certificates beginning in January 1915, I could not find a death certificate for my great-grandmother. I shared my research challenge with Sameera Thurmond,[82] the Chinn descendant Viloria mentioned in her 27 August 2001 message. Sameera and I had subsequently connected. Regarding my great-grandmother's "missing" death certificate, Sameera provided the following insight:

> My guess about the absence of a death certificate for Sarah is that because 1915 was the year in which SC began compiling deaths, civil servants may have done a sloppy job

in the actual recordings (please keep in mind, too, that they were extremely haphazard when it came to Blacks). My great great-grandmother died circa 1927 in Augusta[,] Georgia. Augusta had long been documenting deaths; nonetheless, neither the state [n]or local governments have a record. Additional sloppiness came from the undertakers. If they didn't get around to reporting it . . . well. . . it wasn't recorded. So all kinds of events may have prevented actual recording of the event.[83]

Based on this, I concluded a death certificate was never issued for Sarah Ann.

Less than a year after losing her mother, Nellie lost her little sister, Elouise, on 26 July 1917 in Parksville, Washington Township, McCormick County. The exact date is known because a death certificate[84] was issued in this instance. Elouise was born 1 October 1916. She died due to complication of the bowels. The death certificate identified her parents as Cliff Blair, born in Edgefield, and Sarah Chinn, born in Edgefield. The informant was Elouise's grandfather, Carter Chinn. Reflecting on this latest discovery, I concluded that my grandmother had experienced a similar tragedy to mine: the loss of a parent at a tender age. Sadly, her losses also included a sibling who never reached her first birthday.

In researching my grandmother's family, I searched for any clues to help construct a timeline to fill in the gaps in the absence of any oral history or a family Bible. (I was told a family Bible was lost in a fire in the 1930s and that the event scarred Kittie Tompkins Chinn for the remainder of her life.) One such record which proved to be invaluable was my great-grandfather's World War I Draft Registration Card.[85] He was mistakenly identified as "Clifton" Blair. He registered for the draft on 5 June 1917 in McCormick County. As reported on the registration card, "Clifton" Blair was born in 1894 (the month and day were left blank) in Parksville, South Carolina.

His present occupation was farming. He was employed by W.G. Blackwell of Parksville.

The surname Blackwell was oddly familiar. I began reviewing notebooks, folders, and binders where I had compiled my genealogical research. Ultimately, I found the answer in a letter from Aunt Evangeline from the mid-1990s that contained a reference to a Dr. Blackwell. According to my grandmother, Dr. Blackwell delivered her and her sister and buried their mother Sarah Ann. I wondered if W.G. Blackwell, Clifford's employer, was Dr. Blackwell. A subsequent search on Ancestry.com verified my grandmother's recollection. William G. Blackwell, white male, age 32, was a physician (general practice). He resided in Washington Township, Edgefield County, at the time of the 1910 US Census.[86] Wm. G. Blackwell, white male, age 42, medical doctor (general practitioner) resided in Washington Township, McCormick County at the time of the 1920 U.S. Census.[87] In researching my paternal grandmother's ancestors (the Blair and Tompkins families), I learned they had not physically moved from Edgefield County to McCormick County. Rather, McCormick County was formed in 1916 from parts of Edgefield, Abbeville, and Greenwood Counties.[88]

Continuing my review of my great-grandfather's World War I Draft Registration Card, in response to box 9 — "Have you a father, mother, wife, child under 12, or a sister or brother under 12, solely dependent on you for support?" — "Clifton" Blair answered "2 children." He identified his marital status as single. As to his physical attributes, "Clifton" Blair was tall and of medium build with brown eyes and black hair.

This World War I Draft Registration Card confirmed oral history and vital records. Sarah Ann Chinn Blair died about December 1916. Clifford Blair married Jannie Lou Siegler on 20 December 1918.[89] Thus, Clifford was single (a widower) when he registered for the draft on 5 June 1917. His younger daughter Elouise, born 1 October 1916, was alive at the time he registered for the draft. She died over a month later, on 26 July 1917 as listed on her death certificate. Further, my great-grandfather being described as tall is consistent with Uncle Archie's statement that Clifford Blair was over six feet tall. I never imagined this registration card would be so helpful.

I assumed this World War I Draft Registration Card was the extent of Clifford's association with the military. However, on 25 January 2014, while searching on Ancestry.com for "Clifford Blair" of "McCormick County, South Carolina" for the exact date Clifford was enumerated in the 1920 US Census, I received two new results. (Ancestry.com regularly adds new records to its databases). To my surprise and delight, Clifford Blair surfaced on a database labeled "U.S., Lists of Men Ordered to Local Board for Military Duty, 1917-1918, Select States."

Clifford Blair was supposed to report to Camp Jackson, Columbia, South Carolina, on 24 August 1918. He was among a select group of men to be inducted into military service. Clifford, a farmer, failed to report to Military Authorities. Clifford was not the only person from McCormick County who did not report; four others failed to report.[90] The vast majority of selected men, 16 out of 21, did report. I can only speculate why Clifford failed to report. Maybe he was not notified, or he was too busy harvesting the land in late August. Perhaps he simply forgot.

The Military Authorities didn't forget, however. Apparently, they found Clifford because on 1 September 1918 he was present at Camp Jackson, Columbia, South Carolina, where he was inducted into military service. How did Clifford feel about being inducted into military service? Did he view it as an opportunity to leave South Carolina? Was he apprehensive about fighting in some distant land? Who would take care of his daughter Nellie in his absence? Clifford never had to confront these issues since the Great War ended two months later on 11 November 1918.

Sameera, My Genealogical Guardian Angel

Over the years of researching my Edgefield roots, a helping hand was extended to me on many occasions by my Chinn cousin, Sameera. She visited the South Carolina Department of Archives and History in Columbia and the Edgefield County Archives multiple times. Sameera was my genealogical guardian angel and mentor. In early May 2005, she addressed two sets of envelopes to me. One envelope contained Sameera's handwritten notes copying information directly from the marriage and death registers of individuals bearing my ancestors' surnames. The other envelope contained photocopies of marriage and death certificates. One record was especially priceless: my great-grandparents' marriage license![91] I didn't realize this record existed. On 2 December 1913 in Edgefield, South Carolina, Clifford Blair, age 20, of Parksville married Sarah Chinn, age 18, of Parksville. As excited as I was about having a copy of my great-grandparents' marriage license, my thoughts returned to my grandmother. How did she feel when her father married Jannie? Did she get along with Jannie? I presumed my grandmother was excited with the birth of her half-brother Walter, born 25 January 1919, and heartbroken when another half-brother, Sylvester, died young. Did Sylvester's untimely passing remind Nellie of the mother and sister she no longer had? Was my grandmother anxious when her dad moved the family north?

Employment with the Railroad

I do not know exactly when Clifford grasped the opportunity to work for the railroad other than that it was after he registered for the WWI draft on 5 June 1917 at which time he was still working as a farmer. Apparently, there came a point in his life when Clifford realized his prospects would never improve. Even though slavery had been abolished many years prior, Clifford was, in essence, comparable to the Untouchables of India, resigned to the caste system of Edgefield where blacks, especially those with his darker skin tone, could never rise above sharecropping. Like the famous individuals profiled in Isabel Wilkerson's book, my great-grandfather sought *The Warmth of Other Suns*[92] and a job with the railroad provided that opportunity.

In searching for proof of Clifford's employment with the railroad, I turned to Ancestry.com for assistance. I did not find any record of Clifford working for the railroad in South Carolina. However, when I visited the communities of Parksville and Plum Branch in October 2011, I had visual proof of his opportunity to work for the railroad industry in South Carolina. Railroad tracks dotted the landscape. A search on Google yielded the name of Clifford's probable employer — the Charleston and Western Carolina Railway operated the train lines in this area. Line #1, Augusta, Georgia to Greenwood, South Carolina, stopped in the following locations: SC/NC State Line, Wood Lawn, Meriwether, Clarks Hill, Modoc, Parksville, Plum Branch, Cairo, McCormick, Trickum, Troy, Mill Way, Bradley, Verdery, Inka, and Greenwood.[93] Clifford undoubtedly saw trains arriving and departing from his hometown his entire life, and he ultimately secured a railroad job that carried him north.

From Ancestry.com, I discovered that Uncle Archie was spot on about Clifford living in Richmond, Virginia and the District of Columbia. In 1924, Clifford Blair, colored, was residing at 2209 Bath in Richmond, Virginia. No other Clifford Blair was listed in the Richmond City Directory.[94] His occupation was fireman. This was surprising until I recalled a maternal great-grandfather who also worked for the railroad was listed as a fireman in the Covington, Kentucky City Directory in 1928. Perhaps the fireman position was with the railroad. I searched via Google, and found the answer from the USGen Web Project.

> The fireman's main job was to shovel coal into the firebox of the engine. Early engines burned from 40 to 200 pounds of coal per mile, depending on the quality of the coal and on the engineer. Another job of the Fireman was to keep the cylinders on the drive wheels oiled while the train was underway.[95]

At over six feet tall and of medium build, Clifford Blair definitely had the stature to perform such a labor-intensive, back-breaking job.

I found Clifford Blair, colored, residing at the same address in Richmond, Virginia, in 1925. Once again, no other Clifford Blair was listed in the directory.[96] His occupation was now listed as laborer. In 1926, Clifford Blair was residing in Washington, D.C, at 327 C Street N.W. The directory[97] for the District of Columbia did not identify residents by race, but no other Clifford Blair was listed. His occupation was a porter at Union Station.

Uncle Archie's recollection of Clifford's life was incredibly accurate. Even before substantiating Uncle Archie's recollection about Clifford's places of residence, I was confident when he told me my great-grandfather died in the District of Columbia. When I concluded my conversation with Uncle Archie on 25 January 2002, I visited the Vital Records Division, Department of Health for the District of Columbia. I was thrilled when I finally laid eyes on my great-grandfather's death certificate.[98] He died on 30 January 1926 of pneumonia, and his wife was "Jane" Blair. The unidentified informant did not know the names of Clifford's parents but knew they were born in South Carolina.

My thoughts returned to my grandmother. She had lost her mother, her sister, and now her father. She could not have imagined on her 12th birthday that her father would be dead 29 days later. What's next for Nellie? Would she remain in the District of Columbia with her stepmother and half-brother, Walter? Uncle Archie answered those questions for me. He understood from his mother that after he (Uncle Archie) was born in July 1927, she sent Nellie back to South Carolina. I asked Uncle Archie where in South Carolina and to which family Nellie had been sent, but he did not know.

NELLIE RETURNS TO SOUTH CAROLINA

About two months after this conversation with Uncle Archie, I spoke with Aunt Evangeline. I inquired if she knew what happened to her mother after Jannie Blair sent her mother back to South Carolina. Aunt Evangeline told me that her mother had lived with her grandmother, Kittie Tompkins Chinn. This made sense as my grandmother knew a great deal about her maternal grandparents. Once the 1930 US Census was released, I confirmed where Nellie resided. In 1930, Nellie Blair (15) was living with her maternal grandparents, Carter (67) and Katie T. (64), along with Ben F. Williams (15).[99] Initially, I had difficulty locating my Chinn ancestors, because the transcriber for Ancestry.com interpreted the last name as "Chive."

In researching my grandmother's ancestors, I repeatedly came across the Chinns and the Tompkins, Nellie's *maternal* grandparents. I even connected with two Chinn descendants.

Where were the Blairs, Nellie's *paternal* ancestors? I was determined to find them.

TRACING BLAIR ANCESTORS
THROUGH THE FEDERAL CENSUS

My first step was consulting Aunt Evangeline's notes from the mid-1990s. I reviewed all of this information on the Blairs. My great-grandfather had many siblings. They were Jessie Jones, Sally Jones, Anna Williams, Maggie Young, Elouise Lanham, John Blair, Jim Blair, Frank Blair, Frances Blair, and Jesper Blair. My aunt's notes did not include the names of the parents, however, and the names of Clifford's parents were not listed on his death certificate. Clifford died before the 1930 US Census. To learn the names of his parents, I had to begin with the most recent census when Clifford Blair was alive—the 1920 US Census.

In 1920, I found Clifford Blair (22) living in Edgefield, McCormick County with wife "Genie" (20), daughter Nellie (6), son Walter (4 months[100]), and father Nathaniel (65).[101] I was thrilled to finally learn the name of my 2ND great-grandfather. Nathaniel was listed as a widower in 1920, and the race of each member of this household was black.

A more detailed examination of this census record reveals that Clifford's occupation was farming, his employment field was "own account," and he rented his home. Clifford was able to read and write, as could his wife and father. Neither Clifford's wife nor father worked outside the home. I was pleased to see that Nellie, age 6, attended school. She was fortunate—statewide statistics show that only 48.6% of six-year-old Negro children attended school in 1920.[102]

It is hard, in a vacuum, to assess and understand my ancestors' lives in 1920, so I sought information for additional
insight. Clifford and his family lived in a majority Negro
county. In 1920, the total population of McCormick County
was 16,444 individuals.[103] Of that total, 11,268[104] of those
individuals were Negroes, making up 68.5% of McCormick
County's population. Native-born whites were 31.4% of the
population (5,167 individuals[105]), and only nine foreign-born
whites[106] (or .01%) resided in McCormick County.

In 1920, there were 3,334 homes[107] in McCormick County.
The vast majority of those homes—2,341[108] or 70.2%—were
rented. A further 818 homes[109] (24.5%) were owned, and the
remaining number were of unknown tenure.[110]

My Blair ancestors lived in the second smallest township
in McCormick County. The population of Edgefield Township totaled 1,375.[111] The smallest township, Indian Hill, had
a population of 732. The other townships were: (a) Bordeaux,
including McCormick town (4,041); (b) East Greenwood (1,462);
(c) Mount Carmel, including Mount Carmel and Willington
towns (3,726); (d) Plum Branch, including Plum Branch town
(1,849); (e) Washington, including Modoc and Parksville towns
(1,842); and (f) West Greenwood (1,417).[112] I was clueless about
the precise location of Edgefield Township. Initially, I could
not find a map to help orient me. No historical McCormick
County map (with names of individuals and places like Edgefield and Greenwood) was available through the Tompkins
Library (Old Edgefield District Genealogical Society). Ultimately, I contacted the South Carolina Department of Archives
and History and learned of a 1918 map of McCormick County
that includes Edgefield Township.

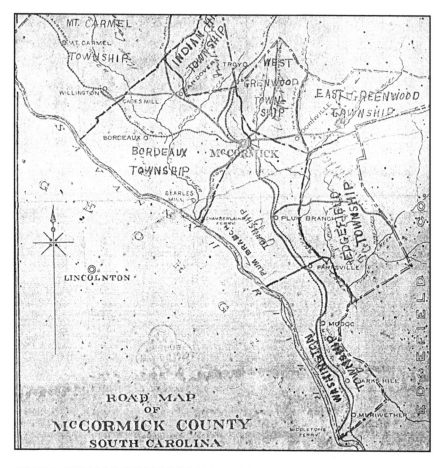

MAP 2. 1918 MAP OF MCCORMICK COUNTY, SOUTH CAROLINA
Courtesy of the South Carolina Department of Archives and History

I was relieved that both Clifford and his father Nathaniel could read and write. In 1920 in McCormick County, the illiteracy rate of males 21 years of age and over was 28.7% (53 Native whites and 979 Negroes).[113] At the macro or state level, the illiteracy rates were alarmingly high, particularly for men in Nathaniel's age bracket. For Negro men, age 65 years and over, the illiteracy rate was 66.9%.[114] It is amazing that Nathaniel was literate. The illiteracy rates among females were worse. For Negro women age 65 years and older, 81.2 %[115] were illiterate!

I returned to the task of tracing my Blair ancestors via the census. In 1910, the Blair family, with Nathaniel (58) as the head of the household, was residing in Plum Branch, Edgefield County.[116] The shift in counties between 1910 and 1920 was due to the formation of McCormick County in 1916,[117] rather than a physical move on the part of the family. Nathaniel's wife was listed as Lucy (50)—I now had the name of Clifford's mother. I am certain she is Clifford's mother, since Nathaniel and Lucy had been married for 35 years (which means they were married in 1875). Five children were living in the household with Nathaniel and Lucy: Anna (25), Walter (21), "Clifus" (15), Maggie (17), and Ella (13). Anna and Maggie were two of the sisters listed in Aunt Evangeline's notes, though her notes omitted Walter as a sibling. I assumed Clifford named his son Walter after his older brother.

There were three pieces of information that caught my eye upon reviewing the 1910 US Census. First, my 2ND great-grandmother Lucy gave birth to sixteen children but only 12 were alive at that time. I reread Aunt Evangeline's notes. Including my great-grandfather, I had the names of 11 of the 16 children. Walter was not on the list, so if I included him I had the names of 12 children. I hoped the names of the other four children would be revealed by other censuses. Second, the race of each member of the household was listed as mulatto. This description threw me for a loop. I have seen Clifford Blair's portrait, and he does not appear to be mulatto.

As I reflected upon Clifford's racial classification, I began to realize that I shouldn't jump to conclusions. My understanding of the word "mulatto" is an individual of mixed heritage (such as one black parent and one white parent). I know from my own family history that skin tone is not always a true indicator of one's racial heritage. For instance, my mother and her full-blooded sister have different skin tones. My mother bears the dark skin tone of their mother; her sister bears the lighter skin tone of their father. Neither daughter's skin tone is a blend of the parents' different hues. Maybe this was the case with Clifford. I do not know if Clifford and his family members received the designation of mulatto because the census taker assumed, based on his visual perceptions, that the Blairs were clearly a mixture of a black and white. Another possibility is the knowledge of the census taker. Local individuals, typically local white males, were selected to handle the task of going door-to-door to collect information for the census. It is possible the census taker knew who "sired" Nathaniel and who "sired" Lucy and that personal knowledge is reflected in the mulatto designation. A third possibility is error by the census taker, and a fourth possibility is that the census taker never actually visited the Blair home and obtained incorrect information from a neighbor. There are too many variables for me to determine why the Blairs were designated as mulatto in the 1910 US Census.

The third matter that grabbed my attention was the issue of literacy. All five Blair children could read and write, but sadly, at that time, neither Nathaniel nor Lucy could. When did Nathaniel learn to read and write? Who taught him? Was Lucy literate before she died? What was the state of literacy among South Carolinians, and especially the black population, in 1910? A *Report of Supervisor of Schools for Adult Illiterates and Night Schools*, authored by Wil Lou Gray, the Supervisor of Adult Schools for the 1918-1919 scholastic year, provides a shameful breakdown.

ILLITERACY IN SOUTH CAROLINA.

The census of 1910 gives the following figures:

Total population in South Carolina   1,515,400

Illiterates (10 years and over)   25% or 276,980
White illiterates (10 years and over)   10.3% or 50,245
Negro illiterates (10 years and over)   38.7% or 226,242[118]

Twenty-three counties registered over 25 per cent. illiteracy: Barnwell, Beaufort, Berkeley, Calhoun, Chester, Chesterfield, Clarendon, Colleton, Darlington, Dillon, Dorchester, Edgefield, Fairfield, Georgetown, Hampton, Kershaw, Lancaster, Laurens, Lee, Marlboro, Union, Williamsburg, York.[119]

Should I be surprised that Edgefield had a high illiteracy rate? The report further discusses the real source of these embarrassing numbers:

THE PROBLEM

The problem in the elimination of illiteracy is largely a negro question. Of the 276,980 illiterates, 226,242 are negroes. The younger generation is taking advantage of their educational opportunities, meager though they are, but what shall be done with this adult group which comprises about one-fifth of the State's population, ten years of age and over, not a member of which can read the Bible or the papers, study the laws which govern him and which protect health, keep accounts, write a letter, or follow a written or printed direction? This whole-sale ignorance has been and is the State's chief burden, for it means a low salary wage which forces a low standard of living, not only for the negroes, but for whites who are compelled to compete with them for a living.[120]

The Civil War had ended in 1865, more than 50 years prior. Could no one appreciate the economic and social consequences of a sizeable population of illiterate individuals? The illiteracy problem among Negroes was a direct legacy of slavery. South Carolina, like other Southern States, forbade educating the enslaved population. And apparently, no concerted effort was made to tackle this problem after the end of the Civil War.

I wish I could determine how Nathaniel became literate between 1910 and 1920. Perhaps he learned how to read and write from his children, or, presuming he attended church, maybe the church had a program to help especially its older members become literate. Maybe the State of South Carolina provided funding to help eliminate illiteracy among the Negro population. Regardless of how it was achieved, I am proud that Nathaniel learned to read and write, and I am in awe of his determination.

Ten years earlier, in 1900, Nathaniel Blair (49), Lucy (45), James (16), Anna (14), Walter (12), Katie (8), Missie (8), Maggie (6), Clifford (5), and Eller (3) were residing in Plum Branch, Edgefield County.[121] At this point, Lucy had given birth to 10 children and all ten were alive. I quickly realized that the twins—Katie and Missie—were not part of the household in 1910, and I assumed they were two of the four deceased children. I also noticed the physical description of every member of the household was black. Why the shift from black to mulatto and back to black? I cannot begin to explain why the race of my ancestors changed from one census to the next.

The 1900 census confirms that both Nathaniel and Lucy were illiterate. The two youngest children, Clifford and Eller, could not read nor write, but their illiteracy is due to non-enrollment in school thanks to their tender ages. Their older siblings, however, could read and write.

I was surprised to learn that Nathaniel and Lucy reported being married for 32 years. If this was true, they would have married in approximately 1868. There is a difference of seven years between the approximate year of marriage per the 1910 census (1875) and the 1900 census (1868). As I continue researching the Blair line backwards in time, I hope to learn which date is more accurate.

The most frustrating part when researching one's ancestors chronologically backwards via the federal census is "the black hole", that void between the 1900 and the 1880 US Censuses due to the destruction of the vast majority of the 1890 US Census. Most of the 1890 census was lost in 1921 due to a fire at a building which housed the records combined with water damage from efforts to combat the fire. The less than one percent of the 1890 census remaining does not include any records from South Carolina. The difficulty caused by the destroyed 1890 census is compounded by South Carolina's lack of vital records (birth, marriage and death) during the 20 year gap between the 1880 and 1900 censuses.[122]

What would the 1890 census have revealed? For me, a researcher of African descent, the 1890 census was unique. With regard to an individual's race or color, this census listed the categories of black, mulatto, quadroon (one-fourth black) or octoroon (one-eighth black). Census enumerators were given precise instructions:

> Be particularly careful to distinguish between blacks, mulat-
> toes, quadroons, and octoroon. The word "black" should
> be used to describe those persons who have three fourths
> or more black blood; "mulatto," those persons who have
> from three-eighths to five-eighths black blood; "quadroon,"
> those persons who have one-fourth black blood; and "octo-
> roon," those persons who have one-eighth or any trace of
> black blood.[123]

This definition may explain why the classification of my Blair ancestors vacillated between black and mulatto. Returning to the 1890 census, why was the issue of the percentage of black blood so important 35 years after the Civil War ended? In "Racial Reorganization and the United States Census 1850-1930: Mulattoes, Half-Breeds, Mixed Parentage, Hindooes, and the Mexican Race," Jennifer L. Hochschild and Brenna M. Powell outline the genesis of the race or color classifications for the 1890 census.

> Rep. Joseph Wheeler (D-AL) proposed in 1888 that data be collected "to ascertain and exhibit the physical effects upon offspring resulting from the amalgamation of human species." The census should therefore "publish the birth rate and death rate among pure whites, and among negroes, Chinamen, Indians, and half-breeds or hybrids of any description or character . . . as well as mulattoes, quadroons, and octoroons." Congressional records say nothing of Wheeler's purpose. However, Carroll Wright, the Commissioner of Labor and acting census superintendent in the late 1880s, supported the inquiry, arguing that "whether the mulattoes, quadroons, and octoroons are disappearing and the race becoming more purely Negro, is a question which can not be settled by observation. It must be settled by statistics, and the sooner the statistics are collected the better." Neither house of Congress discussed the addition, merely noting this addition would be "inexpensive" and was "desired by the scientists."[124]

Although the race classification of my Blair ancestors shifted from census to census, the racial classification of my Tompkins ancestors was consistently mulatto. With the 1890 census, I wondered if their classification would have been quadroon or even octoroon. I will never know the answer. So much happened in that 20 year gap—births, marriages, deaths, and relocations—I know I'm not the only researcher miffed about the destroyed records. To continue my search of my Blair ancestors, I had to leap backwards 20 years to find them.

In 1880, Nathaniel (36) and Lucy (34) were residing in Talbert Township, Edgefield County.[125] There were five children in the household: Josephine (12), John (8), Sallie (4), Jasper (3), and Henry (3 months[126]). Henry's name, however, was crossed out. I discovered Henry died that same year and was listed on the 1880 Mortality Schedule.[127] I realized that, by 1900, Henry had been forgotten because that census reported Lucy gave birth to ten children and all ten were alive. Did Lucy give birth to other children who died very young? Returning my attention to the 1880 census, I noticed that Nathaniel was identified as mulatto. All other members of the household, however, were identified as black.

As in the 1910 and 1900 censuses, neither Nathaniel nor Lucy could read or write. Their daughter Josephine, however, could. The 1880 census did not ask about the years of marriage of the husband and wife, but Josephine's age was listed as 12, which means she would have been born about 1868, the same year her parents married per the 1900 census.

Lastly, on the day of the enumeration for the census, Nathaniel was sick or temporarily disabled and thus was unable to attend to his normal work duties. His condition was identified as "Neuralgia." Interestingly, Lucy is labeled as "Neuralgia guide." Neuralgia is a disease of the nervous system.[128]

Additionally, Nathaniel Blair was listed on the US Agriculture Schedule in 1880 for Talbert Township, Edgefield County.[129] In reviewing this document, I learned Nathaniel did not own the land he tilled. His tenure was identified as "rents for fixed money rental." His farming implements and machinery were valued at $5, his livestock was valued at $10, the cost of building and repairing in 1879 was $10, and the cost of fertilizers purchased in 1879 was $5. The estimated value of all farm products (sold, consumed, or on hand) for 1879 was $125. It is hard to appreciate the historical value of money. Luckily, a calculator available on the website Measuring Worth[130] helps in assessing value.

TABLE 5. CONVERSION OF VALUES FOUND ON 1880 AGRICULTURAL SCHEDULE

COMMODITY OR LABOR	1879	2014[131]
(a) Farming Implements & Machinery (b) Fertilizer	$5	$122 (real price) $845 (labor value-unskilled wage) $1,420 (income value)
(a) Livestock (b) Building & Repairing	$10	$245 (real price) $1,690 (labor value-unskilled wage) $2,830 (income value)
All Farm Products	$125	$3,060 (real price) $21,100 (labor value-unskilled wage) $35,400 (income value)

As listed on the Agriculture Schedule, the third tenure, after "owner" and "rents for fixed money rental" is "rents for shares of products." This category appears to be sharecropping. The American Heritage New Dictionary of Cultural Literacy defines sharecropping as:

> A system of farming that developed in the South after the Civil War, when landowners, many of whom had formerly held slaves, lacked the cash to pay wages to farm laborers, many of whom were former slaves. The system called for dividing the crop into three shares — one for the landowner, one for the worker, and one for whoever provided seeds, fertilizer, and farm equipment."[132]

The American Heritage Dictionary of the English Language defines a sharecropper as "[a] tenant farmer who gives a share of the crops raised to the landlord in lieu of rent."[133]

According to the 1880 US Agriculture Schedule, Nathaniel was not receiving a share of products and was receiving a fixed money rental. It appears my 2ND great-grandfather was not the "classic" sharecropper. Was there a real difference between a tenant who received fixed money rental and a tenant who received a share of the crops? I found an answer to this question from the Learn NC: North Carolina Digital History website, which has an article titled "Sharecropping and Tenant Farming."

> After the Civil War, thousands of former slaves and white farmers forced off their land by the bad economy lacked the money to purchase the farmland, seeds, livestock, and equipment they needed to begin farming. Former planters were so deeply in debt that they could not hire workers. They needed workers who would not have to be paid until they harvested a crop — usually one of the two labor-intensive cash crops that still promised to make money: cotton or tobacco. Many of the landowners divided their lands into smaller plots and turned to a tenant system. During the Gilded Age many African Americans and whites lacked money to buy farmland and farm supplies. They became tenant farmers and sharecroppers.
>
> Tenant farmers usually paid the landowner rent for farmland and a house. They owned the crops they planted and made their own decisions about them. After harvesting the crop, the tenant sold and received income from it. From that income, he paid the landowner the amount of rent owed.
>
> Sharecroppers seldom owned anything. Instead, they borrowed practically everything — not only the land and a house but also supplies, draft animals, tools, equipment, and seeds. The sharecropper contributed his, and his fam-

ily's, labor. Sharecroppers had no control over which crops were planted or how they were sold. After harvesting the crop, the landowner sold it and applied its income toward settling the sharecropper's account. Most tenant farmers and sharecroppers bought everything they needed on credit from local merchants, hoping to make enough money at harvest time to pay their debts.

Over the years, low crop yields and unstable crop prices forced more farmers into tenancy. The crop-lien system kept many in an endless cycle of debt and poverty. Between 1880 and 1900, the number of tenants increased from 53,000 to 93,000. By 1890, one in three white farmers and three of four black farmers were either tenants or sharecroppers.[134]

Before reviewing the 1880 US Agriculture Schedule, I assumed Nathaniel Blair was a sharecropper. I learned about the sharecropping system in grade school and high school, but I do not recall any teacher discussing variations in farm tenancy. Although Nathaniel Blair did not own land, I now understand he was a tenant farmer rather than a sharecropper—a more economically viable position on the farm tenancy ladder. I nevertheless suspect life was just as arduous for a tenant farmer such as Nathaniel Blair. As for his landlord, only one person owned land on the page where Nathaniel was listed: a seventy-five-year-old white woman named Susan Chamberlain.

Having completed my review of the 1880 population and non-population schedules, I had one more population schedule to check: the 1870 US Census, the first federal census listing all Americans of African descent by first and last names. I found Nathaniel (21), Lucy (17), and Josephine (1 month[135]) residing in Washington Township, Edgefield County.[136] The last name, as transcribed[137] by Ancestry.com, is "Blore[138]" instead of Blair. Nathaniel was identified as mulatto, while Lucy and Josephine were identified as black. Neither Nathaniel nor Lucy could read or write. The 1870 census does not inquire about the marriage, but based on Josephine's age, I suspect Nathaniel and Lucy married in approximately 1868.

Since my 2ND great-grandfather is listed on the 1880 Agriculture Schedule, I wondered if he was also listed on the 1870 Agriculture Schedule. I reviewed the agriculture schedule for Washington Township, since Nathaniel Blair resided there in 1870. He is not listed. I found only one Blair on the schedule, a man named Columbus Blair.[139] It was not readily apparent whether he was related or connected to Nathaniel Blair.

TURNING TO STATE RECORDS FOR BLAIR ANCESTORS

After locating my Blair ancestors in 1870, other questions swirled in my head, such as the identities of Lucy's and Nathaniel's parents. Fortunately, my genealogical guardian angel, Cousin Sameera, had already provided some assistance. In an e-mail dated 10 February 2002, Sameera stated:

> I was looking at the SC death index the other day and came across some Blair names in McCormick and Edgefield Counties. Might I suggest that you merely file these names away. While these names may not mean anything to you at this juncture, they may come in very handy as you learn more about your family[140]

Sameera listed the names, dates, ages, volumes, and certificate numbers of eight Blairs who died. Included among those eight names was the following:

BLAIR, Lucy

Died 2/12/1915 – age 52

Vol. 6 – certif. #2579[141]

At the time I received the e-mail from Sameera, I did not know the name of Clifford's mother. But once I had identified his mother from the federal census population schedules, I knew Lucy was alive as of 1910 but deceased as of 1920. Could this Lucy be my Lucy?

I subsequently obtained a copy of the death certificate.[142] Based on this Lucy's age (52) at the time of her death, as well as the place of death (Washington Township), this woman appears to be my 2ND great-grandmother. This was just the beginning of my analysis, however.

If Lucy died at age 52 in 1915, that means she was born about 1863. To determine whether that was the true approximate birth year, I again reviewed each US Census record listing Lucy Blair. In 1870, Lucy was 17 years old, meaning she was born approximately 1853, which would be a difference of ten years compared to the death certificate. In 1880, Lucy was 34 years old, meaning she would have been born about 1846. I paused. Mathematics was never my best subject, but I know it is impossible for any individual to double in age in 10 years. I remember that the federal census records are not 100 percent accurate.

I then checked for Lucy's age in 1900. The 20-year gap due to the destroyed 1890 US Census reared its ugly head again. In 1900, Lucy was supposedly 45 years old. That meant that in 20 years, Lucy only aged 11 years (from 34 to 45). Where can I find that fountain of youth! If Lucy was in fact 45 years old in 1900, then her birth year would have been about 1855.

I finally turned to the last census record listing my 2ND great-grandmother. In 1910, Lucy Blair was listed as 50 years old, suggesting she would have aged only five years in a 10-year period. She continued to dip in that fountain of youth. Maybe I inherited some of those great genes because people often think I am younger than my true age. Based on the 1910 US Census, Lucy's birth year would have been about 1860.

I then compared Lucy's approximate birth year based on her age as recorded in each census: (a) 1853 per the 1870 US Census; (b) 1846 per the 1880 US Census; (c) 1855 per the 1900 US Census; (d) 1860 per the 1910 US Census. There is a 14-year gap between Lucy's oldest approximate birth year (1846) and her youngest approximate birth year (1860). Despite this exercise, I could not begin to state, with any authority, Lucy's approximate birth year. However, considering that the 1870 US Census lists Lucy as a young wife and mother with Josephine being only a month old, I feel this record likely comes closest to documenting Lucy's true age.

The death certificate lists other information about the decedent. This Lucy Blair was married and a housewife. This matches what I know of my 2ND great-grandmother. She was born in Georgia. This was unexpected and contrary to every census record listing South Carolina as her place of birth. Because Edgefield is on the border with Georgia though, it is not impossible for Georgia to have been her place of birth.

Frustratingly, the death certificate does not identify the name of her husband or the names and birthplaces of her parents. Years later, I overcame the hurdle of the limited information on Lucy's death certificate. Thanks to my Aunt Evangeline taking notes as her mother talked about the past, I learned the name of Lucy's younger sister. By tracing Lucy's sister, I ultimately discovered the names of their parents (my 3RD great-grandparents), an approach that I described in an article I wrote titled "In Search of the Elusive Maiden Name."[143]

I am confident this death certificate documenting the passing of a Lucy Blair on 12 February 1915 is, in fact, my 2ND great-grandmother. Why? According to Ancestry.com, there were only three Lucy Blairs in Edgefield County between 1870 and 1910. In addition to my 2ND great-grandmother, there was the daughter of Cain Blair, born about 1906, and the daughter of Jimmie Blair, born about 1907 (Jimmie may be the son of Nathaniel and Lucy, but Cain is unfamiliar to me). Luckily, my 2ND great-grandmother was the only Lucy Blair in her age group.

Having exhausted my search for information about Clifford's mother, I next turned my attention to Clifford's father, Nathaniel Blair. His name was not among the eight Blairs whose death certificates were listed in Sameera's e-mail. In 1920, widower Nathaniel was living with Clifford. When did Nathaniel die? I searched for but could not find a death certificate for him in South Carolina. Did Nathaniel accompany Clifford and his family as they moved from South Carolina to Richmond, Virginia and later to the District of Columbia? I searched for Nathaniel's death certificate in the District of Columbia but found nothing. During one of my many trips to the Library of Virginia in Richmond, I searched the death indices for Nathaniel Blair and could not find a record. I assumed Nathaniel died sometime after 1920 in South Carolina but a death certificate was not issued. I was really disappointed. How would I ever learn the names of Nathaniel's parents?

Enslaved Blairs – My Ancestors?

During a visit in November 2010 to the Tompkins Library, home of the Old Edgefield District Genealogical Society, I learned of a forthcoming book concerning slaves in Edgefield County. Based on the description, the book seemed very promising, and I hoped that perhaps I might learn the identities of Nathaniel's parents. After preordering it, the following spring I received in the mail *Slave Records of Edgefield County, South Carolina* by Gloria Ramsey Lucas.[144] This 432-page book lists the names of slaves recorded in estate inventories, appraisals, sales journals, and other public documents from 1785[145] to 1865.

I searched for my Blair ancestors. On page 39, five transactions are listed where slaves were transferred from a Blair owner to a new owner. Three of the transactions occurred on 13 January 1830, well before any of my known Blair ancestors were born.[146] My 2ND great-grandfather Nathaniel was born sometime between 1844 and 1855.[147] The three transactions in 1830 involved a slave owner named Christopher Blair selling (a) Nat, a Negro man, to Sarah Blair, (b) a Negro woman and children named Tilda, Redman, and Hannah to Caleb Talley, and (c) Violet, Edmund, and Cinda, a Negro woman and children, to Sarah Blair. Because I did not know the names of Nathaniel's parents, I had no way of connecting him to these Blair slaves.

In searching for my ancestors, I periodically turned to the Public Member Trees on Ancestry.com. This is where some subscribers post their family trees online. I hoped someone had Nathaniel listed on his or her tree. In July 2012, I searched for Nathaniel Blair of Edgefield County. There was one positive result. Nathaniel Blair was listed as Cain Blair's father. I had no idea who Cain Blair was, but this public member tree identified the 1870 US Census as the source for this information. Upon reviewing that record, I quickly realized this Nathaniel (70, born about 1800) and Cain (18, born 1852) lived in the same township (Washington) and the same post office (Parks Store) as my 2ND great-grandfather. Three other individuals lived in the household with Nathaniel and Cain, including a woman named Violet (56, born about 1814).[148] The names Nathaniel and Violet seemed rather familiar, but why?

As I suddenly recalled, they were listed in Mrs. Lucas's book, *Slave Records of Edgefield County, South Carolina*. I grabbed the book and flipped to the page listing a Blair slave owner.

In 1830, Sarah Blair acquired Nat (a Negro man) and Violet, Edmund, and Cinda (Negro woman and children) from Christopher Blair. I didn't think it was a coincidence that slaves named Nat and Violet were bought by Sarah Blair in 1830 and that in 1870 a couple named Nathaniel and Violet Blair lived in the same township as my 2ND great-grandfather.

Before exploring the possible connections between my 2ND great-grandfather Nathaniel Blair and the elder couple, Nathaniel and Violet Blair, I realized I had seen this elder Nathaniel Blair in the census records a decade earlier. My first true foray into genealogy was visiting the National Archives and Records Administration in Washington, D.C. During one of those early visits, on 30 December 2001, I consulted an *1870 Index for South Carolina* that was alphabetized by surname and listed mainly heads of household. I found Blair, Nathaniel, 70, male, black, born in South Carolina, living in Washington Township, Edgefield. This index entry provided a citation for finding this individual on the reel: series M593, roll 1494, page 163. At the time, I knew the names of my great-grandfather Clifford Blair and his siblings only, not the names of their parents. I was told the Blairs lived in Plum Branch, so Washington Township meant nothing to me at that time. Nevertheless, I recorded the information on this 70-year-old Blair in case I could later find a connection to my Blairs. Sure enough, a decade later, I realized that this elder Nathaniel Blair might be an ancestor.

I searched for Nathaniel and Violet in the 1880 US Census, but I could not find them, so I turned my attention to Cain. Searching the federal census population schedules, I traced Cain from 1880 to 1920. During this period, he lived in the same township as my 2ND great-grandfather or in a neighboring township. I began to suspect my 2ND great-grandfather and Cain were brothers.[149] Because of the significant gap in years between Cain and the elder Nathaniel, as reflected on the 1870 US Census, I presumed the elder Nathaniel was likely the grandfather of my 2ND great-grandfather and Cain. And that would mean the elder Nathaniel would be my 4TH great-grandfather. I had not traced a branch from Edgefield back so far.[150] I wondered if I might ever trace this line back to the continent of Africa.

I subsequently obtained a copy of the record for the Estate of Christopher Blair, which listed the slaves Nat, Violet, Edmund, and Cinda.[151] The harsh reality for Americans of African descent who are attempting to trace their ancestors before the end of the Civil War, is the necessity of having to review documents pertaining to slaveholding families, if their ancestors were not free people of color. A review of Christopher Blair's estate record did not provide any additional information about the four slaves. There was nothing to glean from this estate record about the slaves' parents, places of birth, or when and how Christopher Blair acquired them. Researching enslaved ancestors is not an easy endeavor.

AN UNEXPECTED DISCOVERY

Having reached what I believed was a dead end, I turned my attention to locating any additional information about my 2ND great-grandfather Nathaniel Blair. During a visit to the Edgefield County Archives on 25 October 2011, I decided to peruse tax records for Nathaniel Blair and other Edgefield ancestors. I found my 2ND great-grandfather listed on the Treasurer's Tax Duplicate of Edgefield County (Washington Township) for the tax year 1879.[152] Next to Nathaniel Blair's name were the initials "PC." Edgefield County Archivist Tricia Price Glenn explained that "PC" stood for "person of color." Although this abbreviation was likely viewed favorably by freedmen, who before the Civil War were counted as three-fifths of a person under the United States Constitution, those in power in Edgefield felt otherwise, as reflected in an article from the 7 March 1872 edition of the *Edgefield Advertiser*:

> As for any remaining Sale-day items, we call to mind none of interest save several fierce and loud tugs-of-war that came off towards sun down, between intoxicated "P.C.s." This is an official Radical abbreviation, and stands for Person of Color. So mind, now, that you always say "a P.C." instead of "a negro." Many of the P.Cs. had become deeply "subjudicated" by means of gentle whiskey, and their blood being up, they fought like tigers. It was interesting![153]

Returning to the tax record listing my 2ND great-grandfather, I noticed a column titled "Date of Payment." Nathaniel Blair had not paid his taxes. Nor had another person of color named Nelson Blair whose name was unfamiliar to me. The only other Blair on this tax record, C. L. Blair, who I deduced was white due to the lack of the initials "PC" next to his name, paid one half of his taxes on 8 October 1880. According to this record, C. L. Blair owned a rather substantial 1,200 acres of land. I was very interested to learn more about this individual and any possible connection he might have to my Blair ancestors.

The Treasurer's Tax Duplicate record further revealed C. L. Blair owned personal property valued at $490[154], and owned real estate valued at $2,380[155], for a total value of all taxable property of $2,870. In contrast, my 2ND great-grandfather owned personal property valued at $60 and owned no real estate for a total value of all taxable property of $60. This Treasurer's Tax Duplicate record is in stark contrast to the 1880 US Agricultural Schedule, which reported $155 as the value of Nathaniel Blair's property. Admittedly, the two agencies were comparing apples to oranges.

While I was reviewing the Treasurer's Tax Duplicate records, I provided my mother, Phyllis R. Kemp, a list of my paternal male ancestors, and she began reviewing other books. At some point, my mother began flipping through *Conveyance Book 1887-1894*. She asked me to come to her table because she had found the name of one of my ancestors. My mother pointed to a name, and I declared with excitement, "Nathaniel Blair!" My mother was perplexed because her finger was not next to that name. Looking at the name by her finger, I cried out once more, "McDuffie Thompkins." McDuffie Tompkins was my 3RD great-grandfather, the father of Kittie Tompkins Chinn, the grandfather of Sarah Ann Chinn Blair, and the great grandfather of Nellie Blair.

The record my mother located is found in *Record of Conveyances of Real Property in Edgefield County*. The transaction occurred on 29 November 1886[156] in Washington Township. My ancestors were two of the five grantees. The five individuals were identified as "Deacons of Colored Baptist Church." The name of the church is not listed on the document. With the assistance of Edgefield County Archivist Tricia Price Glenn, we pulled the deed book listing this conveyance of real property from W. R. Parks to the Deacons of Colored Baptist Church. I learned that the Colored Baptist Church in question was Mount Lebanon Baptist Church, a place of worship familiar to me.

In the 1990s, Aunt Evangeline shared with me that Carter Preston Chinn and Kittie "Thompkins" Chinn were active members of Mount Lebanon Baptist Church in Parksville. According to Aunt Evangeline, both were also buried in the church's cemetery. McDuffie Tompkins's association with the church is not surprising, since his daughter Kittie was an active member, but I had no idea that my Blair ancestors were also active members of the same church.

The day before this discovery, on 24 October 2011, my mother and I visited the cemetery at Mount Lebanon Baptist Church, located in Parksville, McCormick County. The weather that day was picture-perfect—with a beautiful blue sky, no clouds in sight, and the temperature neither too hot nor too cold. It was so bright that I cast shadows on the headstones as I took photographs with my camera phone.

As I walked the grounds of the cemetery, I knew I would not find markers for my 2ND great-grandparents Carter Preston Chinn and Kittie Tompkins Chinn. About 10 years prior, I met a man named Claude Gilchrist through an Ancestry.com message board. Claude lived across from the church. I relayed to Claude that my ancestors were members of this church and were buried there. Claude kindly volunteered to walk the grounds of the church. He subsequently told me that he did not find headstones for either Carter or Kittie, even though they died almost 20 years apart. Claude told me, that, unfortunately, they were buried in unmarked graves.

Despite this knowledge, I nonetheless walked the grounds, hoping to find something alluding to my Chinn ancestors. My efforts yielded nothing. I did find several headstones listing Tompkins, and I recognized some of the names, including one of Kittie's brothers. What I did not expect to find among the deceased, however, were Blairs.

I located and photographed four headstones inscribed with the surname Blair: Clarence Blair and Mamie Tompkins Blair; Ulysses Blair and Elizabeth "Ruth" Dorn Blair; Thomas J. Blair; and Ella W. Blair. These individuals were not familiar to me and so I assumed my Blair ancestors were not members of this church.

My mother locating the deed listing the five colored deacons challenged that assumption, however. I sought more information about my Blair ancestors and Mount Lebanon Baptist Church. In January 2014, via a Google search seeking information about "Mount Lebanon Baptist Church" and "Parksville," I received an unexpected result. According to the *Report of State Officers, Board and Committees to the General Assembly of South Carolina*, John J. Briggs and Thos. (probably Thomas) Robertson petitioned for incorporation on behalf of Mount Lebanon Baptist Church. The location of this place of worship was identified as being near Parksville, Edgefield County. The date of the charter was 30 December 1902. The purpose was "[t]o serve and worship God with the rules, faith and creed of the Baptist denomination." Thereafter, the officers, trustees and deacons were listed. The very last individual named was "N. Blair, Deacon, Parksville, S.C."—my 2ND great-grandfather!

Because this information was recorded in a report to the General Assembly of South Carolina, I submitted an online query to the South Carolina Department of Archives and History in Columbia in search of more information about this petition for incorporation and Deacon N. Blair. About two weeks later, I received a letter confirming that the Archives holds six pages relevant to this petition of incorporation. I promptly ordered the document.

When I received and reviewed the six pages, I learned that an attorney named Edwin H. Folk submitted the petition on behalf of the church in a letter addressed to the Honorable M. R. Cooper, the Secretary State, on 29 December 1902. Attached to this letter were the notice of application for charter printed in the weekly newspaper (the *Edgefield Chronicle*),[157] the declaration and petition for charter, and the file number assigned to the declaration and petition filed in the office of the secretary.[158] I was disappointed that this petition did not include any additional information concerning Deacon N. Blair or the number of members or any other nugget of historical information about Mount Lebanon Baptist Church.

Holding a copy of the original declaration and petition for charter, I reviewed the names of all the officers, trustees, and deacons. Of the original five deacons listed on the deed when two acres of land were purchased from W. R. Parks on behalf of Mount Lebanon Baptist Church in 1886, only Nathaniel Blair was still affiliated with the church. I knew from researching my Tompkins line that by 1900 my 3RD great-grandfather McDuffie Tompkins was deceased.[159] Maybe the other three deacons had also passed or left Edgefield and relocated elsewhere.

December 1902 was an important time for this church. Four days prior to the issuance of the charter, the Deacons of Mount Lebanon Baptist Church purchased an additional three acres of land from W. R. Parks.[160] I had learned of this conveyance about three years prior, during another visit to the Edgefield County Archives on 28 December 2011. Unfortunately, this conveyance does not identify the deacons by name, but I know from the 30 December 1902 charter that Nathaniel Blair was still a deacon at the time. Researching my Blair line has been thrilling as I continue to discover facts about my ancestors' lives that no one recalled.

RESEARCHING BEYOND MY DIRECT BLAIR ANCESTORS

As I considered my next move to find additional information, I remembered that my Blair ancestors did not live on a deserted island but within a particular community within Edgefield County. I decided to search for other Blairs in Edgefield, beginning with the 1870 US Census. Perhaps, through researching other Blairs, I might learn more about my ancestors.

I turned once again to Ancestry.com, searching for the name "Blair" in Edgefield. I also searched for "Blore," since my ancestors were identified as such in 1870. The search yielded a grand total of 17 Blairs and Blores—a tiny sum, thankfully. I would be reluctant to use such a strategy for some of my other paternal lines, since, according to Ancestry.com, there were 190 Holloways, 109 Petersons, and 76 Thompkins and Tompkins in Edgefield in 1870. The 17 Blairs and Blores were as follows:

TABLE 6. BLAIRS/BLORES IN EDGEFIELD COUNTY IN 1870

SURNAME	FIRST NAME	AGE	RACE	OCCUPATION	TOWNSHIP
Blair	Martha	35	White	Without occupation	Springfield
Blair	Sarah	78	White	House Keeping	Washington
Blair	Columbus	48	White	Farmer	Washington
Blair	Huldy	37	White	House Keeping	Washington
Blair	Savannah	7	White	At Home	Washington
Blair	Nathaniel	70	Black	Farm Laborer	Washington
Blair	Violet	56	Black	Keeping House	Washington
Blair	Cain	18	Black	Farm Laborer	Washington
Blair	Ellen	53	White	Not occupied	Gregg
Blair	Hampton	20	Black	Farm Laborer	Gregg
Blair	George	28	Black	Farm Laborer	Hammond
Blair	Mariah	24	Black	Keeping House	Hammond
Blair	Milledge	26	Black	Musician	Shaws
Blore	Nathaniel	21	Mulatto	Farm Laborer	Washington

Blore	Lucy	17	Black	Keeping House	Washington
Blore	Josephine	1/12	Black	------------------	Washington
Blore	Julius	17	Black	Farm Laborer	Washington

In reviewing the list of 17 Blairs and Blores, I immediately recognized that the vast majority, 11 of 17, lived in Washington Township. Seven of the those eleven Blairs and Blores were black or mulatto, while the remaining four were white. One of the white Blairs bears a familiar name—Sarah. There was a Sarah Blair listed in the *Slave Records of Edgefield County, South Carolina*. Based on her age, 78-years-old, she appears to be the same Sarah Blair who purchased four slaves (Nat, Violet, Edmund, and Cinda) from the estate of Christopher Blair in 1830. Two of the formerly enslaved individuals, Nat (the elder Nathaniel) and Violet, continued to reside in the same community with the former slave owner.

As I continued reviewing the list of Blairs and Blores, I noted that the four white Blairs —Sarah, Columbus, Huldy, and Savannah— resided in the same household. The name Columbus Blair was familiar. In searching through my notes and papers, I discovered that he was listed on the 1870 Agriculture Schedule. I knew I had seen the name somewhere else as well, but I could not remember where. I decided to consult the *Slave Records of Edgefield County, South Carolina*. I recalled there were other transactions involving the Blairs besides those between Christopher Blair and Sarah Blair. I soon found what I suspected. On 17 November 1846, James M. Blair sold Rachel, a Negro girl, to Columbus Blair for $526. Since both Sarah Blair and Columbus Blair were documented slave owners, I wondered if the black Blairs and Blores in Washington Township, besides the elder Nathaniel and Violet, were formerly enslaved by Sarah or Columbus.

Before pursuing this possibility, I decided to focus on this Columbus Blair. As usual, I turned to Ancestry.com. I searched for Columbus Blair of Edgefield in the federal census. Besides the 1870 US Census, I only found Columbus Blair listed on the 1900 US Census. I wondered why he didn't appear on the 1880 record.

I decided to search the 1880 US Census database for any Blairs living in Edgefield. Upon reviewing the results, I quickly discovered why I could not find Columbus Blair in 1880. He was identified as C. L. Blair (white male, age 54, residing in Washington Township). His wife was identified as H. A. Blair (white female, age 35). The third member of the household was Sarah Blair (white female, age 87) who was, according to the census, C. L. Blair's mother. I made a mental note that Columbus Blair and C. L. Blair were the same individual.

I returned to the list of the 17 Blairs and Blores in 1870 as one nugget of information intrigued me. Milledge Blair, a 26-year-old black male, was a musician. This struck me as a very unusual occupation, since many blacks in 1870 were farm laborers or kept house. Milledge Blair must have been quite the talented musician to escape toiling the land like the majority of Edgefield's blacks after the Civil War.

In reviewing the list of 11 Blairs and Blores in Washington Township, I noted that with the exception of Julius Blore, they lived in groups: Columbus, Huldy, Sarah, and Savannah; Nathaniel, Lucy, and Josephine; Nathaniel, Violet, and Cain. Julius was the only male living in a household with Mariah Price, Dicie Price, Susan Price, and Elizabeth Lockhart. The census taker noted that Mariah and Dicie Price constituted a family, but the remaining three individuals—including Julius Blore—were each distinct and separate families of one. The final observation I made from reviewing the list of Blairs and Blores residing in Washington Township were the ages of Nathaniel Blore (21), Cain Blair (18), and Julius Blore (17). Because of their closeness in age, I wondered if they were brothers or cousins. I hope further research will yield a definitive answer in the future.

Having completed my review of all Blairs and Blores in the 1870 US Census, where else can I turn for additional information about my Blair ancestors? Once again, Cousin Sameera was a guiding light. She compiled and self-published a book titled *Selected Newspaper Articles from the Edgefield Advertiser, Edgefield Chronicle and The Weekly Monitor in South Carolina Relating to African Americans from the Period of September 1833 to May 1900.* [161] I eagerly searched for Blairs in the index and found one Blair, a man named Milledge Blair. I recognized the name from the 1870 US Census. The 2 October 1879 edition of the *Edgefield Advertiser* reported:

ARREST OF A MURDERER

Sam Stewart, the negro who murdered Milledge Blair, colored man, in November 1876, at the store of Mr. Padgett in "Wosley [?] Town" by cutting his throat from ear to ear was arrested in Newberry a few days ago and brought back to Graniteville by Squire Simms and Mr. Blackwell, the jailor at Aiken.

Stewart will be carried to Aiken and placed in jail to await trial. The cause he assigns for the deed is that Blair was a "Democrat nigger." At the time of the murder he said he had killed one Democratic nigger, and was ready to kill another. He thinks he will get clear.

Not surprisingly, most former slaves supported the Republican Party, the party of President Abraham Lincoln. How did Sam Stewart know that Milledge Blair was a "Democrat nigger?" Perhaps Sam Stewart assumed that Milledge Blair was a "Democrat nigger" based on his occupation as a musician, or perhaps Milledge Blair had publicly identified his party affiliation. It is also possible that someone had falsely suggested to Sam Stewart that Milledge Blair was a "Democrat nigger." I sought a newspaper account of the trial. I searched the *Edgefield Advertiser* newspaper which has been digitized and is accessible via the Library of Congress's Chronicling America (Historic American Newspapers) website, but I found nothing. I decided to search for Milledge Blair, but I again found nothing besides the October 1879 article.

Sam Stewart was captured almost three years after the murder. Why didn't the newspaper publish an article about the murder when it occurred in November 1876? What was happening in Edgefield County in November 1876?

The Election of 1876

In searching Google using the terms "Edgefield" and "November 1876," one of the first results immediately answered the latter question. Jerry L. West wrote a book called *The Bloody South Carolina Election of 1876: Wade Hampton III, the Red Shirt Campaign and the End of Reconstruction*. As I recall from my history classes, the election of 1876 was the first presidential election where the presidential candidate who won the popular vote lost the election. Rutherford B. Hayes, the Republican presidential candidate, won the election of 1876 because he won the vote of the Electoral College. Samuel Tilden was the Democratic presidential candidate who won the popular vote but ultimately lost the election. In my grade school and high school, this disputed presidential election was presented from the macro perspective. Now I needed to learn more about what happened at the micro level in Edgefield County.

I learned from an essay by South Carolina historian Henry H. Lesesne that the "Red Shirt Campaign" was to restore the Democratic Party's control of South Carolina. Leading up to the election of 1876, South Carolina was still under the control of the Republican Party, the party many Southerners despised. According to Lesesne, the architect of the "Red Shirt Campaign" was Martin Witherspoon Gary.

> A fervent secessionist, Gary was elected to the state House of Representatives in 1860. After secession he joined Hampton's Legion, beginning his service as an infantry captain. He served until the war's end, participating in every major engagement in which the Legion fought. By May 1864 he had attained the rank of brigadier general and took command of a cavalry brigade in the defense of Richmond. At Appomattox, he refused to surrender. With some two hundred members of his command, he escaped and joined Jefferson Davis and his cabinet at Greensboro, North Carolina. Gary escorted the party as far as his mother's home in Cokesbury[, Abbeville District], where he turned over his command and ended his career as a Confederate soldier.
>
> Gary capitalized on the reputation he earned in war. He resumed his law practice in Edgefield, began cotton planting, and undertook a series of business and speculative ventures. With a volatile temper and prone to spasms of profanity, he was known as the "bald eagle of Edgefield." Active in Democratic Party politics, in 1876 he was the most uncompromising and outspoken leader of the "Straight-out" faction of the South Carolina Democratic Party, stressing white supremacy and solidarity while vigorously opposing any cooperation with Republicans or black Carolinians. He backed Wade Hampton for governor in 1876. Gary's plan for the 1876 campaign, frequently known in South Carolina as the "Edgefield plan" after its chief advocate, pitted race against race and advocated the use of electoral fraud, physical intimidation, and even murder to keep blacks and other Republicans from voting. Gary organized rifle clubs of white Democrats (the "Red Shirts") to put his plan into action. The statewide violence

and disorder that ensued helped tilt the political balance to the Democrats, ensuring the "redemption" of South Carolina after years of Republican rule.[162]

The Hamburg Massacre

Gary's "Edgefield plan" undoubtedly was welcomed by a good number of whites in Edgefield. Perhaps his rhetoric was an underlying spark of the Hamburg Massacre of 8 July 1876, an event I recalled from a contributor to *Homeplace*, the Old Edgefield District African American Genealogical Society's newsletter that I edited from 2011-2013. I found a summary about the Hamburg Massacre from *The New York Times*'s On This Day article by Robert C. Kennedy:

> In 1876, South Carolina was one of the three remaining states that still had federal troops present, and that had not undergone "redemption." The Democratic Party in the state was bitterly divided, and racial tensions were high.
>
> The Democratic "Fusionists" argued for focusing on local and legislative elections since Governor Daniel Chamberlain was likely to be reelected with support from the black Republican majority. The "Straight-Out" Democrats overtly urged that white supremacy (or "redemption") could triumph if each white Democrat prevented at least one black man from voting through intimidation, bribery, or other means. In May, the Democratic State Convention was unable to agree on nominations for state office.
>
> Racial[] animosity was evident in the town of Hamburg, South Carolina, where the majority black residents complained of unfair treatment and the minority whites responded with charges of harassment. On July 4, the town held an Independence Day celebration, commemorating the centennial of the American republic. Members of the local black militia had gathered for a parade when two white farmers ordered them to disperse so their wagon could pass. Heated words were exchanged, but the white men were allowed to continue on their way.

The next day, one of the farmers appeared in the town court demanding the arrest of the black militia captain, who, in turn, denounced the judge for considering the possibility. The captain was ordered to stand trial for contempt of court on July 8, at which time members of the black militia and a group of armed white men congregated in the town. When the black militia refused to disarm, fighting erupted, and the whites brought a cannon and 100 more men from nearby Augusta, Georgia. Under cover of night, the outnumbered black men attempted to flee, resulting in one being killed and twenty-five captured. Early the next morning, five of the captives were murdered in cold blood, and the property of the black townspeople was ransacked. A young white man was killed during the plunder.

Within South Carolina, the incident strengthened the "Straight-Out" faction of the Democratic Party, which nominated Wade Hampton for governor. They were victorious in the fall elections, and South Carolina joined the ranks of the "redeemed" states . . . Seven white men were indicted for the Ham[burg] murders, but the case against them was dropped after the Redeemers assumed office.[163]

The town of Hamburg was unfamiliar to me. In researching my paternal ancestors, I found them living in the townships of Blocker, Collins, Gray, Ryan, Talbert, Washington, and Wise. I thus consulted a map of Edgefield County surveyed by Isaac Boles in 1871. Hamburg was located along the Savannah River, across from Augusta, Georgia. My Blair ancestors resided in a community along the Savannah River, but was a greater distance from Augusta compared to Hamburg.

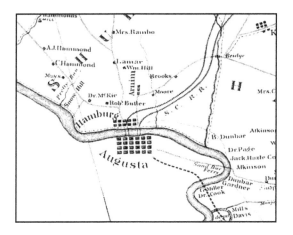

**MAP 3. PORTION OF 1871 MAP OF
EDGEFIELD SHOWING HAMBURG**
Map courtesy of the Tompkins Library, Edgefield, South Carolina

I imagine that the news of the Hamburg Massacre spread quickly among the residents of Edgefield, particularly those communities along the Savannah River. Did my Blair ancestors fear for their future? I wish I knew whether they were determined to fight against white suppression or resigned to whatever might happen. Although this question cannot be answered, I learned the events in Hamburg were discussed in the halls of the United States Congress. On 18 July 1876 Representative Eugene Hale, Republican, of Maine, raised the following during a debate:

> Mr. HALE. Mr. Chairman, this House has been presented this morning a remarkable spectacle . . . The subject-matter before us has been nothing of fancy. It has come up from no desire to "shake the bloody shirt." The gentleman from South Carolina, [Mr. SMALLS, [a Black Republican]] representing a defrauded and murdered race, has offered a practical amendment to the bill before the House, a perfectly germane amendment to a bill which proposes to regulate the movements of the United States Army. The amendment is in these words:

Provided, That no troops for the purposes named in this section shall be withdrawn from the State of South Carolina so long as the militia of that State, peacefully assembled, are assaulted, disarmed, taken prisoners, and then massacred in cold blood by lawless bands of men invading that State from the State of Georgia.

The circumstances calling out this amendment are that at least six men, citizens of the United States, equal citizens with you, sir, and me and the leaders upon the other side; men whom we have undertaken to clothe with all the high privileges and rights that spring from our Constitution and the laws; men whom we have made fellow-citizens with us, have been wantonly and foully murdered. And yet the majority of this House upon a deliberate roll-call have refused to allow sixty minutes debate upon this subject of the slaughter of our fellow-citizens . . . or inquiry into the causes which led to the murder of these six men and for discussion of the means by which we may prevent like occurrences by the presence of the United States armed forces.

The gentleman from Georgia asks why do these things continue to occur! Let me tell him that they will continue just as long as members on that side of the Chamber rise as one man to stamp down the discussion of these atrocities. Let me tell him that so long as the democratic party are led by men in whose neighborhood these scenes are enacted, and who have nothing but good words for the actors in the terrible drama, the raiders and murders in Georgia and South Carolina will go high-handed on their bloody work, and will, as they believe, be protected in it.[164]

Representative Edmund William McGregor Mackey, white Republication of South Carolina, responded, stating in part:

In regard to the Hamburg affair, I think no language too severe can be used in condemnation of it, and I am gratified to see that nearly every democratic paper in the South denounces it. . . .

That particular section of the State where this affair occurred has for years, in my opinion, been a disgrace to the State of South Caro[]lina. Ever since the war that region appears to have been infested with a gang of desperadoes who upon the slightest provocation mur[]der a man with as much coolness as if they were killing a wild boar. Even the murder of white men by white men is not an uncommon occurrence there, and it is looked upon by the rest of the States as the dark corner of South Carolina. The Hamburg massacre is only the outbreak of a lawless spirit which has prevailed in that section for years. It was this spirit of lawlessness and of terrorism which in 1868 at the presidential election actually prevented any polls being opened in Edgefield County, because no republicans could be found to risk their lives to serve as commissioners of elections. It was the only county in the State in which no election was held.[165]

The formerly enslaved residents of Edgefield were denied the first opportunity to exercise the right to vote in 1868. Representative Mackey's comments were supported by the testimony of the following witness on 22 February 1869 for the contested election of S. L. Hoge versus J. P. Reed for the Third Congressional District, South Carolina.

Question. What is your name, residence, and occupation. — Answer. Lawrence Cain. Live at Edgefield Court House. Am a member of the general assembly from that county, and was appointed a commissioner of election for the late general election.

Q. Was there an election for member of Congress held in that County on 3d of November last? If not, why was it not held? — A. Because two of the appointed commissioners refused to serve, for fear that, if they did serve, they would be killed by the democrats, as threats were made against them.

Q. What was the general condition of political affairs in that county during the months of October and November, 1868. — A. Everything was in a very excited condition. Threats of violence were daily made to me. Many of my friends were continually advising me to leave the county, and they were afraid, from the threats, that I would be killed. Daily cases on violence under my observation: republicans being shot and beaten by democrats, of account of their political opinions. This state of things existed throughout the county,

Q. Where were you born and how old are you. — A. In Edgefield county, and have lived there all my life; am 25 years old.

Q. Are you well acquainted throughout the county. — A. Yes. I was one of the registers in that county.

Q. How many registered voters in Edgefield county. — A. At the registration in June, 4,555 colored voters; 2,569 white voters.

Q. How many of the registered voters of that county would have voted the republican ticket, and for Judge Hoge for Congress. — A. At least 5,000. I keep store in Edgefield, and being a representative, persons from every portion of the county come daily to my place for advice, and thus am able to form an accurate opinion of the political views and sentiments of the people of the entire county.[166]

Other comments of Representative Mackey swirled in my head. The citizens of Edgefield County apparently were easily provoked and resorted to violence. A spirit of lawlessness and of terrorism pervaded Edgefield County shortly after the loss of the Civil War. Against this backdrop, my Blair ancestors sought to eke an existence as freed people.

Consulting More Sources for Blairs

The Hamburg Massacre and the results of the 1876 election undoubtedly sent chills down the backs of Edgefield's black residents. I had to set aside my own strong feelings of sadness surrounding those events to resume my search for any Blairs in Edgefield. I turned to *Edgefield County, S.C.: Sifting Through the Ashes of the 1890 Census*. Three Blairs are listed in the index: Sandy Blair, John Blair, and Jake Blair. Sandy Blair is an unfamiliar name—none of Nathaniel and Lucy's children bore this given name—so I turned my attention to John and Jake.

Both are identified as colored individuals who paid the taxable poll for School District No. 28 sometime between 23 June and 27 October 1892. John Blair is also identified on a list of Poll Tax and Personal Property to be Collected for 1895 and is noted as residing in Parksville S.D. Township. I assume "S.D." stood for school district. What is interesting is the comment under the "Notes" column for John Blair, which reads: "left county." This John Blair is also identified on another list as living in Washington Township. The comment under the "Notes" column states: "can't find." Who was this John Blair the tax collector could not locate? Was he perhaps a son of Nathaniel?

My next step was to review Nathaniel Blair's household in 1880. There was a John Blair, age 8, born approximately 1872. Recalling the 1895 tax record noted that John Blair had left the county, I decided to search for a John Blair, born about 1872, in Edgefield County, South Carolina. Among the results was a John Blair (28), living with wife Malinda (27), their two daughters, Lula (12) and Pinkey (10), and a widowed boarder named John Tompkins, (45), all residing in Augusta, Richmond County, Georgia, in 1900. However, this John Blair was born in Georgia, not South Carolina. This individual might not have been Nathaniel's son. Since Edgefield is close to Augusta, it is not impossible for Georgia to be John's place of birth. I reminded myself that Lucy Blair's death certificate stated she was born in Georgia. Further, the presence of a John Tompkins (Tompkins being a familiar Edgefield surname) who was born in South Carolina in this Blair household suggests to me that this John Blair just might be Nathaniel's son.

A closer examination of this census record reveals that John Blair was a laborer for the railroad, much like my great-grandfather Clifford. His wife, Malinda, was a laundress, and John Tompkins was a day laborer. I sought further evidence that this John Blair was the son of Nathaniel Blair and turned to the 1910 US Census. In that year, John W. Blair and his wife Malinda G. Blair were residing in Atlanta, Fulton County, Georgia. John's occupation was a fireman at a cotton mill. I paused when I read this, recalling that Clifford's job as a fireman had involved shoveling coal into the engine. A quick search online confirmed my suspicion that the word "fireman" must have meant something different a century ago: "[A] person who tends or feeds fires: stoker."[167] I assumed that as with Clifford's position with the railroad, being a fireman at a cotton mill required a certain stature and physical strength, traits that allowed both Clifford and John to move from agricultural to industrial work.

According to the 1910 US Census, Malinda continued to work as a laundress. This census states that John Blair and his parents were born in South Carolina, contrary to the 1900 US Census indicating that they were born in Georgia. A review of the 1910 US Census revealed another interesting fact: John, his wife, and his daughters[168] were all identified as mulatto. In contrast, they all were identified as black in 1900. I wondered whether it was a coincidence that Nathaniel Blair and his entire family were identified similarly as mulatto in the 1910 US Census but as black in the 1900 US Census.

My 2ND great-grandfather Nathaniel had another son named Jasper, who was 3 years old in 1880. Searching for Jasper, I discovered another black Blair family in Washington Township. In 1880, a 21-year-old Jake Blair, who was born about 1859, worked as a domestic servant. Jake Blair lived with his brother George Blair (28), his sister-in-law Emma Blair (25), and his nephew John Blair (6).[169] Strangely, I could not find George Blair in 1870, but I did find Jake Blair. He was residing in District 125 of Columbia, Georgia, with his parents, Edward and Emily Blair (both 40), and four younger siblings: Fannie (6), Lennie (4), Elizabeth (3), and William (5 months old).[170] All of these Blairs were listed as having been born in South Carolina. In consulting a map I learned Edgefield County shared a border with Columbia County, so it was reasonable to wonder if these Blairs were related to those in my family.

I finally found Jasper Blair, Nathaniel's son, but not in Edgefield County. At the time of the 1900 US Census, Jasper Blair and his wife, Mary, were residing in Augusta Ward 04, Richmond County, Georgia. Born in September of 1877, Jasper was 22 years old. His occupation was listed as railroad engineer. At the time of the 1910 US Census, Jasper, Mary, and two stepchildren were residing in Bibb County, Georgia. Jasper was a switchman with the steam railroad. It appears that Nathaniel's sons (Clifford, John, and Jasper) all secured employment with the railroad industry.

Neither Jasper's nor John's places of residence were surprising. When I began researching my paternal line from Edgefield County, my search was extremely myopic, focusing on Edgefield and Edgefield only. During those early years, I never looked at a map. I now look back and realize how silly that was. I live in the District of Columbia in a tri-jurisdiction area that includes the Commonwealth of Virginia and the State of Maryland. During my time in the District of Columbia, I have lived very close to Maryland and, at another point, very close to Virginia. In researching my paternal ancestors, I had come to realize it was critical to look at bordering counties and states. Edgefield County, South Carolina, shares a border with Richmond and Columbia Counties, Georgia. The city of Augusta is the closest sizeable city to Edgefield. When I began my quest of tracking my paternal ancestors, I could not have imagined the State of Georgia would be just as important as South Carolina.

A Key Finding From Family Search

Edgefield County, S.C.: Sifting Through the Ashes of the 1890 Census did not provide me any tangible insight into the lives of my Blair ancestors, and I did not know where else to turn. I believed I had exhausted all possible avenues when I learned of a research tool, searching by the names of the parents, on FamilySearch.org. Utilizing this tool, I discovered that two other children of Nathaniel and Lucy Blair had moved to Georgia. Sadly, both of those children died in 1919. In reviewing the death certificate[171] of Francis (Blair) Laster, who died on 4 May 1919 in Worth County, I learned the informant was Walter Blair, presumably Francis's brother. I searched for Walter on FamilySearch.org and found Walter (51) living in Worth County with his wife, Georgia (48), and his son, Nathaniel (23), in the 1940 US Census.[172] In 1930, the individuals residing in the household with Walter (41) were wife Georgia (35), nephew J T Blair (18), nephew Nathaniel Blair (13), and Walter's father, Nathaniel Blair (75).[173] My 2ND great-grandfather was still alive in 1930, which explained why I could not find a death certificate for him in South Carolina, Virginia, or the District of Columbia. He was living in Georgia.

A closer examination of this 1930 census record revealed that Nathaniel could read and write, which was consistent with the 1920 census. Oddly, Georgia is listed as Nathaniel's place of birth and the place of birth of his parents. I don't believe the census taker spoke directly with Nathaniel. Perhaps the census taker assumed Nathaniel and his parents were born in Georgia. I scanned the entire census page that lists Nathaniel Blair. Remarkably, every person on that page was born in

Georgia and every person's father and mother were also born in Georgia. I suspect that the census taker may have taken some short cuts in completing that census return.

Since my 2ND great-grandfather was living with Walter in 1930 but not in 1940, I assumed he died between those years. A quick search on FamilySearch.org confirmed my suspicions. "Nathanel" Blair died on 22 May 1934 in Worth, Georgia.[174] No other information was listed on the transcription. I needed to obtain a copy of his death certificate. Since I assumed Walter was the informant, I hoped he identified his paternal grandparents. If so, I believed I might establish a link between Nathaniel's parents and the slaves Nat and Violet.

Meanwhile, I shared my discovery with Gloria Ramsey Lucas, author and compiler of the *Slave Records of Edgefield County, South Carolina*. The two of us had become friends during my visit to Edgefield in October 2011. When I told her that I had found Nathaniel Blair in Worth, Georgia, in 1930 and that he had died there in 1934, she responded, "Why in the heck did he move all the way down there?" Mrs. Lucas then remarked, "It's close to Florida."

I had failed to consult a map showing the location of Worth County. I assumed Worth County was nearby Edgefield. I couldn't begin to answer her question. My only response was that two of the children had relocated to that county. I began pondering what had attracted these Blair ancestors to Worth County. Did they move directly from Edgefield County to Worth County? Or had they moved from Edgefield County to a nearby county in Georgia, and, while living in Georgia, learned of an opportunity in Worth County? In researching my ancestors, I had come to accept, grudgingly, there are more questions than answers.

I ultimately hired a certified genealogist in Georgia to obtain a copy of Nathaniel Blair's death certificate, as well as records on another 2ND great-grandfather, Jim Kemp. When I received a copy of the death certificate[175], my hopes were dashed. As I suspected, Walter was the informant. In response to the questions about the name and birthplace of Nathaniel's father and the maiden name and birthplace of Nathaniel's mother, the handwritten entries were "don't no." If Walter didn't know the names of his paternal grandparents, how was I supposed to identify them? I wasn't just disappointed, I was annoyed. Where would I go from here?

Genealogical DNA Testing

I provided a saliva sample to 23andMe, a company that conducts autosomal DNA testing identifying the ancestral makeup of each individual as inherited from parents, grandparents, great-grandparents, and more distant ancestors. My initial ancestral composition results revealed I am 71% Sub-Saharan African, 25% European, 3% Asian/Native American and 1% unassigned.[176] This ancestral composition took me aback. I expected the percentages for Asia and Europe to be the reverse. I used to joke that if I had any European ancestry, you couldn't tell by looking at me. My skin tone is a deep dark brown. But as Bryan Skyes observed in his book *DNA USA: A Genetic Portrait of America*,[177] virtually every African American with pre-Civil War roots in the United States has some European ancestry.

In November 2012, I noticed that one of my new DNA matches listed Blair as one of his surnames and listed South Carolina as one of his family locations. Because my mother had also provided a saliva sample to 23andMe, my matches are either marked with the letter "M," meaning my mother's side, or are unmarked, indicating that they did not come from my mother's side and are therefore a match on my father's side. This DNA match listing a Blair surname was a match on my father's side.

I sent this individual a message inquiring if his Blair ancestors lived in the Ninety-Six District, in Edgefield or in Abbeville (which were two of the district created out of the Ninety-Six District in 1785). The individual responded that his direct ancestor William Blair and William's younger brother, George Blair (both born in Ireland), were listed in the Ninety-Six District in the 1779 Colonial Census. His ancestor, William Blair, moved to Newberry County.[178] I replied to his response stating,

> I trace my Blair ancestors to the household of Christopher Blair and his wife Sarah Blair in Edgefield District. Can't find notes of a connection to Newberry. Maybe Christopher Blair is related to someone in Newberry. Are you aware of Christopher and Sarah Blair?[179]

He replied, "Christopher was the son of George Blair who was born in Ireland. That's the connection!"[180]

It is possible that I am related to this individual by some other unknown surname, but what I did learn from my DNA cousin was the connection between the Blair slave owners in Newberry and Edgefield. If these slave owners were related, was there any relationship among their slaves? Perhaps the Newberry and Edgefield Blair slave owners acquire their slaves from the same slave trader. It is even possible that siblings and spouses were divided between the two locations.

My reason for assuming that the Newberry Blairs owned slaves was that during my earliest days of research, on 30 December 2001, I stumbled across a website listing the largest slaveholders by surname and place of residence. Tompkins was identified as a large slaveholder in Edgefield County, South Carolina, and Blair was listed as a large slaveholder in Newberry County, South Carolina. DNA also suggests a possible connection between black Blair descendants with roots in Edgefield to black Blair descendants with roots in Newberry.

In May and June 2016, I exchanged a series of messages with a female researcher with roots in Newberry who is my DNA cousin. Like me, she has an ancestor named Josephine Blair, but her Josephine was born in Newberry County 18 years after my Josephine's birth in Edgefield. This researcher's most senior Blair ancestor is Sam Blair, born about 1820, who resided in Newberry County in 1870.

When I clicked on a result for Sam Blair, Ancestry.com suggested that I review another record — a slave schedule. When I clicked on the link, the result was a 28 year-old black male slave who, in 1860, resided in Newberry, South Carolina. The associated slave owner was George Blair.

I did not know the basis for Ancestry.com selecting this particular record, but since I had been led to George Blair, I quickly searched for any connection to William Blair.

First, I sought to confirm the existence of a George Blair residing in Newberry in 1860. I located a 65-year-old George Blair, who was a married white male, a farmer, and the owner of real estate valued at $4,400 and personal property valued at $58,000. His assets, particularly the personal property value significantly exceeding the real estate value, are indicative of a slave owner.

From a Google search, I learned of a book titled *Sacred to the Memory of the Blairs* by T. W. Blair Sr. and T. W. Blair Jr. According to this publication, George Blair (born 15 October 1794 and died 27 September 1870) was the son of James Blair, who was the son of William Blair (died 1814 in Newberry). That is the same William Blair who was the uncle of Christopher Blair of Edgefield. With genetic DNA indicating connections to both white Blairs and black Blairs of Newberry County, I need to do more research on the Blairs of Newberry.

I decided however to concentrate my research on the Edge-field Blairs, since my ancestors were living in that county. Turning to Google, I searched for any additional clues about the Blairs of Edgefield. One of the results that came up was a message I had posted on the Blair-Family History & Geneal-ogy Message Board on Ancestry.com on 15 January 2002 titled "Blairs of Edgefield, SC."[181] I had forgotten about this message. On 24 January 2002, an individual posted a response:

> MY Blair's
>
> Blair, George and William. I am searching for information on George (b. 1750) and William Blair (b. 1739) in Ireland. Arrived Charleston South Carolina in March or before 1766, possibly Sept. 1765. They were Irish Protestants (pos-sibly Presbyterians) that came and received Bounty Land in Belfast Township of Granville Count[]y, South Carolina [which later became Edgefield]. Have copies of original land grants dated March 1766.
>
> George Blair b 1750, d 1787
>
> + Barsheba
> Children Christopher b 1780 d 1829 Edgefield Dist., SC
> > Gabriel
> > Barsheba
> > Christopher
>
> + Sarah
> Children G W (Washington) b 1808 SC, d 1849 MS
> > Hazle SC
> > Elizabeth SC
> > James b 1814 SC
> > Pulaski (P L) b 1849 SC
> > Sarah SC
> > Christopher SC
> > Columbus b 1824 SC[182]

When I read this message many years ago, it did not mean anything to me. Now, however, I wondered if my ancestors had been pointing me to this Blair slaveholding family, and I had simply ignored their signal.

The genetic DNA match with L. L. does not prove a specific relationship. The DNA match confirms this William Blair descendant and I share common genes, with roots most likely in South Carolina. Along which branch of the family tree, however, is unknown. I thus returned to the research by paper trail. I had no choice but to review once more the Estate of Christopher Blair.

THE ESTATE OF CHRISTOPHER BLAIR

The slaves were listed under "Property," along with animals, furniture, and other personal belongings. It hit me hard to see my ancestors lumped in with the animals and inanimate objects. If slavery wasn't real to me before, it certainly was now.

A Negro male named Nat was valued at $400. A Negro woman named Violet and her two children, Edmund and Cinda, were valued at $600. Sarah, Christopher's widow, purchased Nat for $586 and purchased Violet and the two children for $557.

My next step was to search for Edmund and Cinda. Tracing a woman between 1830 and 1865, particularly an enslaved one, would be very difficult. I did not know how old Cinda was when Sarah purchased her. I decided against searching for Cinda and opted for the "easier" task, searching for Edmund.

RECORDS AT THE SOUTH CAROLINA
DEPARTMENT OF ARCHIVES & HISTORY

In July 2005, I visited the South Carolina Department of Archives & History (SCDAH) for the first time. At the gift shop,

I purchased a Genealogy Starter Kit consisting of six booklets, including the South Carolina Department of Archives & History's *African American Genealogical Research*. From reading this booklet, I learned of state records, including the 1868 voter registration. This voter registration is not available online, so, during a subsequent visit to SCDAH in October 2011, I reviewed the 1868 voter registration for Edgefield County, searching for all my paternal male ancestors (only the men were eligible to vote), including the Blairs.

On the South Carolina 1868 Voter Registration, five "colored" Blairs were listed in the Sixth Regiment Precinct of Edgefield County: Nelson, Hampton, Richard, Natt, and Edmund.[183]

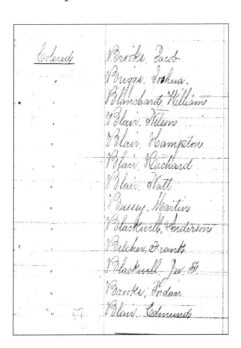

FIG. 11. PORTION OF 1868 EDGEFIELD COUNTY VOTER REGISTRATION (COLORED MEN WITH "B" SURNAMES)
Courtesy of the South Carolina Department of Archives and History

Unfortunately, the voter registration does not provide any other information about the voters, such as their ages or occupations. This "Natt" was likely the elder Nathaniel, not my 2ND great-grandfather who was about 17 years old at the time. Perhaps this Edmund was the same person identified as a child of Violet (and possibly the son of Nat) in the estate papers of Christopher Blair. Edmund Blair, however, was not listed on the Militia Enrollments of 1869. Fortunately, this record set is accessible online via SCDAH's website. I assumed Edmund did not register for the militia because he was older than 45 years or, perhaps, deceased. I could not find him listed on the 1870 US Census.

Turning back to the three remaining black Blairs—Nelson, Hampton, and Richard—I reviewed my notes and papers. I had forgotten that Hampton was listed on the 1870 US Census as residing in Gregg Township. I had also forgotten that Nelson Blair was listed on the tax duplicate list for 1879. I had not seen a Richard Blair mentioned in any record I had reviewed, however, including the Militia Enrollments of 1869. Neither Nelson nor Hampton was listed on the Militia Enrollments of 1869 either, even though both were present in Edgefield after 1869. I am particularly perplexed by the apparent omission of Hampton given that he was 20 years old in 1870, and thus would have been approximately 19 years old in 1869.

On SCDAH's website, the Militia Enrollments of 1869 were described as follows:

> Article XIII of the South Carolina Constitution of 1868 provided for a militia comprised of "all able-bodied male citizens of the State between the ages of eighteen and forty-five years, except such persons as are now, or may hereafter be, exempted by the laws of the United States.

> This series consists of militia enrollment books for individual counties in South Carolina. The enrollments were made between June and December of 1869. County volumes are subdivided by township. The lists of male citizens in each township are divided into two categories, those between the ages of eighteen and thirty and those between thirty and forty-five. Information includes name, age, occupation, place of residence, and race.[184]

The only Blairs listed on the Militia Enrollments of 1869 (and all living in the same community of Rocky Pond)[185] were: "Coin" Blair, colored, 19; Nathaniel Blair, colored, 18;[186] and C. L. Blair, white, 44.[187] "Coin" is obviously "Cain," who lived with Nathaniel and Violet in 1870 and resided in the same community as my 2ND great-grandfather Nathaniel.

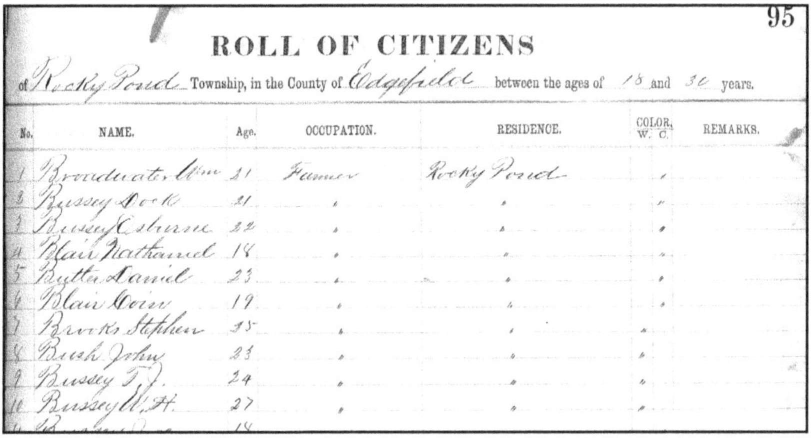
95

ROLL OF CITIZENS

of Rocky Pond Township, in the County of Edgefield between the ages of 18 and 30 years.

No.	NAME.	Age.	OCCUPATION.	RESIDENCE.	COLOR. W.	COLOR. C.	REMARKS.
1	Broadwater Wm	21	Farmer	Rocky Pond		"	
2	Bussey Dock	21	"	"		"	
3	Bussey Osburne	22	"	"		"	
4	Blair Nathaniel	18	"	"		"	
5	Butler Daniel	23	"	"		"	
6	Blair Coin	19	"	"		"	
7	Brooks Stephen	25	"	"	"		
8	Bush John	23	"	"	"		
9	Bussey T. J.	24	"	"	"		
10	Bussey W. H.	27	"	"	"		
11	[illegible]	18					

FIG. 12. 1869 MILITIA ENROLLMENT – ROCKY POND (BLAIR, NATHANIEL)
Courtesy of the South Carolina Department of Archives and History

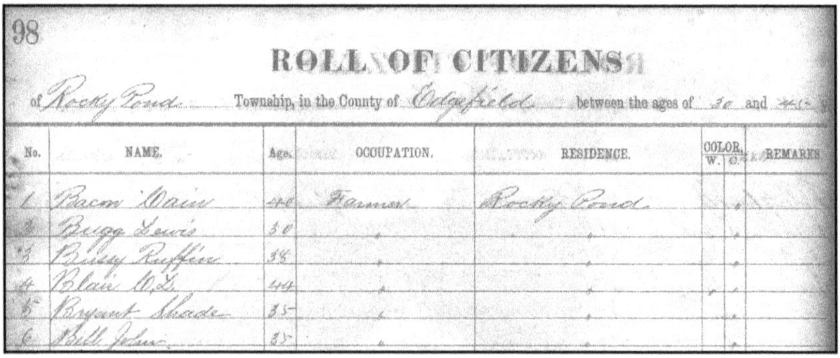

98

ROLL OF CITIZENS

of Rocky Pond Township, in the County of Edgefield between the ages of 30 and 45

No.	NAME.	Age.	OCCUPATION.	RESIDENCE.	COLOR. W.	COLOR. C.	REMARKS.
1	Bacon Wain	46	Farmer	Rocky Pond		"	
2	Bugg Lewis	30	"	"		"	
3	Bussy Ruffin	38	"	"		"	
4	Blair C.L.	44	"	"	"		
5	Bryant Shade	35	"	"		"	
6	Bell John	35	"	"		"	

FIG. 13. 1869 MILITIA ENROLLMENT – ROCKY POND (BLAIR, C. L.)

Courtesy of the South Carolina Department of Archives and History

As I traced my Blair ancestors, I repeatedly came across the names Columbus Blair and C. L. Blair. I knew from Mrs. Lucas's book that Columbus Blair purchased a slave from another Blair, and I knew that Sarah Blair purchased four slaves from her late husband's estate. I also knew from the 1880 US Census and from a post on an Ancestry.com Message Board that Columbus Blair was the son of Sarah Blair.

In mid-July 2012, my mother and I attended the South Carolina Genealogical Society Summer Workshop held at the SCDAH. We had the pleasure of attending a presentation by Scott Wilds called "Using Probate and Equity Court Records in Tracing African-American Slave Ancestry." During the presentation, Mr. Wilds remarked that what a researcher hopes to find is a slave owner who dies young and subsequent litigation among surviving family members. In researching my mother's maternal line from Abbeville County, that very day of Mr. Wilds' presentation, we found an enslaved ancestor under such circumstances. We knew exactly when this enslaved ancestor arrived with the slaveholder's family because one witness gave a ten-year account about who owned which slaves.

I knew at the outset that I would not have such luck with the Blairs. Christopher Blair died in 1829, Sarah Blair acquired the four slaves in April of 1830, and Sarah Blair was still alive in 1880. As such, no records would have been produced concerning the four slaves between 1830 and 1865 unless, for instance, the slaves were transferred to another owner. The fact that Nat and Violet were residing in the same community with Sarah Blair in 1870 suggests she never sold them. Thus far, I had deferred researching the slave-owning Blairs, Sarah and her son Columbus ("C. L.") Blair. Having overturned virtually every stone for information about my direct Blair ancestors and still encountering brick walls, the time had come.

PATERNAL GRANDMOTHER'S LINE

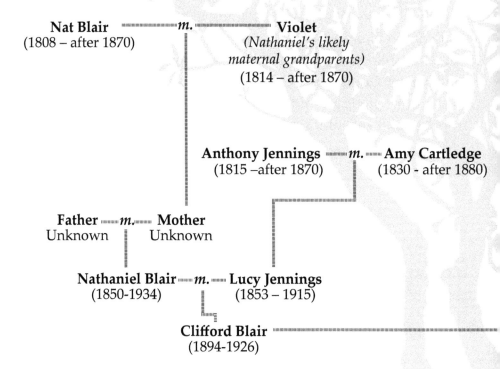

Nat Blair ————— *m.* ————— Violet
(1808 – after 1870)   *(Nathaniel's likely*
                             maternal grandparents)
                             (1814 – after 1870)

Anthony Jennings ——— *m.* ——— Amy Cartledge
(1815 –after 1870)   (1830 - after 1880)

Father ——— *m.* ——— Mother
Unknown   Unknown

Nathaniel Blair ——— *m.* ——— Lucy Jennings
(1850-1934)   (1853 – 1915)

Clifford Blair ————————————————
(1894-1926)

**FIGURE 14. FAMILY TREE OF NATONNE'S PATERNAL
GRANDMOTHER'S LINE**

PATERNAL GRANDMOTHER'S LINE

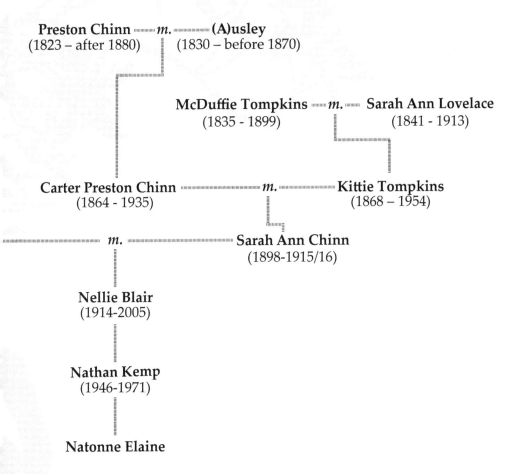

Preston Chinn ⸺ *m.* ⸺ (A)usley
(1823 – after 1880)   (1830 – before 1870)

McDuffie Tompkins ⸺ *m.* ⸺ Sarah Ann Lovelace
(1835 - 1899)   (1841 - 1913)

Carter Preston Chinn ⸺ *m.* ⸺ Kittie Tompkins
(1864 - 1935)   (1868 – 1954)

⸺ *m.* ⸺ Sarah Ann Chinn
(1898-1915/16)

Nellie Blair
(1914-2005)

Nathan Kemp
(1946-1971)

Natonne Elaine

FIGURE 14. FAMILY TREE OF NATONNE'S PATERNAL
GRANDMOTHER'S LINE

CHAPTER 4
TRACKING THE FOOTPRINTS OF MY BLAIR ANCESTORS (CONTINUED)
Natonne Elaine Kemp

I began my quest for information about the slaveholding Blairs by searching for Columbus or C. L. Blair. From the website Find A Grave, I learned that Columbus L. Blair was born on 24 October 1824 and died 22 February 1907.[188] His wife was Huldah Jennings Blair.[189]

I was stunned to learn Columbus's exact date of birth and date of death—South Carolina did not mandate the recording of such information until 1915. Presumably, the Blairs maintained a family Bible and recorded important events, and I wondered whether it still existed.

I have had success using family Bibles while researching my mother's paternal line from Virginia. The Library of Virginia has acquired originals and copies of over 6,800 family Bibles.[190] Such records typically list births, marriages, and deaths, and these family Bibles are particularly important during periods where the Commonwealth of Virginia did not mandate the reporting of vital statistics. I was fortunate enough to find an enslaved 4TH great-grandmother's birth date in the family Bible of the slave owner.[191]

I searched for a comparable collection for the State of South Carolina and discovered, via the South Carolina Digital Library

(University of South Carolina, South Caroliniana Library, Manuscript Division), that South Carolina has a substantially smaller collection of family Bible records.[192] The website allows one to browse individual Bibles. I searched the collection, but I failed to find an entry for the Blair or Jennings surname.

A Shooting During Reconstruction

One Google search revealed that Columbus L. Blair shot a colored man in 1872. This incident was reported on the front page of the Friday morning 12 January 1872 edition of *The Charleston Daily*.

FATAL RENCONTRE[193] IN EDGEFIELD

[SPECIAL TELEGRAM TO THE NEWS.]
Columbia, January 11

A fatal shooting affair is reported from Edgefield. Columbus L. Blair (white) shot and killed Peter Wilkes (colored) on Saturday. The deed is said to have been committed in self defence. Blair was bailed to-day by Judge Moses in the sum of fifteen hundred dollars on the application of Wm. T. Gary. Picket.

ANOTHER ACCOUNT

[From the Edgefield Advertiser.]

On the 6th instant, near Rocky Ponds, on the west side of the district, "a colored man, named Peter Wilkes, was shot and killed by that well-known citizen, Columbus L. Blair, Esq. It seems that Mr. Blair had lent a shot gun to his overseer, a white man by the name of Coleman, who in turn had lent the gun to Wilkes, who was hired on the place. Wilkes having kept the gun an undue time, Mr. Blair sent to request its return, which was refused by Wilkes. Mr. Blair then started in person to see if he could get the gun.

On his way, he met a negro girl bringing him the gun. Taking possession of the gun, he went on to where Wilkes was to query him as to the meaning of his conduct. Wilkes met him in evil spirit and with angry words, and seizing a bed rail advanced and assaulted him. Mr. Blair parried his blows with the gun, which was not loaded, and the barrel of which was soon broken off. After this, Wilkes continuing his assault, Mr. Blair drew his pistol and shot him. From all we can learn and from the testimony of eyewitnesses themselves, this appears to have been an unmistakable case of self-defense.[194]

This incident undoubtedly shocked not only the residents of Edgefield but citizens throughout South Carolina. This shooting occurred while South Carolina was still under the authority of the federal government during Reconstruction following the conclusion of the Civil War. From what little I have studied about the Reconstruction period (1865-1877), federal military authorities had the unenviable task of attempting to transform the role of the newly liberated black population against a backdrop of a hostile white population.

I searched for more information about this shooting and discovered the incident was reported in at least two other newspapers outside the State of South Carolina: the 13 January 1872 edition of the *Augusta Chronicle*, a newspaper in Georgia,[195] and the 14 January 1872 edition of *The Wilmington Morning Star*, a newspaper in North Carolina.[196]

The story as reported in the *Augusta Chronicle* quotes directly from the *Edgefield Advertiser*, but the account of the incident in the *Augusta Chronicle* differs from *The Charleston Daily's* in two ways. First, after the conclusion of the first sentence and before the sentence beginning with "It seems that Mr. Blair had lent a shot gun to his overseer," there is a sentence stating, "We give such particulars of this unfortunate occurrence as we have been able to gather from trustworthy sources." A second difference is the addition of one word in the last sentence of the article. "From all we can learn from the testimony of colored eyewitnesses themselves, this appears to have been an unmistakable case of self-defense."

The difference in reporting, though minor, is significant. Who were those trustworthy sources? In light of the hostility and disdain the editor and writers of the *Edgefield Advertiser* openly displayed about the colored population, I cannot imagine those "trustworthy sources" were colored. Second, by at least one newspaper identifying the eyewitnesses as colored, it suggests that Columbus L. Blair's action was, indeed, a case of self-defense.

The Charleston Daily, the *Augusta Chronicle*, and *The Wilmington Morning Star* all cite the *Edgefield Advertiser* as their principal source of information. I thus searched the *Edgefield Advertiser* for the month of January in 1872 via the Chronicling America (Historic American Newspapers) website. If this shooting was reported in the *Edgefield Advertiser*, no account exists today in the digital collection.

Besides the absence of this incident in the surviving records of the newspaper, I was further fascinated by the *Edgefield Advertiser*'s omission of any references to the legal process stemming from this shooting. According to *The Charleston Daily*, bail was set at $1,500.00. That seems like a lot of money in 1872, especially considering that many southern states had suffered enormous economic loss as a result of the Civil War. According to the website MeasuringWorth.com, the value of that amount ranges from $27,000.00 to $3,130,000.00. In terms of purchasing power, $1,500.00 in 1872 would have carried a relative value of $30,000.00 in 2014. Contrarily, the economic value of that income in 2014 would be $413,000.00. This exercise did not really answer whether the $1,500.00 bail was uncharacteristic or not, however.

I recalled from the Treasurer's Tax Duplicate record of 1879 that "C. L." or Columbus Blair owned 1,200 acres of real estate. Real property wealth cannot be liquidated quickly at full value, so perhaps a bail of $1,500.00 was a hefty amount. However, after reading Stephen Budiansky's *The Bloody Shirt: Terror After The Civil War*, my assumption about economic hardship in Edgefield appeared incorrect:

> The Edgefield district was a prosperous area of large plantations; it had escaped the ravages of war; the soil was light loam and level ground, good for cotton, unlike the sand and red earth of so much of the region; the old wealthy families were wealthy still and carrying on much as before.[197]

Returning to the shooting, I wondered if Columbus L. Blair was ever charged. I searched, in vain, for more information about this incident but found nothing. So I decided to search for information about the victim, Peter Wilkes, and the overseer, Coleman, in 1870, the most recent federal population census to the 1872 shooting.

I found them. Not surprisingly, Peter Wilkes and Coleman lived in Washington Township, Edgefield County, in the area of the Parks Store Post Office. It was the same community where Columbus Blair lived, as well as my 2ND great-grandparents, Nathaniel and Lucy Blair, and their infant daughter, Josephine. I learned that Peter "Wilks," born about 1855, was 15 years old in 1870. He lived with a woman who appears[198] to be his mother and four younger siblings (ages 11, 9, 8, and 7). When Peter "Wilks" was killed in January of 1872, he was likely 16 to 17 years old.

I never got the impression from the newspaper articles that Peter Wilk(e)s, who supposedly met Columbus Blair "with evil spirit and with angry words," was a teenager. The newspaper accounts omitted this information. Columbus Blair was 47 years old in January 1872, nearly three times the age of Peter Wilk(e)s. Could not the loss of life of one so young been avoided?

The shooting of Peter Wilk(e)s by Columbus L. Blair in self-defense reminded me of a 21ST century shooting that received national attention. On 26 February 2012, Trayvon Martin, 17 years old, was shot and killed by George Zimmerman, a neighborhood watch coordinator for a gated community in Florida, allegedly in "self-defense." George Zimmerman legally carried a gun under Florida's Stand Your Ground law that allows residents to use deadly force to defend themselves, even if retreat is possible. Columbus L. Blair happened to be carrying a pistol, which he used to defend himself. Having served as a constable[199] in Edgefield, Columbus knew how to use a pistol. Further, his carrying of a pistol was not unusual apparently. According to Budiansky's The Bloody Shirt, "Edgefield was a place so violent jokes had grown up about it. You could tell a real high-toned Edgefield gentleman, people in South Carolina said, because he was the one with four huge navy-sized revolvers stuck in his belt."[200] The website CSI Dixie describes Edgefield's violent temperament: "The small, rural district of Edgefield, South Carolina was the Deadwood of its day, amassing a reputation for murder and mayhem unique in the nation. Forget the gangs of New York, the toughs in tailored suits strutting about Edgefield's Court House Square were up for almost anything."[201]

My attention returned to the 1872 shooting. I searched for the overseer, Coleman. After searching via Ancestry.com and

FamilySearch.org, the most likely individual was Hozekeah Coleman, a 45-year-old white male. He was a farm laborer. So why did the newspaper account identify Coleman as an overseer?

> Overseers were the middlemen of the antebellum South's plantation hierarchy. As such they occupied an impossible position. The masters expected them to produce profitable crops while maintaining a contented workforce of slaves — slaves who had little reason to work hard to improve the efficiency of the plantation.[202]

Presumably, Coleman managed the plantation for Columbus Blair and oversaw the colored workforce in 1872, seven years after the Civil War ended. The fact that the newspaper labeled Coleman as an overseer is indicative that, from the perspective of those in power, little had changed in the hierarchy of Edgefield's society.

The 1870 US Census shows Hozekeah Coleman resided with John Sumake, a 28-year-old white male working at the saw mill, and 55-year-old Daniel Price, a black male working at a grist mill. I did not expect to find Coleman residing with a black man. Since Daniel Price worked at a mill for grinding grains, Coleman presumably did not oversee him on Columbus Blair's plantation.

Hozekeah Coleman lent the shotgun to a teenager. Apparently Coleman knew Peter Wilk(e)s. Coleman must have had a high enough regard for Peter to entrust him with such a weapon. What did Coleman tell Peter Wilk(e)s upon lending him the shotgun? Was Peter Wilk(e)s aware the shotgun was the property of the landowner, Columbus Blair?

As I read and reviewed the newspaper account, I wondered what had happened to Coleman after the shooting. Did Columbus Blair fire him? If Coleman had a good working relationship with the black community in Parks Store, Washington Township, did the killing of Peter Wilk(e)s affect that relationship in a negative way? Did Coleman feel any guilt or responsibility for entrusting the shotgun to Peter Wilk(e)s?

Turning to Peter, why did he not return the shotgun immediately upon Columbus Blair's request? What were his intentions for keeping it? Once Peter Wilk(e)s realized that Columbus Blair would not tolerate his disobedience, why did he give the unloaded shotgun to a Negro girl to deliver to Columbus Blair? Was this an attempt to appease Columbus Blair? Who was that girl? Was she possibly one of Peter's younger sisters? If so, I can imagine how distraught she was over the killing of her brother.

Was the killing of Peter Wilk(e)s merely an incident where a colored boy didn't know his place? I wondered what the other blacks in the community, including my ancestors, thought. Had nothing changed with the abolishment of slavery for the recently freed black population?

ANOTHER PIECE OF THE PUZZLE

The article described Columbus L. Blair as a well-known citizen. The abbreviation "Esq." meant he was an attorney. My research found nothing to substantiate that Columbus L. Blair practiced law; not once was he identified as an attorney or lawyer by the federal census. If Columbus Blair was not an attorney-at-law, I was puzzled by the use of "Esquire." Possibly, like the word "fireman," the word "Esquire" had another meaning a century ago. According to Dictionary.com, "Esquire" is "an unofficial title of respect, having no precise significance, sometimes placed, especially in its abbreviated form, after a man's surname in formal written address[.]"[203] I made a mental note that Columbus Blair was highly regarded in Edgefield.

If Columbus Blair was well-known, I hoped to find additional references about him in newspapers. That search was not very fruitful; I located mostly references to a case involving him and his mother, Sarah Blair, regarding the distribution of his deceased brother's estate. Otherwise, Columbus L. or C. L. Blair was identified as an adjoining land owner.

I then cast my research net wider. While researching my maternal line from Abbeville, South Carolina, I became aware of a database called ProQuest History Vault: Slavery and the Law.[204] This "collection of archival primary resources" is divided into two series: Series I (Petition to State Legislatures[205]) and Series II (Petitions to Southern County Courts[206]). In reviewing "Race, Slavery and Free Blacks, Series II, Petitions to Southern County Courts, 1775-1867, Part D: North Carolina (1775-1867) and South Carolina (1784-1867)," I found what I believe was a possible reference to Columbus L. Blair. The following is a summary on Reel 22.

> 0029 (Accession # 21385505). Edgefield District, South Carolina. Thomas and Henry Jennings join their sister, Huldah, and her husband in seeking a partition of their late grandfather's estate. During his lifetime, Joseph Jennings conveyed all of his property, including a 370-acre plantation and thirteen slaves, to James Tompkins "in trust nevertheless, that the said James Tompkins & his heirs shall & do permit me, the said Joseph Jennings, during the term of my natural life to be & remain in the full & peaceable occupation, possession & enjoyment of all & singular the said estate." At Jennings's death, the property would be distributed among his heirs. Tompkins has allotted some of the property since Jennings's death, but "the two elevenths of the whole of the said property deeded to your Petitioners

remains yet undivided & undistributed." Therefore, the petitioners pray that the court order Tompkins to make a partition of the remaining property.

I knew from my research that Columbus L. Blair married Huldah Jennings. Perhaps he was her unidentified husband. I am a Tompkins and a Jennings descendant, so maybe one or more of those thirteen slaves were my ancestors. The case description did not identify a year, however.

I turned to the Digital Library on American Slavery.[207] In one of the searchable databases on this website, the "Race & Slavery Petitions Project," I was happy to discover that Petition 21385505 is part of the collection.[208] Through this, I learned the case was filed on 16 April 1855. The digital library listed categories of people (slaves, petitioners, defendants, and other people) associated with Petition 21385505. There are 13 slaves, four petitioners, one defendant, and two other people. I knew three of the four petitioners by name, but what I really hoped to discover was whether the fourth petitioner was Columbus L. Blair, the husband of Huldah Jennings. My assumption turned out to be correct. The petitioners are listed alphabetically by surname—the first petitioner is "Blair, Columbus L." and the second petitioner is "Blair, Huldah Jennings."

I turned next to the 13 slaves. They were Charles, Esther, Hannah, Jerry, Jim ([James]), Lucinda, Patty, Rachel ([the older)], Rachel ([the younger)], Sally, Siller ([Silas]), Tandy, and Wesley. Much to my disappointment, not one name matched any of my known Tompkins or Jennings ancestors.

PROBING DEEPER

My thoughts returned to the shooting of Peter Wilk(e)s. I decided to seek assistance from the Edgefield County Archivist to gain more information about a trial or a verdict.

On 18 February 2014, I sent an e-mail to Tricia Price Glenn and shared with her the news account reported in *The Charleston Daily*. I asked her the following three questions:

> Are there any records reflecting this bail of $1500?
>
> Was Columbus L. Blair indicted? If so, was there a trial? If not indicted, any document stating why he was not prosecuted?
>
> Any sworn statements by witnesses to the incident?[209]

Tricia replied to my e-mail the next day, sharing the following:

FEBRUARY 29, 1872 EDGEFIELD ADVERTISER.
AROUND AND ABOUT TOWN.

> Court will assemble on Monday next, and the term bids fair to be a long one. There is a press of business on hand, for it must be remembered we have had no grand jury since March 1871, and even then a number of cases were continued on account of absence of witnesses. If we mistake not there are as many as eight or ten criminal cases to come before the Court. There are the six men indicted for the shooting of the negro girl at Graniteville—the girl who shot Mr. Brewer's baby. And there is the Blair case . . . As regards the Jury for the coming Term, it is all arranged according to law. We have seen the lists and the names upon each are good ones. Upon the Grand Jury there are 13 white and 5 colored men. Of the 36 petit Jurors 20 are white and 16 colored. It is most earnestly to be hoped that the citizens drawn upon these Juries will be prompt in their attendance.[210]

"And there is the Blair case." That says it all—everyone knew about the case. Tricia shared with me, as reported for the 1872 March Term, The State vs. Columbus L. Blair – Murder No bill.[211]

Perplexed about not finding this information myself, I searched for any and all references to C. L. Blair (instead of Columbus Blair) in the *Edgefield Advertiser*, and located the news account. It was reported in the 7 March 1872 edition that "In the indictment of the State against C. L. Blair, for the killing of Peter Wilkes, the Grand Jury found no bill."[212]

Tricia sent me another e-mail on 19 February 2014 supplementing her earlier e-mail of the same day.

> I just sent you some info. and forgot to put in a message. I attached everything I had on Columbus Blair. I went through the General Sessions Book again and there is no mention of bail – that had to have come from the Advertiser. Sometimes, bail was not put in the book. We unfortunately do not have coroner's records[213] for that time either. As you can see a "No Bill" was found by the Grand Jury which meant they did not find sufficient cause to try him and he was free to go.[214]

When Tricia searched the archival records for Columbus or C. L. Blair, she located a case from the Spring Term of 1850. The Wilk(e)s matter was not the first time the State of South Carolina had brought charges against Columbus Blair. In the case of the State of South Carolina vs Columbus Blair, he was charged with assault and battery, and the jury returned a "true bill" to indict. Unfortunately, unless I personally visit the Edgefield County Archives, I will not learn the circumstances of this assault and battery. Although the Edgefield County Archives has the court case among its collection, the accompanying index was lost some time ago. Thus, Tricia cannot readily locate the case.[215] To my further disappointment, a search for a newspaper account about this 1850 case against Columbus Blair yielded no results.

C. L. BLAIR – A REFLECTION OF EDGEFIELD?

Tricia shared with me another reference, from the 28 September 1871[216] edition of the *Edgefield Advertiser,* where C. L. Blair is mentioned.

MR. EDITOR: -- I have read in your issue of the 21st, an article copied from the Columbia Union over the signature of "An Old Republican," in reference to a Ku Klux outrage said to have been committed in this vicinity within the last month. Since then I have troubled myself no little to ascertain if there was any foundation for the rumor, and am satisfied that the statement is an unmitigated falsehood throughout. I have seen the old colored, man, Sile Robinson, upon whom the outrage is said to have been perpetrated, and he utterly disclaims knowing anything in reference to the reported Ku-Klux disturbance, or having said anything to that effect. And he is willing to sign a paper giving the lie to the whole story.

The colored people in this neighborhood say they are willing to testify that no such outrage has occurred in this section of country; and they further wish me to say for them, that while they are satisfied, and are living in peace and quietness, as they have been doing for a long while, they hope the Party will not disturb the friendly relations existing between them and the whites, by representing the weakest of their race as circulating such libelous and unwarranted falsehoods.

I send you a list of names, of both white and black, who are willing to testify in this matter, should you desire further evidence, viz: Messrs. T. J. Thurmond, Jesse Bailey, P. O. Doolittle, J. W. Glanton, B. F. Glanton, Wm. Parkman, W. J. Holmes, C. L. Blair, Dr. J. H. Jennings, Landon Tucker, E. A. Searles, Starling Freeman, W. Bussey, white, and Sile Robinson, Lewis Gilchrist, Thomas Collins, Alick Hampton, Pleasant Holmes, colored, and could send hundreds of others, if necessary, of both colors, living in the vicinity of Red Oak Grove Church. Wyatt L. Holmes.[217]

This matter was too interesting to bypass, even though my Blair ancestors apparently were not involved. I searched without success for the edition of the *Columbia Union* that printed the story. However, in searching old newspapers for references to "Edgefield" and "Sile Robinson," I found the following in the 28 September 1871 edition of the *Edgefield Advertiser*.

AN OLD LIAR, RATHER.

Last week we copied, from the *Daily Union*, a tremendous farrago of stuff in the shape of a letter dated "Heights Above Hamburg" and signed "An Old Republican." This letter depicted a fearful Ku Klux outrage against a negro family in the Dark Corner. It was intended to fire the negro heart and make the negro brood more fiercely upon what renegades and carpetbaggers term "the wrong of his race."

But to-day we publish a complete refutation of the whole tale. See the affidavit of Sile Robinson and his two sons, hereto annexed.

So, "An Old Republican" turns out to be simply an old liar. But the *Union* will stick up to him. Of that he may be sure!

Edgefield County, S.C.,
Sept. 25th, 1871

We, Sile Robinson and sons John Robinson and Spencer Robinson, do hereby certify that we are informed that certain persons have reported that we are the persons refer[r]ed to in a communication headed "Heights Above Hamburg, SC., Sept. 14, 1871," and published in the Daily *Union* over the signature of "An Old Republican," upon whom a Ku Klux outrage was said to have been committed; that we live near Red Oak Grove, and that no outrage has been committed upon us of any nature whatsoever; that no section of the State can be more free from Ku Klux outrages, as we have not heard of a single act of any organized band of lawless persons.

SILE [his X mark] ROBINSON,
JOHN [his X mark] ROBINSON,
SPENCER [his X mark] ROBINSON,

Witness [signed]

WYATT L. HOLMES
WM. PARKMAN[218]

This "recantation" by Sile Robinson and his two sons is rather suspicious to me. It is remarkable the Robinsons claim (a) Edgefield is free of Ku Klux outrages and (b) they have not heard of a single act of any organized band of lawless persons. I searched for Sile Robinson and his sons in the 1870 US Census to no avail. I wondered whether Sile Robinson and his sons were literate. The fact that their signatures were represented by an "x" or mark suggests not. Even if they could read but not write, did they have the resources or even the luxury of time to purchase and read the *Edgefield Advertiser*? It appears to me this "recantation" was written by someone else whose intention was to refute any allegation of harsh treatment of the formerly enslaved by whites in Edgefield. Despite this effort to deflect such a perception, a historical analysis by Budiansky in *The Bloody Shirt* reveals what the *Daily Union* reported was most probably true.

> Edgefield county's population was 60 percent colored, but Hamburg's was soon 75 percent; within a few years of the war's end its population swelled to eleven hundred. Throughout 1865 and 1866 there were reports of paid killers operating with near impunity elsewhere in Edgefield, especially in rich plantation districts over at the other end of the county toward Edgefield Court-House, the village that served as the county seat. "It is almost a daily occurrence for black men to be hunted down with dogs and shot like wild beasts," a freedman from Edgefield told a government agent in the autumn of 1865. The colored people called them "bushwackers"; an army board of inquiry sent to examine the situation amply confirmed the tales. A band of a hundred men, led by a former Confederate officer, marauded at will through Edgefield county, whipping or killing Negroes who dared to leave the employ of their former masters.[219]

What a frightening place Edgefield was. The freedmen were preyed upon and terrorized. As Budiansky noted in *The Bloody Shirt*, "Edgefield . . . had a reputation as a bastion of the most unregenerate slaveholders in the entire state, the entire South even."[220] I am stunned that in such a hostile environment my Blair ancestors managed to survive.

All of the excerpts from the *Edgefield Advertiser* reflect disdain toward the formerly enslaved population. Not surprisingly, a society built on the institution of slavery was bitter about the loss of its way of life. Blacks, formerly property, were now supposed to be treated as equals. This hostility was apparent to Union forces in Edgefield District, as reflected in a 28 February 1866 letter to Major H W Smith, Assistant Adjutant General from Lieutenant Colonel John Devereux, Subassistant Commissioner at Hamburg.

> Sir
>
> I have the honor to report that in my arrival in this District I immediately put myself in communication with Person most likely to give me reliable information as to the condition of affairs therein also with the military authorities in Augusta Ga. I have elicited many facts of importance and respectfully invite attention to the following points.
>
> 1st The total military force in Edgefield District is nineteen enlisted men of the 25th Ohio Vol commanded by Lieut[enant] Biggerstaff. Seven men are stationed at Edgefield Court House and twelve at Hamburg. Edgefield being one of the largest and most unruly districts in the State[.] This small force is entirely inadequate to inact the proper respect for the United States authority.
>
> 2ND, There are two organized bands of outlaws, one consisting of eight men and the other of thirteen men led by an ex-confederate – Major Coleman. At present raiding this District and committing with impunity the most fiendish outrages on Union Men and Negroes.

> They have murdered a number of Negroes and one White Man without provocation. Robbed and driven from their houses several northern men who have property here. Coleman the leader is a desparate [sic] character. He has exhibited to several persons whom I saw eight ears cut from Colored Persons. He carries them in an envelope and shows them as trophies. This man is a native of Edgefield . . . .[221]

I am speechless. This firsthand account of life in Edgefield, less than a year after the Civil War ended, is chilling. I imagine my Blair ancestors were petrified.

Racial tensions did not subside but persisted. On 23 February 1875, Colonel and Aide-de-Camp Theodore W. Parmele wrote a report to Daniel H. Chamberlain, Governor of South Carolina, about the Condition of Edgefield, stating in pertinent part:

> Dear Sir—During my recent visit to Edgefield County, while engaged in recovering the arms from the State militia in that county, I had, during a stay of three weeks, some opportunity of learning the real causes for the recent troubles there between the white and the colored citizens.
>
> It is obvious to any careful observer who may visit Edgefield County that the majority of the white people are a highly cultivated, industrious, law-abiding class of citizens, who desire peace, and who are satisfied with seeking redress for their grievances only in a lawful manner. So with the colored race. The majority are industrious, respectable, and opposed to any act of lawlessness. There is, however, a disturbing element in the minority of both races. Among the whites a class of men who hold human life at little value, being as reckless in risking their own as they are heartless in taking the lives of others. These men are habitually armed, and ready to resent any assertion of equality as a citizen when coming from a colored man, such action on his part being considered offensive and presumptuous. These de[s]peradoes are beyond the control of the more law-abid-

ing white people, who dare not oppose or condemn them. Among the colored people there is a class who do not wish to labor, and are known as habitual thieves or disturbers of the peace, by making incendiary remarks or suggesting threats in retaliation for acts or language perpetrated or used by white people against them or some one of their race. It can thus be seen that a few lawless or imprudent men of both races have involved Edgefield County in acts which have injured its good name, while a majority of its citizens have been really innocent of any wrong intention.

●•●●●

Capt. Blackwell, who commanded the "Dark Corner Rifle Club," authorized me to make public his statement to me that he was now willing to rent land to twenty colored men, not excepting those who belonged to the militia. Other prominent white men have assured me that the proscription against colored or militiamen is fast dying out and that it will soon be at an end.

I do not think the presence of United States infantry is necessary at Edgefield Courthouse at this time. If mounted patrol could each day pass through such portions of the county as are most disturbed by lawless men, so that all classes of citizens might feel some protection against threat or attack on the public highways, their presence would do good, but even this may not now be necessary, for I believe that the force of public opinion, and a vigorous prosecution of the means provided by the law, will unite to prevent or punish lawlessness hereafter. I have the honor to remain yours respectfully.[222]

Colonel Parmele was undoubtedly an optimist. Returning to the letter to the editor ("An Old Liar, Rather") and the recantation by Sile Robinson and his sons, I noted the market town of Hamburg is mentioned. Even the correspondence from February 1866 mentions Hamburg. These references occurred before the Hamburg Massacre of July 1876. What was special about Hamburg? I found the answer in Budiansky's *The Bloody Shirt*.

> Hamburg offered the freedmen a strength in numbers and a safety in remoteness; Hamburg was a haven, at least a relative haven, a haven by comparison. Within a few years the town was home to hundreds of colored families who had broken free of the life of contracted farm workers, a life scarcely distinguishable from slavery. Among their numbers were schoolteachers, railroad employees, black-smiths; a successful cotton broker, a printer, a clerk of the court; shoemakers, painters, carpenters; a constable. They bought lots and furnished homes. There were several who made considerable investments in farms and other real estate in South Carolina, and in states beyond.[223]

For the formerly enslaved, Hamburg represented the dream of a post-slavery society. But for those unregenerate slave-holders, Hamburg's existence was a threat to a way of life where whites dominated and blacks were subservient. Sadly, Hamburg was doomed because blacks were making lives for themselves apart from that peculiar institution or its post-Reconstruction reincarnation.

The second sentence of the article "An Old Liar, Rather" states, "[t]his letter depicted a fearful Ku Klux outrage against a negro family in the Dark Corner." Also, Colonel Parmele's report to Governor Chamberlain mentioned a "Dark Corner Rifle Club."

I was under the impression that the entire county of Edgefield was a "Dark Corner" based on Representative Mackey's comments in the halls of the United States Congress a couple of weeks after the Hamburg Massacre. But these other references suggest a specific area of Edgefield rather than the entire county. Where was this place in Edgefield?

SHINING A LIGHT ON THE "DARK CORNER"

In researching the name, I discovered the "Dark Corner"[224] was not a particular town or township, but a name given to a region of Edgefield. According to John Abney Chapman's *History of Edgefield County: From the Earliest Settlements to 1897*, "the line commences just above the road leading to Scott's Ferry and extends up the river embracing all that territory between Stevens' Creek and the Savannah River, as far up as Little River, which empties into the Savannah in Abbeville County."[225] This description is so precise that I was able to follow it using the 1871 map of Edgefield County.

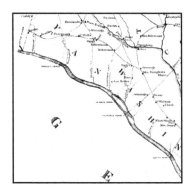

MAP 4. PORTION OF 1871 MAP OF EDGEFIELD CONSTITUTING THE "DARK CORNER"
Map courtesy of the Tompkins Library, Edgefield, South Carolina

According to this map, approximately two-thirds of Washington Township and all of Ryan Township comprised the 'Dark Corner." It appears the Blairs lived in a portion of Washington Township within the "Dark Corner." In the *History of Edgefield County: From the Earliest Settlements to 1897*, John Abney Chapman recounted, "The Dark Corner was first settled by Tuckers, Tompkins, Jennings, Blackwells, Pickets and Searles."[226] I am a Tompkins and a Jennings. My great-grandfather Clifford Blair worked for Dr. William Blackwell, who delivered my grandmother and her sister and buried their mother. My roots in this 'Dark Corner" are deep.

I found confirmation in the 12 August 1857 edition of the *Edgefield Advertiser* that the area of Washington Township where the Blairs resided was part of the "Dark Corner."

PIC NIC AT ROCKY PONDS

There was one of the most extraordinary affairs gotten up at Rocky Ponds recently by those two very respectable gentlemen, Dr. JAMES PRICE and C. H. GOODWIN, whose gentlemanly-like manners are indicative of their prosperity and happiness in this life. We are well acquainted with both of them, and believe that their noble natures and up-right actions, justly entitle them to the hand of some of the fair daughters of the "Dark Corner." They would make good husbands, fond parents and true citizens. And, young ladies, if you should have an "offer," our advice is to take them with[]out hesitation. I will remark, that this Pic Nic was gotten up exclusively for the ladies, and I do not recollect of having seen a drop of the *ardent* about the place—an occurrence never known before in this locality. The gentlemen and ladies of the neighborhood are now roused up to a double degree of diligence in the way of sociality and profound politeness; and are also shaking hands with the temperance cause—as an evidence of which fact we will but allude to the social gather[]ing above noticed, which came off on Saturday the 25th July, at the spring of Mr. EDWARD HOWLE, a worthy citizen and estimable gentleman. The table was furnished with the best of viands in the way of fresh pig and mutton, and a variety of vegetables, well served up under the supervision of Mr. JOHN NORTH, who deserves the best praise for the good manner in which it was prepared.

At the announcement that dinner was ready, I think that about two hundred persons, both male and female, assembled around the table and partook of as fine a dinner as has been given in Edge[]field District this season, and that, Mr. EDITOR, is saying considerable.

After dinner the announcement was made by Mr. C.H. GOODWIN, that as the clouds were indicative off the fall of heavy rain, he would be pleased for the ladies and gentlemen to repair to the well[-]known and familiar "old castle" at the steam mill, which he had the peculiar but most melan[]choly privilege of occupying as a bachelors hall. They accordingly so done, and the young ladies and gentlemen soon after engaged in a social cotil[]lon during the remaining part of the evening, and enjoyed themselves finely. During the afternoon, delicious ice lemonade was ever and anon handed to the ladies and gentlemen present. I would sug[]gest to the ladies if they want a nice thing served up in the way of good lemonades, to get Mr. C. L. BLAIR to make it as he is well qualified to do so, and will cheerfully comply with most any request the ladies may ask of him. All things past of well, and we had a happy and glorious time.

D. M. J.[227]

Rocky Ponds is where Columbus Blair killed Peter Wilk(e)s in January 1872. That tragic event is a stark contrast to this picnic. It appeared that the gentlemen of Rocky Ponds, in the "Dark Corner," were having difficulty attracting wives. From this letter to the editor, I inferred the gentlemen of Rocky Ponds and the "Dark Corner" did not have reputations as refined men of Edgefield. Likely, the reputation was quite the opposite. D. M. J. sought to refute that reputation.

Intrigued by the 'Dark Corner," I searched for additional information. On 21 July 1871, Matthew Calbraith Butler, a military commander (a major general in the Confederate Army) as well as a politician from South Carolina and a resident of Edgefield, testified before a Congressional Committee concerning the condition of affairs in the late insurrectionary states. During his testimony, General Butler mentioned the "Dark Corner."

> *Question.* Now, as to the Ku-Klux organization, you say you have no knowledge of it, but there was a local organization in Edgefield?
>
> *Answer.* Yes, sir.
>
> *Question.* Do you refer to the military company of which you have spoken?
>
> *Answer.* I cannot say it was a military company; it was sort of touching of elbows to be ready for an emergency.
>
> *Question.* When was that organized?
>
> *Answer.* In 1868-'69. It was not a secret organization; it was in the "Dark Corner" of Edgefield, as it was called, very remote from the court-house. The negroes were there burning gin-houses.
>
> *Question.* Was it confined to Edgefield?
>
> *Answer.* Yes, sir.
>
> *Question.* It was not a State organization?
>
> *Answer.* No, sir.
>
> *Question.* Had it a written constitution?
>
> *Answer.* No, sir; it was just an understanding.
>
> *Question.* Is that the only of which you have had any knowledge, in Edgefield County?
>
> *Answer.* The only one.[228]

This testimony solidifies for me that the "recantation" by Sile Robinson and his sons was forged or coerced. According to General Butler, the Ku Klux organization formed in the "Dark Corner," and my Blair ancestors lived in that community.

I cannot help but wonder whether Columbus Blair was part of the Ku Klux Klan. There is smoke—C. L. Blair being listed among those who challenged the reports of the mistreatment of blacks in Edgefield—but I have not uncovered direct proof or fire.

As I continued digging for more information about the "Dark Corner," I stumbled across testimony before Congressional Committees regarding the 1876 election. Jack Picksley, a colored man, was sworn and examined at Columbia, South Carolina, on 10 January 1877.

By Mr. Cameron

Question. Where do you live? —Answer. In Edgefield.

Q. How long have you lived there?—A. All my life.

Q. How old are you?—A. I will be sixty-two years old the 7th of August.

Q. State whether or not you were assaulted by any democrats at any public meeting during the late canvass, and, if so, state the facts in regard to it.—A. I disremember the date, but I think about the 14th October, when there was a mass meeting held at Edgefield Court-House Saturday, late in the evening, about a quarter after sunset, I was going on home quietly, me and another young man, when a company of the red-shirts overtook us and rode on, and when they rode by me they stopped me and jammed me up in the corner of the fence, and I surrendered to them very kindly, and begged them to let me go on; that I was unwell and wished to get home. He asked me if I had a pistol; I told him no, I hadn't had any in forty years, since I had carried a pistol for my master; and he called me a damned liar, and drawed a pistol on me, and searched me, and I happened to have three knives that I carry about this time of the year to butcher with. I had been around Edgefield helping to kill cattle or sheep or anything that comes to hand. He took my knives away from me, and my walking stick, and struck me a lick across the arm; and then ten or twelve men came up and surrounded me, and drawed pistols on me, and would make me say I would vote for Tilden and Hendricks.

By Mr. Merrimon:

Q. Who was the first man that assaulted you?—A. That is Franklin Sharpton; he lives away out in the dark corner.

MR. CAMERON. Go on.

WITNESS. I told him that I didn't know whether I would vote for any person. Said he, "Why?" Said I, "If I cannot vote peaceably and quietly as I always have done, I don't suppose I shall vote at all. At any rate, I am expecting to be murdered the way they are going on now, and I don't expect to live to see my wife and children any more." He cursed and went on a good deal, and finally made me get up behind one of them horses and rode me, as well as I understand, between half and three quarters of a mile. I was right behind the one mile post, and I rode considerably farther than half-way to the other one, and they put me down, and, as the Lord would bless me, it was right at my own gate after dark, and I went on home.

Q. Where were you on the day of the election?—A. At ballot boxes No. 1 and No. 2.

Q. Did you vote?—A: No, sir.

Q. Why not?—A. Well, sir, I was trying to vote from six o'clock in the morning until six at night, and I couldn't get to the polls for no consideration, there was such a crowd of horsemen, and the polls were packed from daylight; in fact, all night Monday night until Tuesday evening. I tried all day to vote, but I couldn't get to vote, and they drawed pistols and guns of all kinds on us that day. I backed up in the crowd several times to try to work in, and finally I had to just go home without it.

Q. Who surrounded the polls in that way?—A. The democratic party.

Q. You were a republican?—A. Yes, sir; and always have been.

Q. What time of day did you first go to poll No. 1?—A. About six o'clock in the morning, and staid there after ten, and none of the colored men had voted. Then we were ordered by the marshal to go to No. 2. I went up there and staid until about half an hour by sun in the evening, and then went to No. 1 again, thinking I would get a chance to vote.

Q. How many went with you to No. 1?—A. Some two to three hundred, and we sent twelve men to try to get in when there was no voting going on and everybody was then standing around on the steps; but they wouldn't let no one come in.

Q. How many republican voters were prevented from voting in the same way you were at Edgefield that day?

MR. MERRIMOM. State what you know of your own knowledge; do not go to guessing about it.

A. I have some idea about it; I think there was not less than five or six hundred. There was a massed crowd there.

BY MR. CAMERON:

Q. It has been stated here that those five or six hundred might have gone to poll No. 2, and might have voted; what is the fact?—A. There was no chance. When we went to No. 2 there was a crowd of horses and horsemen galloping along ahead of us, and striking some of us with sticks. There is men here who have got blood knocked out of their heads. They had to go through all of that to get to the polls, and when we would go there they would back up in such a way on their horses that they wouldn't give us any showing at all, and then when a few would get in the box they would try to test their vote and hinder us all the time they could, and tried in every way to prevent us, and we bore it all and had no fuss nor nothing, and didn't wish to have none. We thought we were voting as quietly as we always did, and didn't try to have no fuss in any way.[229]

I wondered if my 2ND great-grandfather, Nathaniel Blair, and my 3RD great-grandfather, McDuffie Tompkins, were among the five to six hundred colored men obstructed from voting. Were they intimidated? Did they cower in fear and turn away? Or did they stand their ground, determined to exercise their right to vote, a right their fathers and grandfathers never had the privilege to exercise? I cannot know, but I hope and believe it was the latter. As future leaders at Mount Lebanon Church, they may have begun to establish their standing in their community with this election.

In reading the testimony of another colored witness, John Martinborough, it appears Edgefield County preceded Chicago by a century in voting early and often.

BY MR. MERRIMON:

Q. Who is Shepard?—A. Olando Sheppard, United States supervisor there; and after a while we managed to get them out, and I told them, "Well, gentlemen, if you don't intend to let me go on and re-erect this railing I will go away with the box." I just told them that, but at the same time I had no idea of doing it, thinking I might get them out so as to fix the railing. Well, they went out, and with the assistance of the republican manager and one or two other men I got the railing up. About that time—it was about five minutes of six—I swore the clerk, and the polling commenced. There were only three colored men there; that was myself and the other republican manager, and Harris, United States deputy marshal, I think he is.

Well, the democrats voted there, about three hundred of them, all that were around the house, and then about that time they went out and mounted their horses and surrounded the house and hollered, and there was shooting going on, and the democrats came in to vote, and we swore them, ten at a time, and they voted. The majority of the managers of the election had selected a clerk of their own, and the democrats they wanted a clerk, and for quiet's sake I gave them a clerk also—two clerks. Well, they went on voting, and a great many of the democrats who had voted they came back and wanted to vote again. I said, "Well, you have voted before," and a lot of the other men around there said, "These men have not voted and they shall vote," and I could not say anything amongst those men, so I had to let them do it. They drew their pistols out, and their clubs, and were cursing and abusing me, and a great many said that they would do this, that, and the other thing, and I had to let it go. I asked them their names and they would not tell me; they would go to the democratic clerk and whisper their names to him. I don't know how many white men did repeat.

BY MR MERRIMON:

Q. Can you tell us a few of them?—A. I cannot tell you how many did repeat; most all of them repeated.

Q. Give us a few of the men.—A. I don't know their names, as I am a new comer in Edgefield; only been there about two years. A great many of them live away back in Dark Corner, about forty or fifty miles from the village.

BY MR. CAMERON:

Q. Can you give the committee an idea of the number of white men who repeated, as you have here stated?—A. At the box?

Q. Yes.—A. I think at that box there was about, I should say, one hundred and seventy-five repeated. I cannot tell how often they repeated though.

BY MR. MERRIMON:

Q. Do you mean to say that they repeated at that time?—A. I say that they repeated. They voted the first time; of course they were allowed to do that; and a little later in the day they would come again and vote, and so on and so on. I cannot tell how often they repeated. They spoke secretly to the clerk and gave him their names. Some of them I would ask them where they lived and if they were residents of the place sixty days before the election. They would not tell me, and they says, "None of your business;" and they drew their pistols and cursed me and said, "You damned negro radical, you ain't got no business to ask a white man such questions; "and the democrats standing by would say, You needn't answer," and tell me "Don't ask another question or I will hit you with this club,' or "I will shoot you with this pistol." By nine o'clock the white men stopped voting, and I think the first colored man that voted was this United States marshal.[230]

As I reread the testimonies of Jack Picksley and John Martinborough, I thought about the voter intimidation the colored males of Edgefield encountered. White residents, seeking to maintain their position at the apex of society, stuffed the ballot boxes to ensure outcomes favorable to themselves. During the antebellum period, although colored outnumbered whites, the enslaved population was generally kept in check through fear. After the end of the Civil War, a recently-freed black population outnumbering whites could overturn the will of the aristocratic white population, particularly at the ballot box. White Edgefield residents resisted the Yankee invaders and disdained assistance provided to the freedmen. To get back control of their society, whites needed to control affairs politically, at both the county and state levels. Without a doubt, what John Martinborough and Jack Picksley experienced was the implementation of Martin Witherspoon Gary's "Edgefield Plan" to redeem South Carolina by restoring the Democratic Party to power. The white men who threatened these and other black men with pistols were apparently part of the rifle clubs organized by Gary. Colonel Parmele's report to Governor Chamberlain, a year before the 1876 election, mentioned the "Dark Corner Rifle Club," commanded by a Captain Blackwell. The "Dark Corner" appears to have been the epicenter for Gary's "Edgefield Plan." This deduction is supported by the testimony of L. Charlton, a white gentleman called as a witness by G. D. Tillman, candidate for a Congressional seat for South Carolina. The following exchange occurred when Lawrence Cain (a colored man who served in the South Carolina Senate representing Edgefield and who was an 1876 graduate of the University of South Carolina Law School) questioned Mr. Charlton on cross-examination.

> Q. Will you state whether you saw any white men come in on horse-back dressed in red shirts? — A. Yes; I saw some few.

> Q. Did not these men come into town yelling and in quite a threatening attitude, and were they not armed with guns and pistols? — A. They came in clubs of ten or twelve, and cheered a little on the public square; then they scattered off, their horses put away. If any had guns or pistols, I saw none.

> ●●●●●

> Q. About how many Democrats dressed in red shirts came into town that evening? — A. I do not know. Judging from the squads I saw, I suppose from 75 to 100 came in at different times.

> ●●●●●

> Q. Did you see any Republican at the court house precinct on the day of last election that lived a great distance from the court-house that you know? — A. None that I was acquainted with.

> Q. Did you see any Democrats here from the Dark Corner, a distance of 25 miles; from near Saluda River, 25 miles distance; from near Ridge Springs, a distance of 17 miles; or from the neighborhood of Shaw's Mill, a distance of 18 miles? — A. I saw some few white men here from Dark Corner; none from Saluda, or Ridge or from Shaw's Mill that I remember.[231]

While reading about white males using violence to suppress the votes of colored males during the 1876 election, I recalled the killing of Milledge Blair by Sam Stewart. Milledge Blair was murdered because he supposedly was a "Democrat nigger." Against the backdrop of Gary's "Edgefield Plan," Sam Stewart attempted to thwart efforts by whites to "roll back the hands of time." Sam Stewart presumably viewed Milledge Blair as the ultimate betrayer, one whose actions undermined the efforts of the colored population. I wondered if Milledge Blair was, in fact, a Democrat or if someone else, maybe a white man, had merely suggested the possibility of that to Sam Stewart. Unfortunately, the truth has been lost with the passage of time.

Subsequently, the truth about the intentions of the Democratic Party from the "Dark Corner" was publicly revealed. In the 10 June 1890 edition of *The News and Courier*, the Democrats of the Dark Corner boasted:

> That is a very clear and steady light that streams out from the Dark Corner of Edgefield County. The men of 1876 are marching to the front—and the men who followed Wade Hampton and Calbraith Butler and Mart Gary are as true and faithful to the Democratic party now under the leadership of the Blackwells and the Jenningses and Selfs and other true and tried defenders of good and honest government, as they were fourteen years ago. The men of the Dark Corner have never flinched in the face of danger and have never failed to do their duty. They will not be found wanting in the present campaign and are prepared in numbers and resources to stand fast for the State and its best interests.
>
> The Democratic club of the Dark Corner was organized for the campaign on Saturday last. It was organized for the Democratic party and not for the interest of Capt. Tillman; for the purpose of promoting the continuance of white supremacy in South Carolina and not for the sake of advancing the "personal preferences" of any faction; with the distinct object of striving for the good of the State and

not for the glory [of] an ambitious office-seeker . . . [The Democrats of the Dark Corner] pledge themselves anew to work for the preservation of "white or Democratic suprem-acy, which "has proved to be such a great blessing to "our people, both white and black, and for "the common good of all."[232]

The "Dark Corner" has not been forgotten with the passage of time. In his book *Walking Integrity: Benjamin Elijah Mays, Mentor to Martin Luther King, Jr.*, Lawrence E. Carter, Sr. wrote:

> The life of Benjamin Elijah Mays illustrates the ironies of southern history. Born in an area known as the "dark corner" of a county notorious for its extremism, Mays emerged as the great advocate of nonviolence. This area of the South Carolina upcountry has produced many national, regional, and state leaders of distinction. John C. Calhoun, the great defender of slavery; Martin Witherspoon Gary, the "Bald Eagle of the Confederacy"; and "Pitchfork["] Ben Tillman, the agrarian firebrand, all were born in the area. [233]

A POLITICAL FORCE IN THE SHADOWS

Returning to the Democratic Club of the Dark Corner, I won-dered what role C. L. Blair played during the 1876 election. I found him mentioned by John T. Gatson, a white man who was called to testify by George D. Tillman, a Democratic can-didate, who contested the Congressional seat held by Robert Smalls, a Black Republican. Mr. Gaston testified in Edgefield County on 13 April 1877.

> Question. What is your age, residence, and where were you on the 7th of November last, the day of election? — Answer. Thirty-six years old; born near Ridge Spring, and was at Ridge Spring on 7th of November last.
>
> Q. Were the polls opened according to law, and did the voting proceed quietly and orderly during the day? — A.

According to my judgment they did, and the polls were opened according to the law.

Q. Were you present at the box during the whole day?—A. I was on the grounds all day; sometimes at the box and sometimes outdoors.

Q. Were you present when the counting of the vote and the returns were made by officers of the election?—A. I was present when the polls closed, and was asked by the managers to leave the room with the balance of the crowd, and did so.

Q. What manager requested it?—A. First and the supervisor, (the Republican,) after consulting with others; all agreed to leave but the officials.

Q. Was there any dispute or disagreement in regard to the count or signing the returns, as far as you know?—A. None that I heard of.

Q. State if you saw a demonstration made by about two hundred Republican voters that day, and what was said and done about it; give us the full particulars.—A. It was, I suppose, about 10 o'clock a.m.; some two hundred colored men came up the road hollowing and cursing—cheering Chamberlain and cursing Hampton. The crowd had clubs and sticks; one man had a foot-adze, with a long handle to it; two vehicles behind the crowd both had guns in them; the crowd went over to the polls, and I suppose all voted; going to the polls I met them; I told them that they could hollow for Chamberlain, but must not curse Wad[e] Hampton again; if they did, those who did it would be sorry for it; no other man that I know of said anything to them but myself. Robert Watson came up and said to me, "Let them say what they please, for it is the last chance they will ever have to hollow." He went through the crowd patting the men on the shoulder, and telling them to cheer for Chamberlain as much as they please. Mr. Watson is a white democrat, and employs a large number of colored men on his plantation.

Q. Who was the leader of this large crowd, and what was the bearing of this later? — A. It is generally known that George Jackson, the Republican supervisor, was the leader of them, but he was not with them that morning. He arrived there some little time before they came up.

Q. Was not this demonstration intended to intimidate the colored Democratic clubs as well as the whites, and to take possession of the polls, as they had done at previous elections? Did they not say, "clear the way, we are coming," or something to that effect? — A. I fully believe it was intended to intimidate the colored Democratic clubs as well as the white men. Some one hollowed out, "Clear the way, we are coming." It had been their custom before to take possession of the polls at previous elections.

Q. Did they not approach the polls in a threatening and menacing manner, and was there many white men there at any time during the day? — A. They did advance to the polls in a body, crowding around the door, yelling and hollowing, as they did up the road. Do not think there was exceeding one hundred white men there at any one time during the day.

➤•••➤•

[cross-examination by Lawrence Cain]

Q. You stated you had a Democratic club consisting of thirty colored men. Are you certain all of these colored men voted the Democratic ticket? — A. They have all told me so since.

Q. Give the names of the thirty colored men, members of the club. — A. George Bastin, Richard Lott, Sam Archer, Joe Barnes, Sam Holmes, Toney Lightsey, Joe Merrett, Lewis Pompy, Lott Sawyer, William Lee, Peter Weaver . . . Tom Coleman, George Samuels, Columbus Blair, and others.

➤•••➤•

Q. Did you see any white men with pistols or guns there that day? — A. I saw no white men with guns. I saw a few white men with pistols; saw them under the bottom of their coats — their coats being short; did not see any drawn.

Q. You stated that a colored Democrat told you that the Republicans intended to raise a row there that day. Give the name of these colored Democrats. — A. One of them who told me has been killed since, Richard Lott; the other man, Samuel Holmes.

Q. By whom was Richard Lott killed, and for what was he killed? — A. He was killed by a colored Republican. Reports say that it was for going to this man's house after his wife. Other reports say he was killed for being a Democrat; but it is all hearsay with me.

Q. Have you not been informed that he was killed in this man's wife's house? — A. I have heard so. I know nothing of my own knowledge.[234]

Columbus (C. L.) Blair of Rocky Pond, Washington Township, was not a colored man. I turned to Ancestry.com for assistance in researching whether there were two Columbus Blairs in Edgefield. I searched for Columbus Blair in Edgefield between 1870 and 1880. The first result was as expected — the white Columbus Blair living in Parks Store, Washington Township, in 1870. The only other Columbus Blair in South Carolina was a 25 year old black male in 1880 residing in Beaufort.[235] This black Columbus Blair lived in a completely different region of South Carolina, and for that reason, I doubt he was the individual identified by John T. Gatson. There were two Columbus Blairs[236] residing in Georgia in 1870, but these individuals were white.

If this Columbus Blair was not the former slave owner, who was he? I speculated that maybe John T. Gatson had meant to say Milledge Blair, the colored man killed by Sam Stewart for being a "Democrat nigger." If my speculation is true, what a Freudian slip by Mr. Gatson that he would associate Milledge Blair with Columbus Blair. Was Milledge a former slave of Columbus or was there, perhaps, a familial or blood connection between Milledge and Columbus? John T. Gatson's testimony suggested that other colored Democrats faced hostility, such as verbal or physical threats, from colored Republicans.

I decided to search for these other colored men Gaston identified as Democrats at the time of the 1880 federal census. This strategy was imprecise. Although someone may have resided in Edgefield at the time of the 1876 election, there was no guarantee the individual was still alive and living in Edgefield four years later. Nonetheless, I was able to locate three men: Joe Barnes (residing in Meriwether),[237] Sam Holmes (residing in Moss),[238] and George Samuels (residing in Mobley).[239] I located four Tom Colemans, two residing in Aiken[240] (a county created out of Edgefield) and two residing in Edgefield.[241] I also found a nine-year-old Lewis Pompey, residing in Mobley,[242] in a household with a female as the head. This younger Lewis may have been named after a father bearing the same name.

Were these colored men truly Democrats or did John T. Gatson merely make that claim? I had no way of determining the truth.

The election of 1876 was critical. Politically, in the defeated southern states, whites reclaimed their positions of power. The Reconstruction period, which had begun with such promise after the end of the Civil War, was ultimately a failure for the colored population of the South, who lived in fear. Lynching was the ultimate weapon wielded against the colored population. Ida B. Wells, a black journalist from Memphis, Tennessee, sought to raise the consciousness of America about the lynching in the South and to ensure that those black lives lost to the noose mattered. In 1895, Ms. Wells penned *A Red Record: Alleged Causes of Lynching*. She wrote in one particularly pertinent part:

> From 1865 to 1872, hundreds of colored men and women were mercilessly murdered and the almost invariable reason assigned was that they met their death by being alleged participants in an insurrection or riot. But this story at last wore itself out. No insurrection ever materialized; no Negro rioter was ever apprehended and proven guilty, and no dynamite ever recorded the black man's protest against oppression and wrong. It was too much to ask thoughtful people to believe this transparent story, and the southern white people at last made up their minds that some other excuse must be had.
>
> Then came the second excuse, which had its birth during the turbulent times of reconstruction. By an amendment to the Constitution the Negro was given the right of franchise, and, theoretically at least, his ballot became his invaluable emblem of citizenship. In a government "of the people, for the people, and by the people," the Negro's vote became an important factor in all matters of state and national politics. But this did not last long. The southern white man would not consider that the Negro had any right which a white man was bound to respect, and the idea of a republican form of government in the southern states grew into general contempt. It was maintained that "This is a white man's government," and regardless of numbers the white man should rule. "No Negro domination" became the new legend on the sanguinary banner of the sunny South, and under it rode the Ku Klux Klan, the Regulators, and the lawless mobs, which for any cause chose to murder one man or a dozen as suited their purpose best. It was a long, gory campaign; the blood chills and the heart almost loses faith in Christianity when one thinks of Yazoo, Hamburg, Edgefield, Copiah, and the countless massacres of defense-

less Negroes, whose only crime was the attempt to exercise
their right to vote.

Ida B. Wells identified four areas by name. I recognized
Hamburg and Edgefield, but I was somewhat confused since
I had thought that Hamburg was a part of Edgefield. It is on
the 1871 Map of Edgefield County. I decided to research this
matter. When Ms. Wells penned *A Red Record: Alleged Causes of
Lynching* in 1895, Hamburg was part of Aiken County, South
Carolina, which was formed 10 March 1871.[243] Only during
the early years (1865-1871) of the Reconstruction period was
Hamburg part of Edgefield County. When the Hamburg
Massacre occurred in July 1876, Hamburg was part of Aiken
County. This explains why Ms. Wells listed Hamburg separate
from Edgefield. Nonetheless, two of the four localities where
there were "countless massacres of defenseless Negroes" fell
in Edgefield County or what used to be Edgefield County.
This speaks volumes about Edgefield's notoriety.

With the backdrop of this national perspective, the testimonies by colored and white men regarding the 1876 election
struck a deeper and colder chord in me. What particularly
occurred to me when I read John T. Gatson's testimony was
the sharp contrast between his testimony with those of John
Martinborough and Jack Picksley regarding who threatened
whom. John Martinborough described white males hollering
and firing off their pistols, whereas as John T. Gatson charac-
terized the colored men as yelling and cursing. Historically, I
know the testimonies of John Martinborough and Jack Picksley were more accurate, but there is a nugget of information
I gleaned from all three testimonies. They all mentioned one
common fact—the manager of election. This is where C. L.
Blair steps into the light.

In searching for any scrap of information on C. L. Blair, I
utilized the online database of the South Carolina Department

of Archives and History. One of the two results for C. L. Blair revealed that he was a manager of election and polls for Edge-field District in 1859.[244] He was also a manager of election for Parks, Edgefield District, in September 1862[245] and December 1863.[246] As listed in the 14 October 1872 edition of *The Charleston Daily*, C. L. Blair was appointed as a Democrat elections supervisor for Edgefield County, specifically for an area called Red Hill.[247] Consulting the 1871 map of Edgefield County, I found Red Hill in Collins Township, which shares a border with Washington Township; it is located along Blair's Ford.

MAP 5. PORTION OF 1871 MAP OF EDGEFIELD SHOWING RED HILL, BLAIR'S FORD

Map courtesy of the Tompkins Library, Edgefield, South Carolina

C. L. Blair served as manager of election for Washington, Edgefield County, in August of 1900[248] and a manager of election for Modoc in October of 1900.[249] Although I have not located any other records documenting C. L. Blair's service as a manager of election or elections supervisor, I suspect that he continued to serve in such capacities during the intervening years. That would mean he oversaw voting for more than 40 years. He was a man well-connected within Edgefield's political establishment. The testimonies of Jack Picksley and John Martinborough implicate the "Dark Corner" in hostile actions toward the colored population, the same area where C. L. Blair was a manager of election or elections supervisor. Reflecting further, this would mean C. L. Blair likely knew of and condoned Gary's "Edgefield Plan" to restore white control of governance in South Carolina and repress the colored population. This deduction is not far-fetched, especially in light of the following, published in the *Edgefield Advertiser* on 13 April 1864 and 21 April 1864:

> To the Voters of Edgefield District
>
> In the present condition of our country, men of sound judgment and experience should be sent to the Legislature. We therefore nominate our old neighbor, Dr. W. D. JENNINGS, a man suitable for the emergency, hoping he will consent to aid our State by his counsel in the next Legislature.
>
> L. TUCKER
> C. M. FREEMAN
> S. S. FREEMAN
> C. WELLS
> E. A. SEARLES
> JOSEPH PRICE
> E. H. CHAMBERLAIN
> G. C. ROBERTSON
> T. E. JENNINGS
> C. L. BLAIR
> W. L. PARKS
> J. A. TALBERT[250]

Based on the date of this notice, the "emergency" undoubtedly concerned the South's untenable position in its fight against the North. Further, in examining the 1871 map of Edgefield County, I realized that all the endorsers, except for the first, were surnames listed in Ryan Township or Washington Township, prominent surnames from the "Dark Corner."

Besides being a manager of election or elections supervisor for more than 40 years, C. L. Blair was a school district trustee for North Washington in 1893.[251] Almost thirty years prior, C. L. Blair publicly endorsed—via a notice in the *Edgefield Advertiser*—a specific individual, Miss Hattie L. Morgan, whose services were secured as a school teacher.[252] These political or politically-connected positions were not the only seats of influence C. L. Blair held in Edgefield.

FINANCIAL ELITE IN EDGEFIELD

C. L. Blair's footprints extended beyond the political realm. I discovered he was appointed to the Board of Directors for the Greenwood and Augusta Railroad. A meeting was held at Midway on 1 December 1871 that was attended by friends of the Greenwood and Augusta Railroad as well as citizens of Abbeville and Edgefield. As reported in the 6 December 1871 edition of the *Abbeville Press and Banner*:

> On motion of J.D. Talbert, Esq., the following resolutions were unanimously adopted.
>
> *Resolved 1*st, That a committee of twelve be appointed, who shall adopt such measures as may be necessary to secure a charter for a Railroad to be known as the Greenwood and Augusta Railroad.
>
> *Resolved 2nd*, That said committee be authorized to have an immediate survey made and published.
>
> *Resolved 3rd*, That said committee be empowered to raise by subscription, an amount of money sufficient to have said survey made along the proposed route, and for such other purposes as, by said committee may be deemed advisable.
>
> ●•••●
>
> Under the first Resolution the follow[]ing gentlemen were appointed as said committee of twelve—Dr. J. H. Jennings,

Gen. P. H. Bradley, J. D. Talbert, Esq., A. M. Aiken, Dr. N. Merriwether, S. P. Boozer, C. L. Blair, Maj. J. S. White, W. L. Parks, Dr. J. D. Neel, J. G. Shep[]herd and Capt. W. K. Bradley.[253]

Intrigued by this discovery, I sought more information on the Greenwood and Augusta Railroad. Further research revealed that this corporation used convicts to build the railroad in South Carolina and did not treat them well. In my research, I located paperwork titled *Report of the Superintendent of the Penitentiary Together with Other Papers, in Regard to the Condition and Treatment of Convicts Employed on the Greenwood and Augusta Railroad.*[254] On 2 September 1879, Superintendent T. J. Lipscomb issued a report to the Board of Directors of the South Carolina Penitentiary stating in pertinent part:

> GENTLEMAN—Having received a letter from General P. H. Bradley, President of the Greenwood and Augusta Railroad, stating that a great deal of mortality and sickness existed among the convicts leased to that company, I conferred with the Chairman of the Board, showing him the letter. He instructed me to go over there and make an inspection of their condition. . . .

> •••••

> I met the Hon. A. P. Butler, one of the Board of Directors, in Augusta, Ga., about 11 o'clock [on the 21st of August]. We left immediately for the camp on the South Carolina side, in Edgefield County, about nineteen or twenty miles distan[ce], which we reached about 5 P.M.
>
> I found in one end of the stockade nine sick men chained on what was intended to be a straw bed, but the straw was too thin to do much good. I could not stand the awful stench and had to direct the guard to unchain them and bring them out in front of the stockade. I found them in a deplorable condition, all of them complaining of venereal diseases, swollen limbs, &c. I then went to the so-called hospital, where I found three sick—two white men and one black man. They had some straw to lie upon and were

all chained. They were all covered with vermin and fleas—
so much so that I was forced to leave the room. I don't see
how it was possible for a well man to exist in these places
well treated, much less a sick man with no treatment, or
so little that I regarded it as none. They had no change of
clothing, no shoes, no covering of any de[]scription that I
could see. They reported that they had had no medicine
and no medical treatment except one dose of paregoric in
the three days preceding, and their nourishment was fat
bacon and bread. I left the camp and proceeded to where
they were at work on the road, about a mile or a mile and
a half distan[ce]. I found about seventy-five men at work
on the road, clothed in the Penitentiary stripe that I had
sent to General Bradley about five weeks before. It was so
late that I could only look at their condition generally and
postpone the inspection until next morning.

I went next morning to where they were at work, called
the roll and inspected them. I found a great many of them
complaining of vene[]real diseases and swollen limbs, and
almost all with scurvy. They were very dirty in person and
clothing—having no change; some of them said they had
not washed for weeks. I saw no blankets or bed clothing
for them to lie upon or cover with.

I heard great and loud complaint about the cruel treatment of con[]victs by Captain J. J. Cahill and his guard. One
of them, W. H. McGar[]very, No. 3125, showed Colonel
Butler and myself scars upon his head which he said were
caused by blows from a stick in the hands of Captain Cahill,
and persons outside gave the same information. Captain
Cahill himself, in reporting those that were dead, informed
me that the guard had shot one while in shackles and fas-
tened to the gang chain, claiming that he was in revolt. We
heard that Cahill had ordered the guard to shoot him.

The convicts were generally in such a bad condition
that I deemed it my imperative duty to send the Surgeon
of this institution to see them.

The sickness and mortality being so great, I heard that some
of the Directors of the [B]oa[r]d had resigned and Dr. T. J.
Mackey, their surgeon, had ceased to visit the convicts pro-

fessionally. I was informed that he had refused to continue to treat the convicts because his prescriptions were not filled nor his orders as to treatment and nourishment carried out.

●•••●

On 24th September, 1877, [Greenwood and Augusta Railroad] received 100 convicts; on 18th Octo[]ber, 1877, they received 3 convicts; on 31st October, 1877, they received 2 convicts; on 2d May, 1878, they received 65 convicts; on 6th Decem[]ber, 1878, they received 40 convicts; on 7th April, 1879, they received 75 convicts; making, in all, 285 convicts. Of this number 18 were re[]turned to the Penitentiary before I took charge, 38 escaped, 17 were dis[]charged, 7 pardoned, and up to August 1st, according to reports submit[]ted by Captain Cahill, there were 93 deaths. I found when I went there that 21 had died who were not reported, the most of them in August, making a total of 114 deaths.[255]

I was stunned. Forty percent of the convicts assigned to the Greenwood and Augusta Railroad, both black and white, died while in the custody of this corporation. C. L. Blair is not mentioned in the Report. Supposedly, because of the mistreatment of the convicts, some Board members resigned. I wondered if C. L. Blair resigned before this inspection.

The mistreatment of the convicts was so scandalous that the General Assembly of the State of South Carolina responded accordingly on 18 February 1880.

The convicts on the Greenwood and Augusta Railroad were ordered back to the Penitentiary by the following Resolution, passed October 10, 1879, on motion of Governor Simpson:

Resolved, That, in view of the heavy mortality heretofore existing among the convicts hired by the Greenwood and Augusta Railroad, and in view of the fact that Dr. B. W. Taylor, of Columbia, after a thorough individual examination of the convicts remaining with said company, recently made, given it as his decided opinion that the health of said convicts requires that they be removed from said employment, it is the sense of this Board that all the convicts now in the employ of said company, with the exception of the eight reported by Dr. Taylor in good condition, be at once returned to the Penitentiary in Columbia. The eight reported as in good condition to be returned or not, as the com[] pany may desire.

Resolved, That this action above, with the report of Dr. Taylor, be served on General Bradley, the President of the Greenwood and Augusta Railroad, with the Resolution that said convicts be returned at once to the Penitentiary, and that the Superintendent be instructed to receive them.[256]

More than a century later, I applaud the action of the Governor and General Assembly. One perplexing matter, however, is that they chose to give the corporation any discretion at all in continuing to employ the eight convicts in good condition. Dr. Taylor recommended those eight convicts be removed from the employment of the Greenwood and Augusta Railroad. The General Assembly's action is inexplicable.

My search for C. L. Blair was nearly complete. On 20 March 1877, the General Assembly of the Commonwealth of Virginia approved the incorporation of the Jennings Association of the United States of America. C. L. Blair is listed as a director. Section two of this Act defines the objective:

The Jennings [A]ssociation of the United States of America, shall have for its sole object the recovery of such portions of the estates of William Jennings, late of Acton Place, England, and of William Jennings, Senior, of Jennings' Ordinary, Virginia, United States of America, as belongs to such distributees, legatees, devisees, donees, or heirs-at-law of said William Jennings, of Acton Place, London, England, and said William Jennings, Senior, of Jennings' Ordinary, Virginia, United States of America, under the laws of England, or any of the United States of America, or under the laws of any other government. . . .[257]

C. L. Blair's wife, of course, was a Jennings. Those estates must have been sizeable for an association to be formed and to obtain approval of the General Assembly of the Commonwealth of Virginia.

Contemplating C. L. Blair's wealth, besides the 1879 tax duplicate record, I could not find additional information regarding how much land C. L. Blair owned. I discovered from a notice in the *Edgefield Advertiser* published multiple times in late 1846 and early 1847 that Columbus Blair, Applicant, had sued his mother, Sarah Blair, and other Defendants in an action to partition the estate of James M. Blair, Columbus's brother.[258] H. Boulware, Sheriff, Edgefield District, advised:

> BY an Order from John Hill Esqr., Ordinary of Edgefield District, I will proceed to sell at Edgefield Court House, on the first Monday in April next, a tract of land belonging to the estate of James M. Blair, dec'd, situate[d] in the District afore-said, on Steven's creek, waters of the Savannah river, containing four hundred acres, more or less, adjoining lands of James Tompkins, Drury Morgan, Abram Kilcrease, and others. . . .[259]

Although I never found information about how much real estate C. L. Blair owned, through the sale of adjoining properties, I imagine it was a sizeable amount. On 25 March 1863, there was a notice in the *Edgefield Advertiser* titled "Land for Sale." The description included the following: "NINE HUNDRED ACRES Situated on Stevens' Creek, on the Road leading from Augusta to Calhoun's Mill, 28 miles from Augusta and bounded by lands of Dr. J. J. Cartledge, Mrs. Cartledge, C. L. Blair and others."[260] On 26 October 1871, a notice of a Sheriff's Sale of property belonging to the Estate of James Tompkins was posted in the *Edgefield Advertiser*. Four separate tracts would be sold, including "One Tract, containing One Thousand (100[0]) Acres, more or less, known as the Home Tract—

adjoining lands of C. L. Blair, Mrs. Sarah Blair, Jasper Price, W. L. Parks and others."[261] Over twenty years later, on 2 December 1896, another notice in the *Edgefield Advertiser*, under Master's Sale, included this description: "Tract No. 3. One other tract of land known as Rocky Pond tract, situated in the county of Edgefield and State of South Carolina, and lying on both sides of the Augusta and Knoxville Railroad, containing seven hundred, 700 acres, more or less, and adjoining lands of C. L. Blair, Martha B. Bussey, Howle and others."[262] I was unsure whether the Augusta and Knoxville Railroad was the same as the Greenwood and Augusta Railroad, but according to *The Railway News* edition dated 22 May 1880:

> AUGUSTA AND KNOXVILLE.—The stockholders of the Augusta and Knoxville and Greenwood and Augusta Railroads have effectuated a consolidation under the name of Augusta and Knoxville Railroad. Eugene F. Verdery was elected President, and ten directors were elected from Georgia and six from South Carolina. Bonds will be issued to complete the road.[263]

Before its consolidation with the Greenwood and Augusta Railroad, in May of 1877, C. L. Blair was one of the men appointed to the Business Committee for the Augusta and Knoxville Railroad.[264] In light of this appointment, and presuming the Augusta and Knoxville Railroad was a competitor to the Greenwood and Augusta Railroad, I deduced C. L. Blair resigned from the Greenwood and Augusta Railroad before the August 1879 inspection of its Edgefield County work camp. Further, considering the scandalous conduct by certain employees of the Greenwood and Augusta Railroad, it is not surprising that the latter railroad's name was retained when the two merged.

Having exhausted my research of C. L. Blair and learning nothing further about my direct ancestors (although gaining a better understanding of Edgefield in the first 30 years or so after the end of the Civil War), I wondered if I had overlooked any other potential sources of information. Thanks to my cousin Sameera, I soon became aware of another set of records to consult.

SAMEERA'S GUIDING LIGHT

In December 2013, I assembled the last issue of *Homeplace*, the official newsletter of the Old Edgefield District African American Genealogical Society, for which I was editor. Among the matters submitted for possible publication was an extremely lengthy compilation of slaves who were members of various Edgefield churches during the antebellum period (that is, the time before the Civil War). Sameera had created a spreadsheet listing the names of slaves that was over 50 pages in length, longer than the actual issue of *Homeplace* (which was 40 pages). I was unable to include Sameera's entire compilation, but I incorporated as many pages as possible.

I scanned the entire spreadsheet, wondering which church my enslaved Blair ancestors would have attended. During a call with Sameera in November 2013, I inquired if she knew which white churches slave owners and their slaves attended in what is presently McCormick County, but she did not know.

I attempted to identify the Parksville-area churches during the antebellum period on my own without any success. Again, I turned to Sameera. On 17 January 2014, I sent her the following e-mail:

> Good Morning Sameera.
>
> Do you know someone I could speak with about the history of Mount Lebanon Baptist Church and any "white"

churches in the same area before the establishment of Mount Lebanon?

Thank you.
Natonne[265]

Of course, Sameera knew someone. On 22 January 2014, she referred me to Charles Jennings. "He's willing to speak to you. I told him you were related to the Chinns, Kemps, Blairs and possibly the Jennings as well (I just guessed about the last family, though)."[266] Sameera's guess was correct, as I am a Jennings. I wondered if this Charles Jennings was a distant cousin.

That same evening, I called Charles Jennings. After introducing myself and mentioning my ancestral roots at Mount Lebanon Baptist Church, I asked Deacon Jennings if he knew the name of the church that predated Mount Lebanon Baptist Church that slave owners and their slaves would have attended. Deacon Jennings responded that he recalled speaking to an elderly white man years ago who told him that the church servicing what is now Parksville during slavery was called Calliham's Mill Baptist Church. I was not sure if I heard him correctly, so he spelled the name for me.

While I continued conversing with Deacon Jennings, I searched for this church using Google. I did not receive many results. The church was mentioned a handful of times on genealogy message boards. One person posted on the Blackwell Family Genealogy Forum:

> This REV. CHARLES NEWMAN BLACKWELL in 1789 was the Minister of Calliham's Mill Baptist Church which was a member of the Edgefield Baptist Association. That Calliham's Baptist Church was located on Stevens Creek in what is now McCormack [sic] County, South Carolina.
>
> According to Leah Townsend in her book "Baptists in South Carolina," this CHARLES NEWMAN BLACKWELL ministered in 1798 at the Plum Branch Creek Baptist

Church on Plum Branch Creek in Edgefield/McCormack [sic] Counties in South Carolina. That Plum Branch Creek Church was located near the present day town of McCormack [sic], South Carolina.[267]

I should not be surprised by the surname Blackwell. That name has deep roots in the "Dark Corner" of Edgefield.

I relayed this search result to Deacon Jennings and then inquired as to who would have records of this Calliham's Mill Baptist Church. He suggested I check with Furman University in Greenville, South Carolina, the repository of the South Carolina Baptist Historical Collection.[268]

Our conversation then shifted to Mount Lebanon Baptist Church. I sought any additional information about the church's history, particularly any preserved records. Deacon Jennings informed me that there had been a fire in which many of the historical records of the church were lost, which was very disappointing to me.

QUEST FOR INFORMATION

Armed with the name provided by Deacon Jennings, I began my quest for information about Calliham's Mill Baptist Church, hoping it would lead me to my enslaved Blair ancestors. I began with the tip from that genealogy message board, which referred to *Baptists in South Carolina* by Leah Townsend. I searched for this book and author combined with the name of the church but did not receive a result listing the church. I then searched for the author and book and received results confirming the existence of the book. I was puzzled that I could not locate her reference to the church.

When I renewed my research approximately two months later, I mistakenly typed the name "Callahan's Mill Baptist

Church," rather than "Calliham's." To my surprise, I received a result listing Leah Townsend's book.

> The churches of the Savanah River region tended to associate with Georgia groups. Callahan's Mill Church, which was constituted in 1785, entered the Georgia Association sometime before 1792. It had as its pastor 1792-1793, and probably after, Rev. Samuel Cartledge. It was dismissed by the Georgia Association in 1804 to enter the Bethel Association the next year.[269]

According to Leah Townsend, the church was called Callahan's Mill Church, rather than Calliham's. It was surprising to learn of the church's affiliation with the Georgia Association. It was also startling to learn that one of its pastors was a Reverend Samuel Cartledge. In researching my Edgefield ancestors, not only did I discover I am a Cartledge, but I also learned the Cartledge surname has deep roots in Edgefield. That surname was also prominent in the "Dark Corner."

I learned more about the Reverend Samuel Cartledge from a post on New Testament Baptist Church's article "This Day in Baptist History" for 11 September 2013.[270] This historical overview of Reverend Cartledge states that "[h]e moved to South Carolina and became pastor of the Callahan's Mill Church where he served...for over fifty years, until his death in 1843."[271] I realized that the church was once again identified as Callahan's, rather than Calliham's. I was uncertain which name was correct, but this post inspired me to check the Georgia Baptist Association for any records concerning this church.

From the Baptist History Homepage, I learned that J. H. Campbell published a book titled *Georgia Baptist Association*.[272] The website quotes excerpts from this book, including the following reference:

> The Association convened in October, 1792, at Fishing creek. . . . It appears from the minutes of that meeting, that the number of associate churches had increased to fifty-six. Hence there was an increase of twenty-seven churches in four years. The names of these churches are as follows: Shoulder-bone, Buck-eye creek; Callahan's mill, South Carolina . . . .[273]

Because J. H. Campbell had detailed information about the churches that were part of the Georgia Baptist Association, I assumed records existed somewhere, but I was unsure where. A Google search led me to Mercer University in Macon, Georgia. On 25 March 2014, I spoke with Kathryn B. Wright, Research Assistant at the Tarver Library Special Collections at Mercer University. Ms. Wright kindly scanned the pages of the Georgia Baptist Association's minutes on which Callahan's Mill is listed. She also specifically noted the page where Callahan's Mill Baptist Church requested dismissal from the Georgia Baptist Association for geographic reasons.

In reviewing the documents scanned by Ms. Wright, the minutes covering the period from 1792 to 1804 did not identify by name the members of Callahan's Mill, so I cannot state with any certainty whether C. L. Blair's parents or grandparents were members of the church. The minutes do provide a global overview about each church in the association, however, such as the number of whites and blacks.

Seeking more information about the church and its history, I turned to Furman University's website for possible records. One can browse the South Carolina Church Records on Microfilm database and then search for church records by the name of the church, by county name, or by date organized. A search by church name under both Edgefield and McCormick Counties listed twenty-four and four Baptist churches respectively, but Callahan's Mill was not one of them.[274] Since the records weren't there, I began wondering whether any records had survived.

Stumped by the lack of records on Callahan's Mill Baptist Church, I turned to Tonya A. Guy at the Tompkins Library, home of the Old Edgefield District Genealogical Society. I asked Tonya if she had ever heard of Callahan's Mill Baptist Church. She had. When I asked her what became of that church, she told me that it actually still exists—it became Parksville Baptist Church. The Old Edgefield District Genealogical Society does not have any records for either name, so she referred me back to Furman University.

I was surprised that Furman University had not noted the name change, since Parksville Baptist Church was one of the four churches listed in McCormick County. Now, knowing Parksville was Callahan's Mill, I reviewed the information on Furman University's website. Under the column for "Coverage," it states "1856-1984 (scattered), 1922-1984 (scattered)." Callahan's Mill was established in 1785, but the earliest year of surviving records is 1856. I was so disappointed. In contrast, for instance, there are records for Edgefield First Baptist Church from 1823, the year it was established, until 1941.

Based on the limited records for Callahan's Mill, I did not believe it was worthwhile reviewing the microfilm, but then I recalled that Edgefield has a Baptist Association and wondered what records, if any, this organization might have on Callahan's Mill.

In April 2014, I spoke with Jackie Ridings, Ministry Assistant from the Edgefield Baptist Association, regarding any records they may have on Callahan's Mill Baptist Church. I explained I was researching the Blair family and believed they were members of this church. I identified three specific Blairs: Christopher Blair, Sarah Blair, and Columbus or C. L. Blair. On reviewing her material, Ms. Ridings told me that neither

Christopher Blair nor Columbus (C. L.) Blair was listed as a member. She did, however, see the name Sarah Blair. I was too thrilled and requested a copy of the booklet she had consulted.

Ms. Ridings was able to copy 16 pages from *The History of Calliham's Mill: Parksville Baptist Church, 1785 – 1985, Parksville, South Carolina*,[275] which included the title pages and history through 1923, as well as a list of members between the years 1856 and 1876. This document clarified that the church was actually named Calliham's and not Callahan's.

I first reviewed the years 1856-1876. I scanned the lists of men, but neither Columbus nor C. L. Blair was listed. To my delight, Sarah Blair[276] was listed among the female members of the church. Deacon Jennings had told me that slaves typically attended the same church as the slave owner. If Sarah Blair was a member, that meant that Nat, Violet, Edmund, and Cinda were likely members.

The photocopied pages contained another list of members of the church for the year 1883, again subdivided into male and female members. As before, Columbus (C. L.) Blair was not listed but Hulda Blair, the wife of C. L. Blair,[277] was. How odd that C. L. Blair's mother and wife were members of the church, but he, apparently, was not. Speaking of Sarah Blair, I presume she was deceased in 1883. Since she was alive at the time of 1880 US Census, I extrapolated that she must have died after that census but before the 1883 membership list. Considering Sarah Blair was born about 1793-1795, she would have lived close to ninety years.

The bicentennial booklet provides a historical overview of the church. Information I learned from other sources is confirmed in the booklet.

> The Calliham's Mill Baptist Church of Christ was constituted in the year of 1785 under the care of Reverend John Thomas and Reverend Samuel Cartledge. The Reverend

John Thomas was the first known preacher of the church. Reverend Thomas was succeeded by Reverend Charles Blackwell who was the church's itinerant minister in the year 1789. In this year the church already had a membership of 80. The Reverend Samuel Cartledge was called to preach at Calliham's Mill Church in 1790, and he preached there for around fifty-three years.

●•••●

In 1790, the year that Reverend Cartledge came to this church there was a membership of 80. As early as 1792, this church was in the Georgia Baptist Association with 82 members and its only associational delegate was Mr. Edmund Cartledge. In addition to the pastor, Reverend Cartledge, the church was represented at the meetings of the Georgia Baptist Associations in 1803 by John Price and Allen Robertson. There was a membership of 97 in that year.

William Cox was the delegate at the Georgia Association meeting in 1804 when Calliham' Mill church asked for dismission so it could enter the Bethel Association. The church had at this time a total membership of 93.[278]

This booklet also contains a list of some black members with their owners,[279] yet Sarah Blair is not among the slave owners listed. I therefore cannot say with absolute certainty that my enslaved ancestors were members of this church.

In reviewing the booklet, I found an interesting nugget of information: "Records in the Edgefield County Court House show that William Robert Parks, son of W. L. Parks, deeded the land of the present [Parksville] church site and adjoining cemetery to the Parksville Baptist Church."[280] W. R. Parks is the same individual who sold two acres of land to the five colored deacons (including my direct ancestors Nathaniel Blair and McDuffie Tompkins) on behalf of Mount Lebanon Baptist Church.

Not surprisingly, there was tension between blacks and whites after the Civil War. As noted in the booklet: "During the early history of the church, Blacks were included in the membership and until a few years after the Civil War they were still included as members. The last record of Blacks in the church according to the Edgefield Baptist Association was the year 1868 in which there were 48 Blacks and 49 Whites."[281] It did not take long for blacks and whites to segregate voluntarily on the basis of race. What is sad is that this voluntary segregation on the basis of race among churches in Edgefield and McCormick Counties largely persists today, more than 150 years after the Civil War.

The bicentennial booklet was invaluable. I could not help but think about the list of black members with their owners' names. If the compilation in the booklet was not complete, perhaps there were additional records identifying slaves and their slave owners. I decided to order the microfilm of Parksville Baptist Church's records[282] from Furman University after all.

When I reviewed the microfilm, I found no document listing Sarah Blair and the slaves she owned. I was deflated, but that did not deter me from reading the church's history. I found the following report of interest:

September 6th 1856

The Church of Christ at Calliham's Mill in conference proceed to business.

•••••

3rd Bro. S. Cartledge reported Nat servant of Bro. A. B. Kilcrease as being in disorder by gambling and fighting and was appointed to see him and report against to [next] conference.

State of the church since last Association:

Baptized 0
Received by letter 1
Restored 0
Dismissed 2
Expelled 7
Dead 2
No. of Whites 61
No. of Blacks...................................71

Total .... 132[283]

Approximately one month later on 4 October 1856, Nat, servant of Brother A. B. Kilcrease was expelled for gambling and fighting.[284] What caught my eye about these entries were the slave Nat and Brother A. B. Kilcrease. Brother Kilcrease was an adjacent neighbor of Sarah Blair. Did they each have a slave named Nat or was this the same person?

Lewis, a servant of Brother James Tompkins was expelled "for quit[t]ing his wife and taking up with another Woman."[285] Another servant, Milly, was expelled for bastardy.[286]

In reviewing the records, I noticed that before the Civil War, black members equaled or exceeded the number of white members.

TABLE 7. CALLIHAM'S MILL BAPTIST CHURCH'S MEMBERSHIP BY RACE, 1857-1864

Date	Number of Whites	Number of Blacks
5 September 1857	68	68[287]
4 September 1858	55	68[288]
3 September 1859	56	67[289]
1 September 1860	56	72[290]
6 September 1862	57	71[291]
3 September 1864	55	66[292]

However, approximately 15 years after the Civil War, on 4 September 1871, there were 55 whites and 0 blacks.[293]

In reviewing the post-Civil War minutes, two notations caught my attention. The first, dated 6 October 1872, states:

> Moved that we have nothing more to do with the negroes in no shape nor form. They are away from our Church and let them stay away. There will be no more negroes restored in no case.[294]

What happened to "love they neighbor as thy self"? Those Negroes used to be part of Calliham's Mill Baptist Church, and for most of the church's history, the Negro members outnumbered the white members. Maybe, the formerly enslaved population wanted to establish their own church, with members of their own communities as leaders. This apparently did not sit well with their former owners who, in turn, symbolically, washed their hands of those colored members.

A notation in the church's minutes dated 31 May 1873 provides some additional information about this split along racial lines.

> On application of some of the colored people to the church for restoration with an eye of getting letters to constitute a church among themselves, we authorize the clerk to give them a list of the names of the colored people on the church record that they may select from it such names as they are willing to receive as members.
>
> Done in conference
> W. R. Parks, Clk   Rev. G. W. Bussey, Modr.[295]

Coincidentally, Mount Lebanon Baptist Church was established in 1873, under a bush arbor, according to Deacon Jennings. Although the minutes from Calliham's Mill Baptist Church fail to identify any of the colored people or the church by name, I believe the colored people likely included my ancestors Nathaniel Blair and McDuffie Tompkins on behalf of Mount Lebanon Baptist Church. Considering how white society cited the Bible to justify the enslavement of blacks (using the Old Testament story of Noah and his son Ham), it is remarkable that, upon being freed, colored men like Nathaniel Blair and McDuffie Tompkins did not reject Christianity as their religion. Since the parents, grandparents, and great-grandparents of the recently emancipated were stripped of their names, language, culture, and heritage upon being brought to the shores of the United States, however, Christianity was the only religion they knew.

What survives from Calliham's Mill are just scattered records. Although I do not have hard evidence my enslaved Blair ancestors were members of Calliham's Mill Baptist Church, because Sarah Blair[296] was a member and assuming my enslaved Blair ancestors attended church, then they were members of Calliham's Mill, which was *their* church until after the Civil War.

GLEANING MORE FROM ADDITIONAL GOVERNMENT RECORDS

Having exhausted researching all available church records for information, I returned my attention to records generated by the government.

When a family researcher thinks of the census, one typically thinks of the federal census. Individual states, however, also mandated censuses of their populations. South Carolina mandated a census in 1875, but records for Edgefield County did not survive. Fortunately, there are census reports for Edgefield County in 1869, though it is not available online. During a visit to the South Carolina Department of Archives and History in 2005, I purchased this entire census return for Edgefield. Since both my paternal grandparents were born in Edgefield, I considered this a wise investment for future research.

The 1869 South Carolina State Census identified the heads of household by name only. Individuals in each household were counted in the following categories: (a) the number of children between the ages of six and 16 by race and sex; (b) the number of males over 21 by race; and (c) the number of persons of all ages by race and sex. In reviewing this census for Edgefield County, I noticed households composed as follows: of whites only, of colored people only, and of both whites and colored people.

Within the entire Edgefield census, I located one Blair family with C. L. Blair listed as the head.[297] His household consisted of (a) two colored males between six and 16, (b) three colored females between six and 16, (c) one white male over 21, (d) three colored males over 21, (e) one white male of any age, (f) 11 colored males of any age, (g) three white females[298] of any age, and (h) 11 colored females of any age. The colored Blairs vastly outnumbered the white Blairs at twenty-two to four. As such, I deduced my Blair ancestors were still residing on the property of the slaveholding family in 1869.

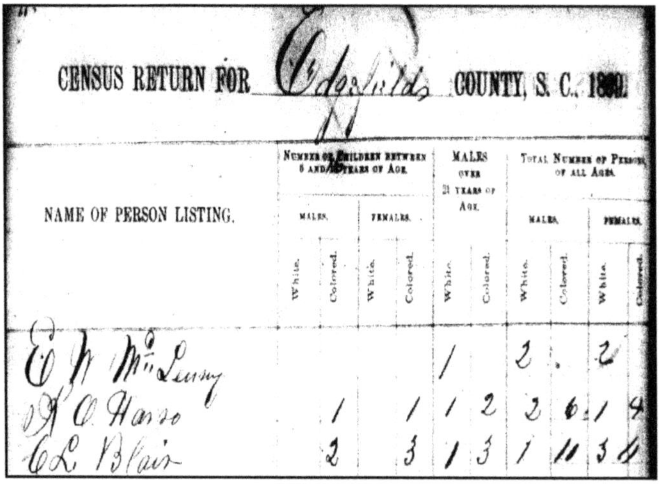

CENSUS RETURN FOR Edgefield COUNTY, S. C. 1869.

NAME OF PERSON LISTING.	Number of Children between 6 and 16 Years of Age: Males, White	Males, Colored	Females, White	Females, Colored	Males over 21 Years of Age: White	Colored	Total Number of Persons of all Ages: Males, White	Males, Colored	Females, White	Females, Colored
E. W. McLenny					1		2		2	
A. O. Harro		1		1	1	2	2	6	1	4
C. L. Blair		2		3	1	3	1	11	3	11

FIG. 15. 1869 SOUTH CAROLINA CENSUS RETURNS, EDGEFIELD – C. L. BLAIR AND HOUSEHOLD

Courtesy of the South Carolina Department of Archives and History

Recalling there were 17 Blairs in Edgefield in 1870 (six whites, one mulatto and 10 blacks), I wondered what had happened to the other 11 colored Blairs counted in the 1869 census. Genetic DNA testing provided a clue. Besides providing a saliva sample to 23andme, I also provided one to Ancestry. One of my DNA matches lists Blair and Cartledge on her family tree. Upon further examination, I discovered these ancestors were a couple, Lucy Blair (born about 1842) and Sam Cartledge (born about 1835). This Lucy Blair was born approximately eight years before my 2ND great-grandfather Nathaniel Blair. I have no idea whether this Lucy Blair and Nathaniel were blood relatives. I do not know if this DNA match, who Ancestry identifies as my 5TH to 8TH cousin, matches me on the Blair line or the Cartledge line. When I searched for this couple in 1870, I found them living next door to Columbus Blair.[299] I have learned from experienced genealogists, such as Char Margo Bah of Virginia, that former slaves often were recorded as living close to their former slave owners in 1870 and 1880. Sam and Lucy Cartledge had seven children, six of whom were alive in 1869. It is possible Sam Cartledge and his family were eight of the 11 colored persons residing with Columbus (C. L.) Blair. This is mere speculation, of course, particularly considering that on the other side of Columbus Blair (and his family) was a white Cartledge family headed by Thomas Cartledge.[300] Were Sam Cartledge and Lucy Blair slaves of Columbus (C. L.) Blair, or slaves of Thomas Cartledge? If the slave schedules of 1850 and 1860 had identified every slave by given name, instead of omitting this information, I could likely answer this question.

In 1870, there were 17 Blairs[301] in Edgefield. Eleven of those Blairs lived in Washington Township (six black Blairs, one mulatto Blair, and four white Blairs). As I reflected upon the Blair household in 1869, especially considering that there seemed to be only one Blair slaveholding family in Edgefield, I realized I could trace the Blair family backwards in time.

According to the 1860 US Census Slave Schedule for Edgefield, Sarah "Blas"[302] [Blair][303] owned 19 slaves and her son C. L. "Blas" [Blair][304] owned 10 slaves.[305] Among Sarah Blair's slaves, the eldest was a 52 year old male and the second eldest was a 46 year old female. I compared the ages of the elder Nathaniel and Violet in 1870 with the 1860 slave schedule. Per the 1870 US Census, the elder Nathaniel was born approximately 1800, but the 1860 US Census Slave Schedule indicates his birth year as approximately 1808. Although there is a gap of eight years, mistakes were inevitable since South Carolina did not mandate the recording of births during this period. Possibly the slaveholding family knew when the elder Nathaniel was born, but by the time of the 1870 US Census, either the census taker or the elder Nathaniel estimated his age. Regarding Violet, her birth year per the 1870 US Census and the 1860 US Census Slave Schedule is the same, approximately 1814. These dates, cross-referenced with the ages on the census, establish that the enslaved 52-year-old man and 46-year-old woman were indeed my Nat and Violet.

All slaves on the 1860 US Census Slave Schedule for Sarah "Blas," except one, were described as black. One slave, a 10-year-old male, was described as mulatto. This slave might be my 2ND great-grandfather Nathaniel. The 1869 Militia Enrollment lists Nathaniel as 18 years old, but in 1870 Nathaniel was 21 years old, born about 1849. Nathaniel is identified as mulatto in 1870 and 1880.

According to the 1850 US Census Slave Schedule, Sarah Blair owned 13 slaves.[306] The eldest male was 43; the eldest female was 38. The variation in ages between 1850 and 1860 is not significant. I believe these two eldest slaves are Nat (the elder Nathaniel) and Violet.

Going back to the 1840 US Census,[307] Sarah Blair resided in a home with five other whites. She owned seven slaves, including one male slave between 24 and 35 (probably Nat) and one female slave between 24 and 35 (probably Violet). The remaining five slaves were two males under 10, one male between 10 and 23, and two females under 10. Recalling that Sarah Blair purchased Nat, Violet, Edmund, and Cinda in 1830, I suspect Edmund is the male between 10 and 23. Slave-era research frequently requires deducing from the available evidence. Maybe two of the male slaves under 10 were Hampton, Richard, or Nelson, those unknown colored Blair males on the 1868 Voter Registration. I eliminated Hampton Blair as a possibility, since the only individual I found with that name was 20 years old, born about 1849-1850, living in Gregg County, Edgefield in 1870.

I next searched for Nelson Blair, but I could not find him in the 1870 or 1880 censuses. In 1900, however, I found a Nelson Blair, 60 years old, born in February 1840 and residing in Militia District 129, Columbia, Georgia, with wife Callie Blair (32) and stepdaughter Bessie Dunn (11).[308] I reviewed the original census record to ensure the ages were correct as listed, and not typographical errors by transcribers at Ancestry.com, and the transcription was correct. According to this census, Nelson was born in Georgia, as were his parents. In 1910, Nelson Blair, 71 years old, born about 1839, was residing in Washington Township, Edgefield.[309] This census record states that Nelson was born in South Carolina and that his parents were born in Virginia. With such contradictory information about the places of birth between the 1900 and 1910 US Censuses, I was not sure what to believe, but I felt it was not a coincidence and believe that this is the same Nelson Blair on the 1868 Voter Registration.

I don't have a clue where Nelson Blair was in 1870 and 1880. Maybe he was avoiding the census takers, or maybe he was transient during the time the census takers made their visits. A third possibility is that Nelson went by a different surname after emancipation in 1870 and 1880. Regardless of the real reasons for his omission from the censuses in 1870 and 1880, I was thrilled to ultimately find him.

Finally, I searched for Richard Blair, born in Edgefield County, South Carolina, between 1830 and 1840. There were no results for Richard Blair meeting my criteria, but another result listed a 45 year old black male named Dick Blair, born approximately 1835 in South Carolina, and residing in Bonham, Wilcox County, Alabama in 1880.[310] Dick is a nickname for Richard, so it is possible that this "Dick Blair" in Alabama is the missing Richard Blair, but I have no additional information that would confirm this. Researching black Americans, especially from the late-antebellum period until 1900, can be exceedingly frustrating.

I returned to the seven slaves owned by Sarah Blair as listed in the 1840 US Census. Cinda, daughter of Nat and Violet, could have been under 10 years old or older than 10 years old. Although the ages of the Nat, Violent, Edmund, and Cinda were not identified by the Estate of Christopher Blair, I assumed the family unit (Violet with her children, Edmund and Cinda) were listed in descending age, which would mean Cinda was the youngest individual.

In 1830, Sarah Blair acquired the four slaves from her husband's estate. During an initial search on Ancestry.com, I could not locate any Blairs in Edgefield. Her absence from the census was perplexing, so I searched for any Sarah living in Edgefield. The closest result was a Sarah Blake, a white female between the ages of 50 and 59 but because this Sarah Blake lived by herself, I knew she was not the Sarah Blair who had multiple children, including Columbus, who would have been about six years old. I was stumped.

Several months later, I tackled the 1830 US Census again. The only place Sarah Blair resided after the death of her husband Christopher was Edgefield. She had to be listed somewhere on the 1830 US Census.

I decided to search for Sarah Blair by the last name "Bla*." The use of an asterisk allows a researcher to receive results with names beginning with the letters "Bla." I received results with several surnames beginning with "Bla," including Black, Blackwell, and Bladen. I paused when I saw the next two results: Washington Blaes and Eliz Blain. First, I reviewed Washington Blaes, whose name Ancestry.com alternatively transcribed as Washington Blain. I quickly deduced that this Washington Blain was Washington Blair, a son of Christopher and Sarah Blair, who was also known as George Washington or "G. W." Washington Blair's household consisted of three whites and one male slave between the ages of 10 through 23.[311]

I then reviewed the result for Eliz Blain. This woman was the head of household. Seven other whites resided in the home. More importantly, this Eliz Blain owned four slaves: a male between the ages of 10 through 23, a female between the ages of 10 through 23, a male under 10, and a female under 10.[312] I deduced this Eliz Blain was, in all likelihood, Sarah Blair. Maybe Eliz or Elizabeth was her middle name. In researching my ancestors, I have seen instances where a census taker identified an ancestor by a middle name rather than a first name. Those four slaves are almost certainly Nat, Violet, Edmund, and Cinda.

Ten years prior, in 1820, Christopher Blair was the head of household.[313] Nine free white persons and two slaves were in the household. There was a female slave between 14 and 25 years old, too old to be Violet. The other slave was a male under 14. This slave might be my 4TH great-grandfather Nat if his birth year was about 1808.

Ten years earlier, in 1810, Christopher Blair apparently did not own any slaves.[314] That census did not specifically inquire about the number of slaves in the household, however. Was Nat a part of Christopher Blair's household as an infant? If not, when and from whom did Christopher Blair acquire Nat?

In researching Christopher Blair's parents, I found his mother, Bershaba Blair, in the 1790 US Census,[315] his father, George Blair, listed in 1779-1780[316] as residing in the Ninety-Six District, and, in 1766, George Blair was listed in Charles Town,[317] the pre-Revolutionary War name of Charleston.[318] None of these records mention slaves.

George Blair, purportedly from Ireland, fought on behalf of the colonies against the British during the American Revolution. He was granted bounty land, 100 acres in Belfast Township in Granville County, on 1 June 1767 from the Governor in Council of South Carolina, as an incentive and reward for his military service.[319] Ironically, South Carolina was a province at this time, so the grant of land was from "George the Third by the Grace of God, of Great Britain, France and Ireland, King, Defender of the Faith."[320] Belfast Township, also known as Londonborough Township,[321] is located in present-day Greenwood and McCormick Counties, but prior to these counties' formations, this land was in Edgefield District.

THE BLAIR IN ME

Having traced the Blair slaveholding family to the time when that line arrived on America's shores, I realized I could not state whether Nat and Violet were born in America or elsewhere. I did not know if they were brought directly to South Carolina from some place in Africa or came to South Carolina from Maryland, Virginia, or the West Indies. From whom did Christopher Blair acquire Nat and Violet? Who were Nat's parents? Did he have any siblings? These same questions apply to Violet. I knew the country of origin for the Blair line, which was Ireland, but I could not begin to identify the homeland of Nat or that of Violet. Although I have researched and turned over many stones, I could not progress any further. I resigned myself to pressing forward and working with what I had gathered, despite so many unanswered questions.

I returned my attention to the 1869 South Carolina State Census. Were those colored Blairs more than "former" property of C. L. Blair and Sarah Blair? It appears that at least one colored Blair may have been sired by a white male. The research paper trail suggested such a connection to an unidentified white male. My 2ND great-grandfather Nathaniel was described as mulatto on three of the five censuses while he resided in South Carolina. And there was one mulatto male slave, approximately Nathaniel's age, listed on Sarah Blair's slave schedule in 1860. The question I could not answer was whether the unidentified white male was a Blair or not. And if a white Blair had sired Nathaniel, who was his mother? If a white Blair sired Nathaniel, then I carry the Blair gene, which would explain at least some of the European ancestry found in my DNA profile.

Since that initial Ancestral Composition, 23andMe, has updated its analysis. This company now claims I am 20.9% European, with my largest component being 10.3% British and Irish. 23andMe defines this population as follows:

> When modern humans first arrived in the regions known as Great Britain and Ireland tens of thousands of years ago, these two regions were physically joined to one another.

> Today the peoples of the islands of Great Britain and Ireland
> descend from Celtic, Saxon, and Viking ancestors.[322]

This analysis suggests to me that I might be a Blair, but in a way I never imagined. Based on my skin tone and what I knew of my heritage, I knew I was majority African and believed I was about a quarter Native American. The fact that I am more European than I imagined or what my skin tone reflects is still a fact I am processing. Americans tend to judge people like the covers of books, and my skin tone is my cover. I have periodically encountered white individuals who judge me by my appearance and make snap judgments about who they perceive me to be. But once they open the cover and engage in a conversation with me, they realize their assumptions were wrong. Now knowing my true genetic heritage, I want to learn about my entire heritage, including "Kiss me, I'm Irish."

THOSE BLAIR ROOTS

In tracking the footprints of my Blair ancestors, I have learned more than I expected when I began this journey. Many questions remain unanswered, apparently forever forgotten or lost with the passage of time. As I reflect upon this journey, my thoughts turn to my grandmother Nellie Blair, daughter of Clifford, granddaughter of Nathaniel, 2ND great-granddaughter of Nat and Violet. She lost her father, Clifford, in late January 1926. According to Clifford's death certificate, his body was shipped back to South Carolina for burial. Presumably, there was some type of memorial service in the District of Columbia that Nellie, her stepmother, and her half-brother Walter attended before Clifford's body was sent to South Carolina.

By early February 1926, Nathaniel Blair had undoubtedly relocated to Worth County, Georgia, to the home of his son Walter. At least two of Clifford's siblings had predeceased him. Several siblings had moved to Georgia, and one had relocated to Virginia. Josephine Blair Jones and Sallie Blair Jones remained in the Parksville area. They probably made arrangements to have Clifford buried at Mount Lebanon Baptist Church. They didn't have money, however, for a marked grave.

I presume that at least a graveside service was held for Clifford and that word spread in the community about Clifford's untimely death. Some neighbors probably stopped by to pay their respects. As I reflect about Clifford's return to his native home, I imagine the following happened.

> At some point, his sister Josephine noticed a young woman with a girl, presumably her daughter, standing at a distance, and she appeared to be explaining something to her child.
>
> Seventeen years later, a young lady filled out an application for a social security number. She wrote her name, date of birth in 1920, and place of birth, McCormick County, South Carolina. She paused before writing the names of her parents. In her mind's eye, she remembered accompanying her mother to the cemetery at Mount Lebanon Baptist Church.
>
> "Mommy, why are we here?"
>
> Her mother explained, "The man you never knew and now will never know, your father, has died."
>
> With tears in her eyes, the daughter turned to her mother and cried "My father? You said daddy died before I was born."
>
> "Yes, child. I did say that. It is too complicated for you to understand now."
>
> Stunned by this revelation, the daughter asked, "What's my daddy's name?"
>
> The mother answered, "Cliff Blair."
>
> Having recalled that painful day, the young lady resumed filling out the application. She listed Cliff Blair as her father and L[] H[] as her mother.

This young lady, as I discovered thanks to the addition of the US, Social Security Applications, and Claims Index, 1936-2007 on Ancestry.com, was C. L. W.

With the unexpected discovery of a child probably sired by Clifford out of wedlock, I can't help but wonder whether my grandmother knew she had another sibling.

EPILOGUE 1
A GUIDE TO HELP YOU FIND YOUR ANCESTORS: STARTING WITH THE KNOWN, UNCOVERING THE UNKNOWN
Edna Gail Bush

●•••●

Maybe your interest has been piqued by some family oral history concerning a missing ancestor, a probable lynching, or an ancestor who took part in a significant historical event. My mother used to collect the funeral programs of family and friends, starting with the death of her mother in 1945. They were kept in shoe boxes. I remember being fascinated by the life histories in the programs and became hooked on genealogy. In any case, genealogy has become a popular hobby for many people. Today, with the use of DNA testing, many questions about genetic admixture are either confirmed or eliminated. This tool has opened up many possibilities to finding distant ancestors.

Where do you start? Start with what is known—usually that will mean yourself, your parents, and your grandparents. Name your parents, including your mother's maiden name, places and dates of birth, schools and churches attended, military service, date and place of marriage, children (full names and the dates and places of birth), occupations, hobbies or interests, memberships in organizations, dates and places of deaths and burials. For your parents and grandparents, identify any siblings. If possible, list the names of the siblings' spouses and their children. Compile the same information for these individuals as you did for your parents and grandparents. Gather as much information as possible, working backwards toward the 1870 census. You may want to try and complete a five-generation chart within this time frame. Initially, you may be faced with some blanks for names and birth years, but that is to be expected. At the 1870 point, look for information about your ancestors in the following places:

- Your immediate family records—Family Bibles, funeral programs, wills, family burial sites
- Interview senior relatives
- Try to verify family oral history and lore
- Federal, state and county census records
- Historical newspapers[323] in the state and county of your ancestors
- Military records (including World War I Draft Registration Cards)[324]
- School records
- Prison records
- Tax records
- Vital records, including birth and death[325] as well as delayed birth records[326]
- Marriage records
- Deeds, property records, and land records
- Historical church records in the states and counties[327] of your ancestors
- Historical records maintained by churches
- Coroners' inquisitions/inquests
- State archives, county archives, and genealogical societies[328]
- Court records, estate inventories and appraisals, will transcripts of known slaveholders, civil cases
- 1850 and 1860 Slave Schedules (part of the federal census)
- Mortality Schedules (1850-1880, part of the federal census)
- Agricultural Schedules (part of the federal census)
- Freedman Bank records

- Freemen's Bureau Labor contracts
- Historical books for the state and county of your ancestors
- Local historical societies in the states and counties of your ancestor
- Free websites, such as FamilySearch.org and HeritageQuest through participating libraries
- Posting messages on message boards such as Ancestry (Rootsweb), Afrigeneas, and GenForum
- City directories
- Blogs and websites of other genealogy enthusiasts and certified genealogists
- Congressional and state legislative records
- Search engines like Google
- A hired certified genealogist

This last checkpoint, hiring a genealogist, may be a rewarding option. I turned to a genealogist to help me work past a frustrating brick wall when I couldn't find the first Edna. Within ten hours of searching, the certified genealogist presented my probable ancestors. When I saw the record listing my 3RD great-grandmother and her children, names I immediately recognized, I knew I had hit pay dirt. The genealogist's report also suggested areas for further study, including court records. As a result, I found the documentation that was presented in my chapter concerning the tug of war over the control of my ancestors between various trustees and the Burton family.

Assess your genealogical goals. Do you hope to find the ancestor who survived the transatlantic voyage? To find out who enslaved your ancestors? To discover whether your ancestors were enslaved individuals, free people of color, or Native Americans? Whatever your goals, I hope these tips will help guide your way.

EPILOGUE 2
RECONNECTING THE EDGEFIELD BRANCHES
Natonne Elaine Kemp

•••••

Individually, we toiled and scaled the brick wall of slavery, identifying our enslaved Edgefield ancestors and those who "owned" them. Collectively, we collaborated on this book, sharing our successes and disappointments as we tried to learn more about those ancestors who persevered before us. Our efforts do not end with the publication of this book, but shift to another phase.

Genetic DNA testing has altered the genealogical landscape. It may confirm a familial connection already established by paper trail research, identify a previously unknown relationship, or raise doubts about a purported familial relationship. Edna Gail Bush ("Gail") and I have found it invaluable in discovering our connections to others we mutually know.

To my knowledge, Gail and I have no blood connection. As the editor of *Homeplace* for three years, I had the pleasure of reading and editing her submissions for publication. Her articles listed Edgefield townships and surnames unfamiliar to me. In 2014, however, Sheila Hightower-Allen (a cousin of Gail's) sent an e-mail stating that Gail and I are related per the website GEDmatch.com, which "provides DNA and genealogical analysis tools for amateur and professional researchers and genealogists."[329] Individuals who have tested with a genetic DNA company such as Ancestry, FamilyTree DNA, or 23andMe can upload his or her raw data to GEDmatch. This website will assign a kit number to that raw data. The beauty of this website is that an individual can learn who is a DNA cousin regardless of which DNA testing company others have used. I had uploaded my 23andMe raw data to this website.

I subsequently misplaced Sheila's e-mail, and she could not recall how she determined Gail and I were related. In using GEDmatch, I often select "one-to-many matches," where I enter my assigned kit number and GEDmatch produces a list of other kit numbers I match at a certain threshold level (7 cMs or above). As for cMs, they are described as follows:

> The centiMorgan (cM) values for DNA segments are measurements of how likely the segment is to recombine as it passes from parent to child. Segments with higher cM values have a greater probability of recombining in any one generation. Therefore, when you share DNA segments with larger cM values with a match, your common ancestors are likely to come from generations that are more recent.[330]

As GEDmatch explains on the page of one-to-many matches, "[t]o qualify as a 'match' in the genealogical time frame, results must have a largest Autosomal segment that has at least 700SNPs[331] and be a least 7 cM."[332] Presently, I have 2,000 DNA matches. With each DNA match GEDmatch lists, among other things, the total cMs you share with a DNA match, the largest cM you share with a DNA match, and the generation or distance of the DNA match. For instance, my mother's kit number is 1.0 generation from me, and my brother's kit number is 1.2 generations from me. Outside of my immediate family, my closest DNA matches are two Chinn cousins.

Gail's name does not appear on my list of DNA matches. So I turned to another tool available on GEDmatch: one-to-one comparison. When I compared Gail's kit number to mine, using the default setting of 700 SNPs and 7 cMs, no shared DNA segments were found. I then began adjusting the minimum segment cMs size to a lower level—first to 5 cMs and then to 3 cMs. At 3 cMs, Gail and I matched on two segments. I'm guessing this is how Sheila discovered that Gail and I are related.

I recall learning about autosomal DNA testing from a webinar. The presenter stated that unlike Y DNA testing (which identifies a male ancestor from the past who passed genes from son to grandson to great-grandson and so forth) or mitochondrial DNA ("MTDNA" which identifies a female ancestor from the past who passed genes from her daughter to her granddaughter to her great-granddaughter and so forth), autosomal DNA is a combination of genes a child inherits from his or her parents, grandparents, great-grandparents, et cetera. Unless one is an identical twin, the combination of genes each child inherits from the same set of parents and earlier generations will vary. Autosomal DNA does not prove the exact relationship, but this test can establish a geographic connection. For the two of us, Edgefield is our geographic connection.

Genetic DNA testing is helping to confirm relationships, but gaps of knowledge still exist. For instance, through the traditional paper trail research, Gail knows that Lee Bush is a cousin on her Bush line, and I know that Lee Bush is a cousin on my Peterson line. Gail, Lee Bush, and I tested with Ancestry DNA. Lee Bush appears as a cousin to Gail, but, oddly, he does not appear as mine. I assumed that whatever combination of genes I inherited from my father did not include identifiable genes from the Peterson line. Yet, to my delight, Lee Bush appears as a DNA cousin on GEDmatch and at the expected generation (5.2). Lee and I are fourth cousins; our common ancestors are our 3RD great-grandparents, Josh(ua) Peterson and Laura

Holloway. Lee is a descendant of their son Felix, and I am a descendant of their daughter Sarah Ann.

The analysis is not as straight forward in another example, however. Through the traditional paper trail research, I learned that Travis Gordon and I are cousins on the Peterson line. Our common ancestors are Josh(ua) Peterson and Laura Holloway. Travis is a descendant of their son Nathan, and I am a descendant of their daughter Sarah Ann. Gail, meanwhile, had no knowledge of any connection to Travis Gordon.

For reasons unknown to us, Ancestry selected Travis Gordon's DNA sample for extensive analysis. Gail and I received "hints" of connections with Travis. To my surprise, Ancestry claims Travis and I share three connections. In addition to the known connection on the Peterson line, Ancestry revealed a connection on the Lovelace/Loveless line (Sarah Ann Lovelace—a different Sarah Ann) and a connection on the Holloway line (Carrie Holloway). My connections to Travis are on my father's paternal line (Holloway and Peterson) and my father's maternal line (Lovelace/Loveless).

Surprisingly, Gail, who had no known connections to Travis Gordon, is connected to him along seven lines: (a) Gail's maternal 3RD great-grandparents, Coleman and Edna Burton Coleman; (b) her maternal 3RD great-grandparents, Griffin and Eliza Palmore; (c) her paternal 2ND great-grandparents, Caesar Bush and Easter Weaver; (d) her paternal great-grandparents, Henry and Annis Watson West; (e) her maternal great-grandmother, Emma Reed Medlock; (f) her paternal great-grandparents, Alfred and Laura Stevens Bush; and (g) her maternal great-grandfather, Yancy Harris (this is a mystery, because Yancy Harris was stepfather to Gail's grandmother Edna).

Stunned by the number of common ancestors she shares with Travis, Gail spoke with an Ancestry representative for an explanation. The representative had never heard of two individuals, identified by Ancestry as distant cousins, sharing so many connections. But she assured Gail that those connections are based on the DNA, with the specific identities based on Gail's and Travis's family trees.

For individuals of African descendant with deep roots in a specific geographic area, genetic DNA testing has revealed a porthole to slavery, and, more specifically, breeding among the enslaved population. As outlined in her maternal chapter, Gail discovered female ancestors who were "breeders." After exchanging information with Travis and conducting additional research, Gail determined one of Travis's male ancestors (Sidney Gordon) had four female partners during and after slavery. With these four women, he sired at least twenty-seven children. For historians and social scientists, genetic DNA testing may be of value in studying slave communities.

Gail and I are already aware of the value of genetic DNA testing. And, thanks to Gail's cousin Sheila Hightower-Allen, who has been distributing kits, more individuals with roots in Edgefield are having their genetic DNA analyzed.

Not everyone who provides a saliva sample knows the identities of his or her parents. Some adopted individuals have turned to genetic DNA testing to learn their biological heritage. For some other individuals, the identity of only a father is unknown. In April 2017, a new DNA cousin appeared on my page. Ancestry identified him as a first cousin and listed him above my known maternal great aunt. Because this new first cousin and I share over 60 DNA matches, I knew he was a match on my father's side, and thus an Edgefield descendant. Because he was such a close match, I assumed he was a child or grandchild of one of my father's siblings. When I began communicating with this individual, he revealed that he did not know the identity of his father. I turned to Aunt Evangeline for assistance. She does not recognize this individual or the name of his mother. Presently, we are stumped. In time, however, due to the closeness of the kinship, I have no doubt that his connection to me will be revealed.

In general, anyone providing a saliva sample to a genetic DNA company should know (or make an effort to learn) the names of their parents, grandparents, great-grandparents, and 2ND great-grandparents, as well as the siblings of their parents, grandparents, great-grandparents, and 2ND great-grandparents. By compiling such information, one may be able to identify a common ancestor with a DNA match, particularly those matches identified as fourth cousins or closer.

If a DNA cousin sends you a message, particularly someone identified as a first to third cousin, please be courteous and respond. By sharing information about the known branches, we can reconstruct the Edgefield branches, not only those who migrated north and west after the Civil War, but even those branches stretching back to the antebellum period, which slavery tore asunder.

I have spent the last decade researching my maternal and paternal lines. My mother's roots are in Abbeville, South Carolina, as well as multiple counties in Virginia. Unlike Edgefield, which has the second best archival collection after Charleston in the State of South Carolina, Abbeville lost many records, particularly after fires at the courthouse. Also there is no organized genealogical or historical society in Abbeville. Meanwhile, while various counties in Virginia have historical or genealogical societies, I have not experienced a sense of community among family researchers, particularly among family researchers of African descent. The DNA cousins on my maternal line do not seem as willing or eager to share information. I cannot explain why.

Edgefield is different. It calls out to us. We are drawn to it. There is something about Edgefield.

EPILOGUE 3
WHAT WAS DONE IN THE DARK IS NOW IN THE LIGHT
Edna Gail Bush

▸•••◂

For people of color in America with a known history of enslaved ancestors, it is difficult to find and learn about our people beyond a certain point. Captured Africans were brutally beaten, some to death, when they refused to answer to their new names or when they spoke in their native tongues or tried to hold on to their cultures. I can't imagine living through such cruelty and disrespect.

What was done to enslaved African girls and women from the time of the Middle Passage through the Jim Crow years was never expected to be revealed. The sexual abuse that began on the slave ships resulted in the first generation of mixed race children in the new land.

Young mixed race children were trained by their black mothers to never mention or question why their skin was so much lighter than their siblings or other black children on the plantation. Husbands, who tried to protect their wives from the sexual assaults committed by the masters or their sons or any white men, were beaten, sold, or killed. The white men never saw a time when their sexual abuse would be revealed. A floodlight of proof by DNA is now connecting black Americans to their relatives with European roots.

Years ago, I began my search with the hope of finding my African ancestors. To date, I've only found one connection. She was Margaret Medlock, born about 1782 in Africa and enslaved by the Samuel Medlock family until 1865. In the 1880 United States Federal Census, I found her living in Ward Township of Edgefield. She is surrounded by many of my Medlock ancestors. My exact connection to Margaret is unknown, but I do know that she had many children during slavery, including twins Dave and John Medlock in the early 1800s (twins run in the Medlock family). To date, she is the only known African in my family who survived the horrendous Middle Passage. Autosomal DNA testing has helped me to connect with other descendants of Margaret's all over the US. She is considered the Mother of all black Medlocks in the United States.

An unexpected result of DNA testing is the number of connections with European-descended relatives that have led me to more than five slaveholders and counting in my family tree. DNA now supports that Allen Young Burton, the slaveholder of my direct maternal line, is also my probable 4TH great-grandfather. DNA matches for both my sister and I show many white Burton matches originating in Henrico County, Virginia. Remembering Cousin Little Joe's family lore about the first Edna being part "Indian and white," I had to find definitive proof, so I, with help from my sister, delved deeper.

The most fascinating and illuminating Burton DNA match was found on my sister's Ancestry.com list. Ancestry identified this match as a 5TH-8TH cousin connected to Burton ancestry. This match traces his ancestry to Francis Burton, born 1560, in Newcastle, York, England. His children were Byron, Ralph, Robert, Thomas, John, Anne, and Richard, all born in England. The second generation through Richard (born about 1595) and his wife, Katherine, listed their children as: Frances,

John, Judith, Thomas, Robert, Samuel, and Richard. The third generation, through Richard and Katherine's son John (born about 1632) and his unknown wife were the following children: John, Robert, Benjamin, William, Mary, Rachel, and Ann, all born in Henrico County, Virginia. The fourth generation, through John and his wife's son Robert (born about 1660) and his wife, Mary Nowell, had many children like the prior generations, but it was through their son Nowell, born in 1690, a member of the fifth generation, that I began to see movement from Henrico County. Nowell and his wife, Judith Allen, had seven sons and one daughter. For the sixth generation, their son Noel (born in 1730) and his wife, Joan, had moved from Henrico County to Mecklenburg, Virginia, where Noel died in 1763. Due to the fact that Noel died before his father and away from the rest of the family in Henrico County, little is known about his widow and their children. However, a note in the Ancestry.com community Rootsweb states: "It is…by the preponderance of evidence that Richard Burton and his siblings were the children of Noel and Joan Burton. This seventh generation includes: Robert (born in 1752, and died in 1813 in Mississippi); Hutchins (born in 1755 and died in 1820 in Georgia); Richard Burton (born in 1759, my probable 5TH great-grandfather, who died in 1840 in Edgefield County, South Carolina); Allen (born in 1760 and died in Edgefield County, South Carolina in 1807); and Young Nightingale Burton (born in 1761 and died in Mecklenburg).

Their mother, Joan, must have experienced hard times raising her sons alone. Recorded in 1769 in the Mecklenburg County, Virginia, court orders, book 2, page 189, it states that "the church wardens of St. James Parrish bind out Richard Burton to John Lynch according to law." By 1776, evidence shows that Richard Burton enlisted in the Revolution in South

Carolina under a Georgia general.[333] Then, in 1781, Richard represented the estate of his brother Young Nightingale Burton in Virginia.[334]

Sometime in the early 1790s, Richard married Mary Johnson and they had three children, representing the eighth generation: Allen Young Burton, Richard Johnson Burton, and Martha Burton. Allen Y. Burton owned twenty-three enslaved men, women and children—more than likely, several of those children were his. My 4TH great-grandmother, Nellie, was the senior female on the plantation and the probable mother of those children. Burton was neither married nor had any legal issue. He may have tried to protect his children in his will by stating that they were to be kept together for the benefit of his parents, sister, and brother.

My sister's DNA revealed 11% ancestry from Great Britain, and mine showed 7% from Great Britain. The overwhelming majority of Burton matches for both of us points to origins in England to Henrico County, Virginia. Based on the family lore that the first Edna was "part white," our DNA matches support that Allen Y. Burton, slaveholder, was our 4TH great-grandfather.

The Burton branch wasn't the only one that DNA highlighted to me. I have 11 fourth to sixth cousin Stevens/Stephens matches and 33 distant Stevens/Stephens matches, the majority of them appearing within the past year, as if my Stevens ancestors were shining a floodlight on the path to show me this truth to find a previously unknown branch.

There were several matches that piqued my curiosity. I noticed they were managed by the same person, so I sent her a message about our connection. Apparently, this European-descended match was curious about how I matched her and her family members. As previously mentioned in my earlier chapter, she confirmed our connection as 4TH cousins two times removed. It turned out that her ancestor and my new-found 2ND great-grandfather were brothers. In this way, she gave me confirmation that Elisha Stevens Jr. was the father of my great-grandmother Laura Bush. This also confirms the folklore from Cousin Annabelle Bush Nipper that the slave-holder gave her grandmother Laura to Alfred to marry when she was 14 because she looked too much like the slavehold-er's children with his wife. This reminds me of a famous quote I came across by Mary Boykin Chestnut in 1861. She was the wife of South Carolina Senator James Chestnut. Mary observed,

> Who thinks any worst of a Negro or mulatto woman for being a thing we can't name? God forgive us, but ours is a monstrous system, a wrong and an iniquity! Like the patri-archs of old our men live all in one house with their wives and their concubines, and the mulattoes one sees in every family exactly resembles the white children…every lady can tell you who is the father of all the mulatto children in everybody's household, but those in her own she seems to think drop from the clouds, or pretend so to think.

Mary Boykin Chestnut's peer Frances Anne Kemble also observed the increasing occurrence of mixed race children of white men. She stated: "The white man's blood and bones have begotten this bronze race, and bequeathed to it in some degree, qualities, tendencies, capabilities, such as are the inheritance of the highest order of human animals…because nobody pretends to deny that throughout the South, a large proportion of the population is the offspring of white men and colored women."

I am so grateful to all my new Stevens cousins for their help and for being open to sharing knowledge and family lore. One Stevens cousin, who is also descended from Elisha Stevens Jr., told me that our unknown slave 2ND great-grandmother was not allowed to raise her children, which is why they never knew her name. She was a house servant, and her duties to serve the plantation master and his family were more important. Her children were given to a slave nurse to raise.

Researchers should be aware that not all European DNA matches will be so open or helpful. I have another high 4TH cousin match who was somewhat hostile after I identified myself as a black woman. She shut down when I asked her questions about our obvious connections to several family lines in Edgefield. There are many people like her who want to deny the truth of DNA testing, but DNA does not lie.

My Stevens ancestry is now complete, showing the line of descent as follows:

Generation 1: Josiah Stevens

- slaveholder
- born 1728
- Germany to North Carolina, US
- married 1 – Catherine Boren; married 2 – Sarah Hobby

Generation 2: Elisha Stevens Sr.

- slaveholder
- 1750-1834
- Edgefield, South Carolina
- married Elizabeth Fleek
- born 1756
- Germany to Granville, North Carolina

Generation 3: Elisha Stevens Jr.

- slaveholder
- 1784 -1871

- Edgefield, South Carolina
- with unknown slave woman

Generation 4:

WILSON	EDMUND	HANNAH	LAURA	ELIAS	GABRIEL
Abt.1835	1837	1839	1849	1850	1861
			married Alfred Bush, my great-grandfather		

Generation 5: My grandfather Elbert Bush

- married Minnie West

Generation 6: My father Abner Bush

Generation 7: Me, my siblings, and eight first cousins

This verifies the range of my match (5TH-8TH) with the European-descended Stevens relatives.

I found an interesting bit of information on my 2ND great-grandfather Elisha Stevens. In *Our Saluda County Ancestors: Volume 1* by Mary B. Parkman and Betty Anne W. Turkett, on page 44, "Marion Witt tells the story that she (Sarah) was 16 and he (Elisha) was 50 when they married." Elisha had to establish legal children; he and Sarah had nine. But I believe that he had many other mulatto children, because many of my DNA matches do not seem to connect to any of the above siblings of my great-grandmother Laura. Since he did not marry until he was 50, who were the other enslaved women with whom he probably had children? A clue may lie in the other 4TH cousin Steven matches. My research continues to explore those lines.

DNA testing has been like repeated lightning strikes for me. Following yet another branch of my family tree, both my sister and I have discovered many DNA matches of Bush ancestry that started in Essex, Virginia. One of my male Bush matches also tested in the 5TH-8TH distant cousin range, and his ancestry was traced to Edgefield County, South Carolina.

When my brothers were tested, their Y-DNA only showed ancestry with men with the surname New, who originated in England before moving to Virginia and then further south. I began to believe that the Bush blood must have come through a female. My paternal 2ND great-grandmother, Easter Weaver, was found in only one census. In 1880, she lived in the household of her son Alfred Bush. She was noted to be 88 years old and a mulatto. My DNA matches with Alfred, a 5TH-8TH cousin who traces his ancestry to and shines the spotlight on a descendant of John Bibby Bush.

John Bibby Bush (1706-1748) lived his whole life in Essex, Virginia. He and his wife, Susannah Spencer, had five children: Richard, Bibby, Elizabeth, Barbara, and Thomas. Richard (1725-1803) and his wife, Mary Prescott Bush, in turn, had Bibby Bush. The name Bibby came from his 3RD great-grandmother, Elizabeth Bibby (1650-1725). Bibby Bush (1751-1812) and wife Mary Herrin (1752-1828) had many children, among them Herrin W. Bush (1776-1828), whose first wife was Martha Lott (1773-1850) and then, after she died, Elizabeth DeLoach. Most southern landowners of their time were slaveholders. I have two black matches in the fourth cousin range along with two black and fourteen white matches in the distant cousin range. All of the white matches originated in Virginia. My sister has thirty-four distant Bush matches, thirty-one of which are white, and we share six of those thirty-four matches. A distant black

Bush match that we share traced her own ancestry back to my 2ND great-grandmother Easter Weaver and a white male in the John Bibby Bush line, similar to my distant white Bush match. Because of this, I am certain that my mulatto 2ND great-grand-mother, Easter Weaver, was fathered by a Bush male in the Bibby Bush line. This would explain why my great-grandfather changed his name from Wever in 1870 to Bush by 1880, joining black half-brothers who carried the name.

DNA testing has been a real eye opener for me. Finding the truth of my ancestry through DNA was more than I ever expected. I am a descendant of African and Native American enslaved people, and slaveholders. I have always believed that racism is a waste of time and energy, but now I believe this even more so. As an American with roots stretching back to the colonial period, I support the words of one of my favorite people, educator Jane Elliot: "There is only one race, the human race."

ENDNOTES

＊••••◀

CHAPTER 1

1   Fox Butterfield, *All God's Children* (New York: Harper Perennial, 1995, 1996), xvii.

2   Orville Vernon Burton, *In My Father's House Are Many Mansion*(University of North Carolina Press, 1985) 289.

3   James T. Bacon, Editor, "Edgefield District in Bad Odor," *Edgefield Advertiser* (Edgefield, South Carolina), 19 December 1866, p. 2, col. 3; digital images. *Chronicling America* (http://chroniclingamerica. loc.gov) Historic American Newspapers.

4   Simkins, Francis Butler, *Pitchfork Ben Tillman, South Carolinian*, Southern Classics Series; Louisiana State University Press, 1944; Published in Columbia, South Carolina by University of South Carolina Press, 2002.

5   Bela Padgette Herlong, Carol Hardy Bryan, Charles Reneau Andrews, *Where Our Paths Crossed, The Old Edgefield District Settlement of Mount Willing*, (Cumming, GA.: Mount Willing Press, 2011) vol. 1, 123.

6   Gloria Ramsey Lucas, *Slave Records of Edgefield County, South Carolina* (Edgefield, SC: Edgefield County Historical Society, 2010) 412.

7   Ibid, 12.

8   "A Promise Fulfilled," *Civil War Times Magazine* (December 2009) 34.

9   James T. Bacon, Editor, *The Negro Code*, Edgefield Advertiser, November 22, 1865, image 1, columns 1, 2 and 3; Chronicling America website.

10   James T. Bacon, Editor, "The True Negro Question," *Edgefield Advertiser* (Edgefield, South Carolina), 8 November 1865, image 2, column 3; digital images, *Chronicling America* (http://chroniclingamerica.loc.gov) Historic American Newspapers.

11   Testimony of John Picksley, former slave, Deposition, 1866, Freedmen's Bureau microfilm roll 142, p. 670.

12   Estate papers of Alfred Bush, 1887-1888; Edgefield County Probate; pkg. 117-4773, FR 708-719, D. 199, Laura Bush, Administrator, 1887-1888, South Carolina Department of Archives and History, Columbia, S.C.

13   Title Deeds to Real Estate: Michael W. Clark to Alfred Bush, 1874; Jackson Holmes to Alfred Bush, 1874; H. T. Wright to Alfred Bush, 1883, Edgefield Archives, Edgefield, South Carolina.

14   Old Edgefield District Genealogical Society, Tompkins Library. Family Surname files for Clark, Holmes, and Wright families.

15   1870 United States Federal Census, Spring Grove Township, Edgefield County, South Carolina; Roll: M593_1495; p. 489B; Image 114655; Family History Library Film: 552994, [database online], Provo, UT, Ancestry.com Operations, 2009.

16   1850 United States Federal Census, Edgefield District, Edgefield, South Carolina; Roll: M432_852; p. 90A; Image: 185, [database online], Provo, UT, Ancestry.com Operation, 2009.

17   1870 United States Federal Census, Spring Grove, Edgefield, South Carolina; Roll: M593_1495; p. 492B; Image: 114893; Family History Library Film: 552994,[database online], Provo, UT, Ancestry.com Operations, 2009.

18   1880 United States Federal Census, Ward Township, Edgefield County, South Carolina; Roll: 1228; FHF 1255228; p. 435C; Enumeration District: 064, [database online], Provo, UT, Ancestry.com Operations, 2010.

19   1900 United States Federal Census, Xenia, Greene, Ohio; Roll: 1272; p. 24A; Enumeration District: 0098; Family History Library microfilm: 1241272, [database online], Provo, UT, Ancestry.com Operations, 2004.

20   Hendrik V. Booraem, *The Early History of Johnston,* The Edgefield County Historical Society, 1993.

21   Elizabeth Rauh Bethel, *Promiseland, A Century of Life in a Negro Community,* University of South Carolina Press, 1997, 1981.

22   South Carolina Death Records, 1821-1961; Wise Township, Edgefield County, South Carolina; File 4072; Registration District 1813; Registered 2; Adam Bush died 21 February 1931; [database online], Provo, UT, Ancestry.com Operations, 2008.

23   Edgefield County Probate, Estate Papers of Alfred Bush, 1887-1888; Laura's request dated 6 February 1888; Box 117, pkg. 4773; FR 708-719; D 199, SCDAH, Columbia, South Carolina.

24   Ibid. Eldred's note to Arthur Tompkins; estate papers, 9 March 1888.

25   John C Sheppard, 82nd Governor of South Carolina, 10 July 1866 to 30 November 1866; Wikipedia, online encyclopedia, accessed 10 December 2015.

26   Edgefield Archives, Edgefield County, South Carolina; Court of Common Pleas, Judgement Roll 11946, loose papers; Laura Bush vs Della Bush Hammond, 1896-1897.

27   1900 United States Federal Census, Shaw Township, Edgefield County, South Carolina; Roll: 1526; Page 2A; Enumeration District 0121; FHL microfilm: 1241526; [database online], Provo, UT, Ancestry.com Operations, 2004.

28   Edgefield Archives, Edgefield County, South Carolina; Court of Common Pleas, Judgement Roll 11946, loose papers; Laura Bush vs Della Bush Hammond, 1896-1897; Della's sworn testimony.

29   Ibid. Laura's sworn testimony.

30   Ibid. Michael W. Clark's sworn testimony.

31   Edgefield Archives, Court of Common Pleas, Edgefield County, South Carolina; Decree 13 August 1897 for Roll # 11946.

32   Ibid. Deposition of property.

33   Edgefield Archives, Edgefield County, South Carolina; Equitable Home Company vs Eldred "Elliot" Bush, et al; Judgement Roll 12589, loose papers, filed October 1912.

34   Ibid.

35   Edgefield Archives, Edgefield County, South Carolina; Court of Common Pleas, Master's Report file; Equitable Home Co vs Eldred " Elliot" Bush, et al; Eldred Bush's sworn testimony.

36   Ibid. Arthur S. Tompkins's sworn testimony.

37   M.P. Well's sworn testimony.

38   Calvin Bush's sworn testimony.

39   J.D. Eidson's sworn testimony.

40   Edgefield Archives, Edgefield County, South Carolina; Decree: property to be sold first Monday in December 1912; Judgement Roll 12589.

41   Ibid.

42   1940 United States Federal Census, Pickens, Edgefield, South Carolina; Roll: T627_3806; Page: 2A; Enumeration District: 19-12. [database online], Provo, UT, Ancestry.com Operations, 2012.

43   Oral interview with Cousin Elizabeth Harrison Hill, Parkchester, NY 1995.

44   Kopf, Dan. *The Great Migration*: The African American Exodus from the South; priceonomics.com, 28 January 2016. Accessed 12 February 2016. 1910-1940 1.6 million blacks left the south, 12.7% from South Carolina to New York alone.

45   The Spirit Filled Life Bible, Jack W. Hayford, Litt. D., Executive Editor, Thomas Nelson, Inc., 2002; Psalms 90:12.

46   Ibid. Matthew 7:24-25.

47   W. E. B. DuBois, quote: "The slave went free; stood a brief moment in the sun; then, moved back again toward slavery" in *Black Reconstruction in America*, Harcourt, Brace and Cack Company, NY, 1935.

48   Online website, the meaning of Sankofa, (http://www.people.tribe. net), accessed 9 May 2007.

●•••●

CHAPTER 2

49   Verse from a song by Dar Williams quoted in prologue of *St. Mary's Well*, by Carol Kenny, Sole Sentinel Press, December 2009.

50   Mount Canaan Baptist Church, Trenton, South Carolina, founded in 1868. From church website, church history accessed 10 January 2015.

51   South Carolina Will Transcripts, 1782-1855, database and digital images, South Carolina Department of Archives and History (SCDAH); accessed by Nancy A. Peters, Certified Genealogist, 2013; copy of original will purchased from Edgefield Archives, Edgefield, South Carolina.

52   Ibid. Will Transcript of Allen Y. Burton, 1840, p. 2.

53   Lucas, *Slave Records of Edgefield County, South Carolina*, 68.

54   1850 United States Federal Census, Edgefield District, South Carolina, Slave Schedule, Richard J. Burton, manager; [database online], Provo, UT, NARA M432, roll 1009, Ancestry. Com Operations, Inc. 2014. Accessed 1 October 2014.

55   Race and Slavery Petition Project, Edgefield District, 1853, PAR # 21385334; Richard J. Burton and sister Patsy Burton asked the court to appoint "some reliable person" to replace N. L. Griffin, deceased. They requested B. C. Bryan be appointed their trustee to manage the estate. Accessed 5 November 2014.

56   Edgefield Archives, Equity Court Record, April 1854, petition to appoint W. F. Durisoe as Trustee as requested by Richard J. Burton and Patsy Burton. Based on complaint against B. D. Bryan. 23 enslaved named; 900 acres.

57   *Edgefield Advertiser*, 27 July 1859, image 2, 135 acres for sale; *Edgefield Advertiser* (Edgefield, South Carolina), 24 October 1860, image 3, 250 acres for sale; digital images, *Chronicling America* (http://chroniclingamerica.loc.gov) Historic American Newspapers.

58   Edgefield Archives, Equity Court Papers, Edgefield County, South Carolina, 1858; O.P.H. Burton and Others vs W. F. Durisoe, sworn testimony of Mark Etheredge, p. 3.

59   Ibid. Sworn testimony of John Huiet, p. 4.

60   Ibid. Sworn testimony of James Swearingen, pp. 5 & 6.

61   Ibid. Sworn testimony of debts owed to Mr. Goode, Mr. Frazier, Dr. Mims, B. C. Bryan, Lodrick Hill, Mr. Penn and Mr. Nicholas, p. 6.

62   Edgefield Archives, Equity Court Papers, p. 3, O.P.H. Burton vs W. F. Durisoe, request of the Trustee to sell a slave, " And the trustee,

W. F. Durisoe, prays that he be allowed to sell one of the negroes for cash to meet the previous liability."

63   Edgefield Archives, Equity Court Papers, 14 January 1858, Chancellor Wardlaw granted partition of the Burton estate for sale.

64   Edgefield Archives, Equity Record, Book KKK, pp. 60-63, Lucinda Burton to G. M. Roper, D. R. Durisoe and W. F. Durisoe, sale of eight Negroes, 27 December 1859.

65   1860 United States Federal Census, Edgefield District, South Carolina, slave schedule, Mrs. L. Burton, manager; NARA microfilm publication M 654, roll 1230.

66   Edgefield Archives, Coroner's Report, Miscellaneous Papers, Accidental death of Richard J. Burton, Jr., December 1866; on the morning of 28 December 1866, Richard Jr. and his brother Allen went hunting. After a while, Allen returned and told his mother Lucinda that Richard Jr. had accidently shot himself.

67   1880 United States Federal Census, Pickens Township, Edgefield County, South Carolina; Roll 1228; FHL 1255228; p 15B, enumeration district: 044, Ancestry.com [database online], Provo, UT, Ancestry.com Operations, 2010.

68   Freedman's Bureau Office Records 1865-1872, Aiken (sub-assistant commissioner – Edgefield District); Labor Contracts A-K, Roll 42; Eliza Burton, image 63; Family Search. Org. Accessed 15 June 2015.

69   Ibid. Alfred Burton, image 67; Family Search. Org. Accessed 15 June 2015.

70   1880 United State Federal Census Mortality Schedules, 1850-1885, SCDAH, Columbia, South Carolina; Archive roll #1; census place: Ward Township, Edgefield County, South Carolina; # 467 Carolina Christie and her infant son Peter Christie Jr., #116 died of Typhoid fever.

71   Medlock-Bush Family Collection: group picture of Palmore ancestors, picture of Victoria Palmore, and picture of Maria Jeannette Coleman.

WHERE MATERNAL ANCESTORS RESIDED BETWEEN 1870-1940 AND OTHER VITAL RECORDS

1870 United States Federal Census, Edgefield District, South Carolina, Shaw's Creek Township, p. 444-A, dwelling 298, family 319, Edna Coleman; digital image, Ancestry.com; microfile M593, roll 1494.

1870 United States Federal Census, Edgefield District, South Carolina, Saluda Division, dwelling 787, family 797; Isaac Bacon; Roll M593 1495; p. 404A, Image 107971, FHL Film 552994; [database online, Provo, UT; Ancestry.com Operations, 2009.

1870 United States Federal Census, Edgefield District, South Carolina, Saluda Division, dwelling 788, family 798; Eliza Burton; Roll M 593 1495; p. 404 A, Image 107964; FHL Film 552994; [database online], Provo, UT; Ancestry.com Operations, 2009.

1870 United States Federal Census, Ward 6, Grant Parish, Louisiana, Roll 593_513; p. 121 A; Image: 118568; FHL Film 552012, Daniel and Susan/Sukey Cranshaw, [database online] Provo, UT: Ancestry.com, Inc. 2009.

1870 United States Federal Census, Ward 6, Grant Parish, Louisiana, Roll 593_513, p. 1198 Image: 118485; FHL Film 552012, Seaborn and Betsy Burton; [database online], Provo, UT: Ancestry.com Operations 2009.

1870 United States Federal Census, Spring Grove, Edgefield District, South Carolina, p. 493 A, dwelling 338, family 360, Peter and Carolina Christie and Nelly Timmerman; NA microfilm publication M593, roll 1495, digital image, Ancestry.com.

1870 United States Federal Census, Spring Grove, Edgefield District, South Carolina, p. 493 A,
Dwelling 337, family 359, Caesar Walker; NA microfilm publication M 593, roll 1495, digital image, Ancestry.com.

1880 United States Federal Census, Silverton Township, Edgefield District, p. 232 A, dwelling 156, family 167, Ellen Lewis household; digital image, NA microfilm publication T9, roll 1218; Ancestry.com.

1880 United States Federal Census, 2nd Ward, Grant Parish, Louisiana; Roll 453; FHL Film: 1254453; p. 278 A; Enumeration District 027, Seaborn and Betsey Burton; Image 0767, [database online] Provo, UT; Ancestry.com Operations, 2010

1880 United States Federal Census, 2nd Ward, Grant Parish, Louisiana; Roll 453; FHL Film 1254453; p. 278 A; Enumeration District 027, Image 0767, Daniel and Susan Cranshaw, [database online], Provo, UT; Ancestry.com Operations, 2010

1880 United States Federal Census, Gregg Township, Aiken County, South Carolina; Family 515; Roll 1218, Family History Film: 1255218; p. 71 C; Enumeration District: 004; Elbert and Maria Jeannette Coleman, [database online], Provo, UT, Ancestry.com Operations, 2010.

1880 United States Federal Census, Wise Township, Edgefield, South Carolina; Roll: 1228; Family History Film: 1255228; p. 455C; Enumeration District: 065; Noah and Annis Coleman Palmore; [database online], Provo, UT, Ancestry.com Operations, 2010.

1880 United States Federal Census, Gregg Township, Aiken County, South Carolina; Roll: 1218; Family History Film: 1255218; p. 71C; Enumeration District 004; Joseph and Anna Blaylock Coleman, [database online], Provo, UT, Ancestry.com Operations, 2010.

1900 United States Federal Census, Gregg Township, Aiken County, South Carolina; Roll: 1515; p. 19A; Enumeration District: 0026; FHL microfilm: 1241515; Elbert and Maria Jeannette Coleman; [database online], Provo, UT, Ancestry.com Operations, 2004.

1900 United States Federal Census, Gregg Township, Aiken County, South Carolina; Roll: 1515; p. 16A: Enumeration District: 0026; FHL microfilm: 1241515; Nancy Edna Hammond, Isabella Cheatham and Laura Vanderhorst; [database online], Provo, UT, Ancestry. com Operations, 2004.

1900 United States Federal Census, Gregg Township, Aiken County, South Caroline; Roll: 1515; p. 19A; Enumeration District: 0026; FHL microfilm: 1241515; Joseph and Anna B. Coleman, [database online], Provo, UT, Ancestry.com Operations, 2004.

1910 United States Federal Census, Aiken, Aiken County, South Carolina; Roll: T624_1447; p. 19B; Enumeration District: 0001; FHL microfilm: 1375460; Isabella Cheatham;[database online], Provo, UT, Ancestry.com Operations, 2006.

1910 United States Federal Census, Greenville, Ward 6, Greenville, South Carolina; Roll: T624_1461; p. 4B; Enumeration District: 0032; FHL microfilm 1375474; Frank and Victoria Palmore Croft;[database online], Provo, UT, Ancestry.com Operations, 2006.

1916 South Carolina Death Records, 1821-1961, Gregg Township, Aiken County, South Carolina; File # 31596, Registration # 18; Registration District 2-B; death of Joseph Coleman, 1 May 1916.

1920 United States Federal Census, Gregg Township, Aiken County, South Carolina; Roll T625_1682; p. 21B; Enumeration District: 7; Image: 812; Anna B. Coleman;[database online], Provo, UT, Ancestry.com Operations, 2010.

1920 United States Federal Census, Gregg Township, Aiken County, South Carolina; Roll T 625_1682; p. 21B; Enumeration District 7; Image 812; Dwelling 439; Family 439; Laura Vanderhorst household; [database online], Provo, UT, Ancestry.com Operations, 2010.

1920 Ibid. Dwelling 433; Family 433; Julian and Katie Coleman Fair.

1920 Ibid. Dwelling 437; Family 437; Maria Jeannette Coleman in household of Julia Davis.

1930 United States Federal Census, Gregg Township, Aiken County, South Carolina; Roll: 2184; p. 13B; Enumeration District 0009; Image: 820.0; FHL microfilm: 2341918; household of Laura Vanderhorst; [database online], Provo, UT, Ancestry.com Operations, 2002.

1930 United States Federal Census, Asheville, Buncombe, North Carolina; Roll 1675; p. 21B; Enumeration District 0001; Image: 281.0; FHL microfilm: 2341409; Anna B. Coleman household; [database online], Provo, UT, Ancestry.com Operations, 2007.

1930 United States Federal Census, Washington, Washington, D. C.; Roll: 293; p. 9B, Enumeration District 0045; Image 334.0; FHL microfilm: 2340028; household of Julian and Katie C. Fair; Maria Jeannette Coleman;[database online], Provo, UT, Ancestry.com Operations, 2002.

1932 North Carolina Death Certificates, 1909-1976, Buncombe County, North Carolina; Registration District 11-2065; certificate 508; death of Anna B. Coleman, 22 August 1932; [database online], Provo, UT, Ancestry.com Operations, 2002.

1940 United States Federal Census, Warrenville-Graniteville, Aiken County, South Carolina; Roll: T627_3782; p. 12A; Enumeration District 2-12; household of Edna Medlock; [database online], Provo, UT, Ancestry.com Operations, 2012.

1958 South Carolina Death Records, 1821-1961; Registration District 204; State file # 58-001297; death of Laura Glover Vanderhorst, 20 January 1958; [database online], Provo, UT Ancestry.com Operations, 2008.

South Carolina Delayed Birth Records, 1766-1900 and the city of Charleston, SC Births 1877-1901 for Charlie Lewis, born 18 August 1887, son of Ellen Lewis, a daughter of Edna; [database online], Provo, UT, Ancestry.com Operations, 2007.

●•••●

CHAPTER 3.

72   According to the author's mother, Phyllis R. Kemp.

73   Natonne Elaine Kemp, "Stumbling Without the 1890 Census," *Quill* XXVII:2 (2011): 23-27, XXVII:3 (2011): 47-51, XXVII:4 (2011): 71-72.

74   Besides Bernice Bennett, Sheryl Kemp Bailey and her husband, Harris Bailey, were researching the Kemp line. The author learned about the distribution of slaves owned by Henry J. Kemp, who died in 1844, from Mr. Bailey in 2005. Via an e-mail Mr. Bailey attached a chart outlining the distribution of slaves by the name of the slave and the name of the new slave owner.

75   This Blair portrait came into the author's custody, possession, and control in 2014.

76   Evangeline Kemp Marshall, text message to the author, 16 August 2016. Aunt Evangeline wrote that Clifford's son Walter was 6'4" ("He was very tall[,] could hardly fit in his cab and yes he was taller than [your] dad.").

77   natoplato, "Chinn-SC," *Ancestry*, Message Boards, 11 July 2001 (http://boards.ancestry.com/surnames.chinn/277/mb.ashx): accessed 25 March 2013.

78   msyee581, "Re:Chinn-SC," *Ancestry*, Message Boards, 27 August 2001 (http://boards.ancestry.com/surnames.chinn/277.1/mb.ashx): accessed 25 March 2013.

79   Natonne, "Re:Chinn-SC, *Ancestry*, Message Boards, 27 August 2001 (http://boards.ancestry.com/surnames.chinn/277.1.1/mb/ashx): accessed 25 March 2013.

80   Viloria Arttaway is the author's fourth cousin. They share a common ancestor, Preston Chinn, their 3rd great-grandfather. This common ancestor is on Viloria's and the author's paternal lines. Through genetic DNA testing, Viloria and the author learned they are also cousins along their respective maternal lines.

81   Photographer unknown; photograph in the custody of Viloria Arttaway.

82   Sameera Thurmond and the author are third cousins, once removed. Sameera is a 2nd great-grandchild of Preston Chinn, whereas the author is a 3rd great-grandchild of Preston Chinn.

83   E-mail from Sameera V. Thurmond to the author of 10 February 2002 (note: Ms. Thurmond's computer generated an incorrect date, i.e., 3 January 1995).

84   South Carolina State Board of Health, Death Certificate for Elouise Blair, 26 July 1917, File No. 14194, South Carolina Department of Archives and History.

85   Registration State: *South Carolina*; Registration County: *McCormick*; Roll: *1877674*, card for Clifton Blair. (Source Information: Ancestry. com. *World War I Selective Service System Draft Registration Cards, 1917-1918* [database on-line]. Provo, UT: Ancestry.com, 2002) accessed 4 June 2005.

86   1910 United States Census, Washington Township, Edgefield County, South Carolina; p. 2A, dwelling 23, family 23, lines 6-9; 16 April 1910; National Archives Microfilm T624, Roll 1459. (Source Information: Ancestry.com. *1910 United States Federal Census* [database on-line]. Provo, UT, USA: Ancestry.com Operations Inc., 2006) accessed 30 June 2013.

87   1920 United States Census, Washington Township, McCormick County, South Carolina; p. 10B, dwelling 19, family 19, lines 93-96; 13 January 1920; National Archives Microfilm T625, Roll 1702. (Source Information: Ancestry.com. *1920 United States Federal Census* [database on-line]. Provo, UT, USA: Ancestry.com Operations Inc., 2010) accessed 30 June 2013.

88   Michael E. Stauffer, *The Formation of Counties in South Carolina* (South Carolina Department of Archives & History, 3rd printing 1998) 19.

89   McCormick County, South Carolina, Marriage License, Clifford Blair to Jannie Lou Siegler, 20 December 1918, Clerk of Court, McCormick County Courthouse.

90   Three other farmers (Henry Talbert, Thomas Williams, and Miller Hermon) and a railroad fireman (Abe Tompkins) did not report.

91   Edgefield County, South Carolina, Marriage License, Clifford Blair to Sarah Chinn, 2 December 1913 (the author does not know from where Sameera obtained copy).

92   Isabel Wilkerson, *The Warmth of Other Suns: The Epic Story of America's Great Migration* (Vintage Books, 2010).

93   "South Carolina Railroads – Charleston & Western Carolina Railway" (http://www.carolana.com/SC/Transportation/railroads/sc_rrs_charleston_western_carolina.html) accessed 2 January 2014.

94   *Hill Directory Co.'s Incorporated Richmond City Directory* (1924) p. 441 (listing Blair, Clifford (c)). (Source Information: Ancestry.com. *U.S. City Directories, 1821-1989* [database on-line]. Provo, UT, USA: Ancestry.com Operations, Inc., 2011) accessed 11 April 2013.

95   "Railroad Job Descriptions," The USGen Web Project (http://www.usgennet.org/usa/ne/topic/railroads/job.html) accessed 12 May 2013.

96   *Hill Directory Co.'s Incorporated Richmond City Directory* (1925) p. 356 (listing Blair, Clifford (c)). (Source Information: Ancestry.com, *U.S. City Directories, 1821-1989* [database on-line]. Provo, UT, USA: Ancestry.com Operations, Inc., 2011) accessed 11 April 2013.

97   *Washington City, District of Columbia, City Directory* (1926) p. 291 (listing Blair, Clifford). (Source Information: Ancestry.com. *U.S. City Directories, 1821-1989 (Beta)* [database on-line]. Provo, UT, USA: Ancestry.com Operations Inc., 2011) accessed 10 April 2013.

98   District of Columbia, Death Certificate for Clifford Blair, 30 January 1926, File No. 296733, Vital Records Division, D.C. Department of Health.

99   1930 United States Census, Washington Township, McCormick County, South Carolina; p. 2A, dwelling 25, family 25, lines 35-38; 9 April 1930; National Archives Microfilm T626, Roll 2205. (Source Information: Ancestry.com. *1930 United States Federal Census* [database on-line]. Provo, UT, USA: MyFamily.com, Inc., 2002) accessed 9 September 2006.

100   As listed on the census, the age is reported as "4/12."

101   1920 United States Census, Edgefield Township, McCormick
County, South Carolina; p. 8B, dwelling 91, family 91, lines 30-34;
15 January 1920; National Archives Microfilm T625, Roll 1702.
(Source Information: Ancestry.com. *1920 United States Federal
Census* [database on-line]. Provo, UT, USA: MyFamily.com, Inc.
2005) accessed 14 September 2006.

102   United States Census Bureau, *Population of South Carolina,
1790 to 1920* (http://www2.census.gov/prod2/decennial/doc-
uments/06229686v38-43ch2.pdf) accessed 15 September 2015,
Contents—South Carolina. Population. Composition and Characteristics of the Population. Table 21—School Attendance, By Single
Years From 5 to 20, For the State: 1920.

103   Ibid., Population. Number and Distribution of Inhabitants. Table
2—Population of Counties by Minor Civil Divisions: 1920, 1910,
and 1900 (McCormick County). Footnote 21 notes "McCOR-
MICK.—Organized from parts of Abbeville, Edgefield, and Greenwood Counties in 1917."

104   Ibid., Population. Composition and Characteristics of the Population. Table 9—Composition and Characteristics of the Population,
for Counties: 1920 (McCormick). There is a footnote after McCormick, noting this County was organized since 1910.

105   Ibid.

106   Ibid.

107   Ibid., Population. Composition and Characteristics of the Population. Table 24—Ownership of Homes, For Counties and Places
Having 10,000 Inhabitants or More: 1920 (McCormick).

108   Ibid.

109   Ibid.

110   The table lists "180 " homes" as "tenure unknown." Based on the
reported data, the author determined the number of homes identified as "tenure unknown" should be 175 (3,334 [total homes] –
2,341 [rented] – 818 [owned]).

111   Ibid., Population. Number and Distribution of Inhabitants. Table
2—Population of Counties by Minor Civil Divisions: 1920, 1910,
and 1900 (McCormick County).

112   Ibid.

113   Ibid., Population. Composition and Characteristics of the Population. Table 9—Composition and Characteristics of the Population, for Counties: 1920 (McCormick).

114   Ibid., Population. Composition and Characteristics of the Population. Table 22—Illiteracy of the Population 10 Years of Age and Over, By Age Periods, For the State: 1920.

115   Ibid.

116   1910 United States Census, Plum Branch Township, Edgefield County, South Carolina; p. 20A, dwelling 237, family 238, lines 1-7; 10 May 1910; National Archives Microfilm T624, Roll 1459. (Source Information: Ancestry.com. *1910 United States Federal Census* [database on-line]. Provo, UT, USA: MyFamily.com, Inc. 2005) accessed 14 September 2006.

117   "McCormick County—est. 1916—named for Cyrus Hall McCormick, inventor—county seat, McCormick." Stauffer, *The Formation of Counties in South Carolina*, 22.

118   While admittedly shameful, from a national perspective, South Carolina had the third worse rate of illiteracy among the Negro population in 1910. Louisiana had the highest rate of illiteracy among Negroes, 48.4%, followed by Alabama at 40.1%. United States Bureau of the Census (Cummings, John & Hill, Joseph Adna). *Negro Population of the United States, 1790-1915* (New York, Kraus Reprint, 1969), 415; digital images, *Google Books* (https://books.google.com : accessed 3 May 2016).

119   South Carolina State Dept. of Education, *Fifty-First Annual Report of the State Superintendent of Education of the State of South Carolina, 1919* (Columbia, South Carolina, Gonzales and Bryan, State Printers, 1920), 181; digital images, *Google Books* (https://books.google.com : accessed 3 February 2016).

120   Ibid., 183-84.

121   1900 United States Census, Plum Branch Township, Edgefield County, South Carolina; p. 6A, dwelling 69, family 69, lines 35-44; 4 June 1900; National Archives Microfilm T623, Roll 1526. (Source Information: Ancestry.com. *1900 United States Federal Census* [database on-line]. Provo, UT, USA: MyFamily.com, Inc., 2004) accessed 14 September 2006.

122 A few localities have vital records during this twenty year period. South Carolina mandated marriage licenses on 1 July 1911 and mandated birth and death certificates on 1 January 1915.

123 Jennifer L. Hochschild & Brenna M. Powell, "Racial Reorganization and the United States Census 1850-1930: Mulattoes, Half-Breeds, Mixed Parentage, Hindoos, and the Mexican Race," *Studies in American Political Development*, Harvard University, Department of Government, Spring 2008, 15 n.64 (quoting U.S. Bureau of the Census, *Measuring America: The Decennial Censuses From 1790 to 2000.* Washington, D.C.: Government Printing Office, 2002), 27.

124 Ibid., 15-16 (*see* endnotes 66 and 67).

125 1880 United States Census, Talbert Township, Edgefield County, South Carolina; p. 389D, dwelling 67, family 67, lines 10-16; 3 June 1880; National Archives Microfilm T9, Roll 1228. (Source Information: Ancestry.com and The Church of Jesus Christ of Latter-day Saints. *1880 United States Federal Census* [database on-line]. Provo, UT, USA: MyFamily.com, Inc., 2005) accessed 14 September 2006.

126 As listed on the census, the age is reported as "3/12."

127 1880 US Census Mortality Schedule, Talbert Township, Edgefield County, South Carolina, p. 1, line 11; South Carolina Department of Archives and History; Columbia, South Carolina; Archive Roll Number 1; Census Year: 1880. (Source Information: Ancestry.com. *U.S. Federal Census Mortality Schedules, 1850-1885* [database on-line]. Provo, UT, USA: Ancestry.com Operations, Inc., 2010) accessed 10 September 2013.

128 1880 Sickness on Day of Enumeration Codes (https://usa.ipums.org/usa/volii/80sick.shtml) accessed 7 February 2016.

129 Selected U.S. Federal Census Non-Population Schedules, 1850-1880. Census Year: *1880*; Census Place: *Talbert, Edgefield, South Carolina*, Archive Collection Number: AD271; Roll: 10; Page: 3; Line: 10; Schedule Type: *Agriculture* [database on-line]. Provo, UT, USA: Ancestry.com Operations, Inc., 2010; accessed 18 April 2014.

130 *Measuring Worth* (https://www.measuringworth.com/uscompare) accessed 3 May 2016.

131 The most recent full year of annual computations and observations from government agencies available to Mea*suring Worth.*

132 Sharecropping. Dictionary.com. *The American Heritage® New Dictionary of Cultural Literacy, Third Edition.* Houghton Mifflin Company, 2005 (http://dictionary.reference.com/browse/share-cropping) accessed: 18 April 2014.

133 Sharecropper. The Free Dictionary.com. *The American Heritage Dictionary of the English Language, Fourth Edition.* Houghton Mifflin Company, 2009 (http://www.thefreedictionary.com/sharecropper) accessed 18 April 2014.

134 "Sharecropping and tenant farming." LEARN NC: North Carolina Digital History/North Carolina in the New South/Changes in agriculture (http://wwwlearnnc.org/lp/editions/nchist-newsouth/4698) accessed 26 July 2014.

135 As listed on the census, the age is reported as "1/12."

136 1870 United States Census, Washington Township, Edgefield County, South Carolina; p. 160, dwelling 9, family 10, lines 38-40; 1 September 1870; National Archives Microfilm M593, Roll 1494. (Source Information: Ancestry.com. *1870 United States Federal Census* [database on-line]. Provo, UT, USA: MyFamily.com, Inc., 2003) accessed 14 September 2006.

137 Ancestry.com hired individuals to transcribe the handwriting of records, such as the United States Federal Population Schedule, which are accessible on its website. When one enters given names and/or surnames in the search field, the results for the population schedules are the names as transcribed. One should **always** look at the original record because there may be a discrepancy between the given name and/or surname as listed on the original record and as transcribed.

138 Family Search lists the surname as *"Blare."*

139 Selected U.S. Federal Census Non-Population Schedules, 1850-1880. Census Year: *1870*; Census Place: *Washington, Edgefield, South Carolina*; Archive Collection Number: AD263A; Roll: 5; Page: 1; Line: 15; Schedule Type: *Agriculture.* [database on-line]. Provo, UT, USA: Ancestry.com Operations, Inc., 2010; accessed 18 April 2014.

140 E-mail from Sameera V. Thurmond to the author, 10 February 2002 (note: Ms. Thurmond's computer generated an incorrect date, i.e., 3 January 1995).

141 Ibid.

142   South Carolina State Board of Health, Death Certificate for Lucy Blair, 12 February 1915, File No. 2579, South Carolina Department of Archives and History.

143   Natonne Elaine Kemp, "In Search of the Elusive Maiden Name," *Homeplace* VI:2 (2012): 14-18.

144   Gloria Ramsey Lucas, *Slave Records of Edgefield County, South Carolina* (Edgefield, SC: Edgefield County Historical Society, 2010).

145   Edgefield County was formed out of the Ninety-Six District. "[The 1785 act] gave Ninety-Six District the counties of Spartanburg, Union, Laurens, Newberry, Abbeville and Edgefield." Stauffer, *The Formation of Counties in South Carolina*, 9.

146   The other two transactions occurred in 1846 and 1847. James M. Blair sold Tom, a Negro man, to Jas. Tompkins and James M. Blair sold Rachel, a Negro girl, to Columbus Blair.

147   Nathaniel Blair's approximate birth year varies with each census: (a) in 1870, his birth year was about 1849, (b) in 1880, his birth year was about 1844, (c) in 1900, his birth year was about 1851, (d) in 1910, his birth year was about 1852 and (e) in 1920, his birth year was about 1855.

148   1870 United States Census, Washington Township, Edgefield County, South Carolina; p. 163B, dwelling 71, family 75, lines 29-33; 2 September 1870; National Archives Microfilm M593, Roll 1494. (Source Information: Ancestry.com. *1870 United States Federal Census* [database on-line]. Provo, UT, USA: Ancestry.com Operations, Inc., 2009) accessed 7 July 2012.

149   The author has no direct evidence of familial ties between Cain and the younger Nathaniel. They were close in age. Per the Militia Enrollments of 1869, Cain was 19 years old; Nathaniel was 18 years old. Per the 1870 US Census, Cain was 18 years old and living with his presumed paternal grandparents. The younger Nathaniel was 21 years old, married, with a child, and the head of his household. Nathaniel and Cain may have been brothers or cousins. In each census between 1870 through 1920, Cain was described as black. In contrast, in three of the five censuses between 1870 and 1920, the younger Nathaniel was described as mulatto.

150   For one other Edgefield branch (the Tompkins) the author knows the identity of a 4th great-grandmother. But this ancestor was residing in the home with her son and grandchildren, so no research was conducted to identify this individual.

151   Estate of Christopher Blair, recorded 7 April 1930, Box No. 3, Package No. 80 (Edgefield County Archives, Edgefield, SC).

152   The author possesses a two-page copy of this record. Unfortunately, the author failed to record the official title of this publication as well as the page numbers.

153   "Sale-Day Notes and Court Items," *Edgefield Advertiser* (Edgefield, South Carolina), 7 March 1872 edition image 3; digital images, *Chronicling America* (http://chroniclingamerica.loc.gov) Historic American Newspapers (accessed 18 October 2014).

154   According to *Measuring Worth.com*, the real price of C. L. Blair's personal property is $12,000 in 2014 (accessed 3 May 2016).

155   Real estate is a physical asset considered in calculating an individual's wealth. In 2014 C. L. Blair's real estate would be valued at $674,000 as income value or economic status. However, as economic power, in 2014, the real estate would be valued at $4,370,000, according to *Measuring Worth.com* : accessed 3 May 2016.

156   This deed was recorded in April of 1887.

157   "**Notice of Application for Charter**. Notice is hereby given that the undersigned will on the 29th day of December, 1902, make application to the Secretary of State of South Carolina, and file with him a petition for a Charter for the 'The Mount Lebanon Baptist Church,' a church located near the town of Parksville, Edgefield, S.C. John J Briggs, Thomas Robertson. Members of said church and authorized to apply for certificate of Incorporation. Dec. 24th, 1902."

158   SC Secretary of State, Corporations Division, Eleenosynamy File #145, Box 1.

159   His wife Sarah Tompkins is identified as a widow in the 1900 U.S. Federal Census.

160   *Title to Real Estate (Edgefield County)*, bk. 19, p. 610 (located 28 December 2011).

161   Sameera read through multiple reels of the *Edgefield Advertiser* before this historical newspaper became accessible online via the Library of Congress's website, "Chronicling America – Historic American Newspapers," (http://chroniclingamerica.loc.gov).

162   Lesesne, Henry H. "Gary, Martin Witherspoon (1831 – 1881)" (http://www.scencyclopedia.org/gary.htm) accessed 19 April 2014.

163   Kennedy, Robert C. "On This Day: August 12, 1876" (http://www.
      nytimes.com/learning/general/onthisday/harp/0812.html) accessed
      19 April 2014).

164   U.S. Congress, *Congressional Record, The Proceedings and Debates of
      the Forty-Fourth Congress, First Session*, Vol. 4 (Washington, D.C.:
      Government Printing Office, 1876), 18 July 1876, 4:4711-4712;
      digital images, *Google Books* (https://books.google.com : accessed 31
      May 2017).

165   *Cong. Rec.*, 44th Cong., 1st sess. (1876), 4:4712.

166   The Miscellaneous Documents of the House of Representatives
      for the First Session of the Forty-First Congress. 1869, "Papers
      in the Case of S. L. Hoge v. J. P. Reed, Third Congressional Dis-
      trict, South Carolina, (Washington: Government Printing Office,
      1869), 47; digital images, *Google Books* (https://books.google.com :
      accessed 8 July 2017).

167   http://www.merriam-webster.com/dictionary/fireman (accessed 27
      February 2016).

168   In the 1900 US Census, Pinkey was identified as a daughter of John
      and Malinda Blair. In the 1910 Census, Pinkie L. Sellers was identi-
      fied as a stepdaughter of John Blair.

169   1880 United States Census, Washington Township, Edgefield
      County, South Carolina; p. 2, dwelling 12, family 12, lines 14-17;
      2 June 1880; National Archives Microfilm T9, Roll 1228. (Source
      Information: Ancestry.com and The Church of Jesus Christ of Lat-
      ter-day Saints. *1880 United States Federal Census* [database on-line].
      Provo, UT, USA: MyFamily.com, Inc., 2010) accessed 2 June 2015.

170   1870 United States Census, District 125, Columbia County,
      Georgia; p. 16-17, dwelling 1029, family 1080, lines 36-40, 1-2; 11
      August 1870; National Archives Microfilm M593, Roll 145. (Source
      Information: Ancestry.com. *1870 United States Federal Census* [data-
      base on-line]. Provo, UT, USA: Ancestry.com Operations, Inc.,
      2009) accessed 2 June 2015.

171   Georgia State Board of Health Certificate of Death for Francis
      Laster, 4 May 1919, File No. 4636.

172   "United States Census, 1940," index and images, *FamilySearch*
      (https://familysearch.org/pal:/MM9.1.1/K75C-CM5: accessed 3 Sep-
      tember 2012), Walter Blair, 1940.

173 "United States Census, 1930," index and images, FamilySearch (https://familysearch.org/pal:/MM9.1.1/38N3-RMM: accessed 3 September 2012), Walter Blair, 1930.

174 "Georgia Death Index, 1933-1998," index, *FamilySearch* (https:// familysearch.org/pal:/MM9.1.1/V43D-1JQ: accessed 3 September 2012), Nathanel Blair, 1934.

175 Georgia Department of Public Health, Death Certificate for Nathanel Blair, 22 May 1934, File No. 14432 (copy obtained for the author by certified genealogist Barbara Smallwood Stock).

176 Over time, with more individuals testing, geneticists have been able to define, with more precision, the identification of various ethnicities. As of 3 May 2016, my ancestral composition is 78.6% Sub-Saharan African, 20.9% European, .4% East Asian & Native American, <.1% Oceanian and .1% unassigned.

177 Bryan Skyes, *DNA USA: A Genetic Portrait of America* (Liveright, 2012).

178 Message from "L.L." to the author via 23andMe, 17 November 2012.

179 Message from the author to "L.L." via 23andMe, 2 December 2012.

180 Message from "L.L." to the author via 23andMe, 2 December 2012.

181 The author, "Blairs of Edgefield, SC, *Ancestry*, Message Boards, 14 January 2002 (http://boards.ancestry.com/surnames.blair/1581/ mb.ashx) : accessed 25 March 2013.

182 [g], "Re: Blairs of Edgefield, SC," *Ancestry*, Message Boards, 24 January 2002 (http://boards.ancestry.com/surnames.blair/1581.1/ mb.ashx) : accessed 25 March 2013.

183 1868 Voter Registration, Edgefield County, p. 172 (South Carolina Department of Archives and History, Columbia, SC) (copy obtained via mail on 3 November 2011).

184 SCDAH's South Carolina Archives Series Description: Militia Enrollments, 1869 (http://www.archivesindex.sc.gov/onlinearchives/Terms/Series/SeriesDescriptions/S192021.html : accessed 20 April 2014).

185 At the time of the 1870 US Census, a township named Rocky Pond did not exist. The author believes this name derived from a post office. Included in the book *South Carolina Postal History and Illus-*

trated Catalog of PostMarks 1760-1860 by Harvey S. Teal and Robert J. Stets (H.S. Teal and R.J. Stets, 1989) are two maps of Edgefield District (pages 70, 72) showing where post offices were located. To this author's untrained eye, the Rocky Pond post office was located in the same area as Washington Township on the 1871 map of Edgefield County, SC surveyed by Isaac Boles.

186   Militia Enrollments of Men Between The Ages of 18 and 30 for Edgefield County, Rocky Pond Township, p. 95 (accessible online via South Carolina Department of Archives and History's website, http://www.archivesindex.sc.gov/onlinearchives : accessed 31 March 2013).

187   Militia Enrollments of Men Between The Ages of 30 and 45 for Edgefield County, Rocky Pond Township, p. 98 (accessible online via South Carolina Department of Archives and History's website, http://www.archivesindex.sc.gov/onlinearchives : accessed 31 March 2013).

•••••

CHAPTER 4

188   Find A Grave.com, (http://www.findagrave.com), summary of Columbus L. Blair's headstone, Modoc Cemetery, McCormick County, South Carolina (accessed 23 October 2014).

189   Ibid.

190   "Historically, Virginia family Bible records have been an important source for vital statistics. These records contain birth, death, and marriage dates and sometimes other personal and family information. Centralized recording of vital statistics did not begin in Virginia until 1853. Even after 1853, this information was not always reported or forwarded to the Bureau of Vital Statistics, and during the period 1896-1912 the reporting of births and deaths was not required.

Over the years, The Library of Virginia has acquired originals and photocopies of over 6,800 family Bible records. These materials have been cataloged and are searchable as part of the Archives and Manuscripts Catalog. In late 1995, The Library of Virginia began a project to scan the pages that constitute the Bible record collection." *Family Bible Records*, Library of Virginia (http://www.lva.virginia.gov/public/guides/bible.htm) accessed 24 April 2014.

191   "Identifying the Virginia Slave Owner – Part 3" by the author, *Searching Family History* (http://www.searchingfamilyhistory.com/ identifying-the-virginia-slave-owner-3.html) accessed 24 April 2014.

192   "Family Bible Records," *University Libraries Digital Collection* (http://library.sc.edu/digital/collections/famrec.html) accessed 24 April 2014.

193   Rencontre, a French word, means "a hostile meeting or a contest between forces or individuals." (http://www.merriam-webster. com/dictionary/rencontre) accessed 15 February 2014.

194   "Fatal Rencontre in Edgefield," *The Charleston Daily* (Charleston, South Carolina), 12 January 1878, vol. XVI – no. 1878, p. 1; digital images, *Chronicling America* (http://chroniclingamerica.loc.gov) Historic American Newspapers.

195   "Homicide It Edgefield District," *Augusta Chronicle* (Augusta, Georgia), 13 January 1872, p. 3; digital images, *Genealogy Bank* (http://www.genealogybank.com) online subscription archives : accessed 19 January 2014.

196   *The Wilmington Morning Star* (Wilmington, New Hanover, North Carolina), 14 January 1872, vol. 9, issue 97, p. 2; digital images, *Newspapers.com* (http://www.newspapers.com).

197   Budiansky, Stephen. *The Bloody Shirt: Terror After The Civil War*, (Plume, a member of Penguin Group (USA) Inc. 2009), 42.

198   The 1870 US Census does not identify the relationship between the head of the household to other individuals residing in the home.

199   Committee on Accounts, Reports and Resolutions of the General Assembly of the State of South Carolina (Columbia, S.C., I.C. Morgan, 1850), 172 (http://www.carolana.com/SC/Legislators/Doc-uments/Reports_and_Resolutions_of_the_General_Assembly_of_ South_Carolina_1850.pdf). "C. L. Blair, Constable, allowed ["4.28]" (accessed 29 July 2016).

200   Budiansky, *The Bloody Shirt*, 53.

201   CSI Dixie, Edgefield County, SC at https://csidixie.org/numbers/ counties/edgefield-county-sc (accessed 21 March 2016).

202   *Overseer and Driver*. Dictionary of American History/2003/Oakes, James. (http://www.encyclopedia.com/doc/1G2-3401803120.html) accessed 9 October 2014.

203 Dictionary.com (http://dictionary.com/browse/esquire) accessed 14 July 2017.

204 "ProQuest History Vault: Slavery and the Law," database, *The University of Texas at Austin, University of Texas Libraries* (https://www.lib.utexas.edu), description of database (accessed 7 May 2016).

205 Ibid. ("[O]ffers access to important but virtually unused primary source materials that were scattered in state archives of Alabama, Delaware, Florida, Mississippi, Missouri, North Carolina, South Carolina, Tennessee, Texas, and Virginia. The collection includes virtually all extant legislative petitions on the subject of race and slavery.")

206 Ibid. ("[W]ere collected from local courthouses, and candidly document the realities of slavery at the most immediate grassroots level in southern society. It was at county courthouses where the vast majority of disputes over the institution of slavery were referred. The petitions that were filed provide some of the most revealing documentation in existence on the functioning of the slave system.")

207 The University of North Carolina Greensboro. *Digital Library on American Slavery*. Database. https://library.uncg.edu/slavery : 2014.

208 Accessed 15 February 2014.

209 E-mail from the author to Tricia Price Glenn of 18 February 2014.

210 E-mail from Tricia Price Glenn to the author 19 February 2014 at 10:48 a.m.

211 Ibid.

212 "Sale-Day Notes and Court Items." *Edgefield Advertiser* (Edgefield, South Carolina), 7 March 1872; digital images, *Chronicling America*, (http://chroniclingamerica.loc.gov) Historic American Newspapers : accessed 18 October 2014.

213 Upon learning about the website *CSI Dixie*, the author forgot about Tricia's remark. Unable to find records for Peter Wilk(e)s and Milledge Blair, and noticing a gap in the years of the inquests (24 December 1869 to 27 September 1877), the author sent an e-mail to Tonya A. Guy, Director of the Old Edgefield District Genealogical Society and Director of the Tompkins Library. Ms. Guy responded,

"Unfortunately, the Coroner's Records for Edgefield are missing from 1869 to 1877. We do not know why exactly, but many of our records are missing during this time. Edgefield was under federal rule during Reconstruction and we think that the records may have been taken somewhere when the federal government left. We just don't know for sure, but they are missing."

E-mail from Tonya Guy to the author of 16 March 2016 at 8:58 a.m.

214   E-mail from Tricia Price Glenn to the author of 19 February 2014 at 10:54 a.m.

215   The author subsequently requested assistance from the current Edgefield Archivist, Tonya A. Guy, who consulted the *General Sessions Index, 1884-1859,* and learned Columbus Blair was not prosecuted for assault and battery. E-mail from Tonya A. Guy to the author of 26 January 2017 at 11:18 a.m. There are no additional records identifying the individual(s) Columbus Blair purportedly assaulted and battered or whether the alleged assault and battery were committed in the line of duty. E-mail from Tonya A. Guy to the author of 1 February 2017 at 9:01 a.m.

216   Tricia Price Glenn identified 21 September 1871 as the date the letter to the editor was published in the *Edgefield Advertiser.* A subsequent search on the Chronicling America website revealed the letter to the editor was published in the 28 September 1871 edition of the *Edgefield Advertiser.*

217   E-mail from Tricia Price Glenn to Natonne Kemp of 19 February 2014 at 10:48 a.m.

218   "An Old Liar, Rather." *Edgefield Advertiser* (Edgefield, South Carolina), 28 September 1871, vol. XXXV – no. 40, p. 2; digital images, *Chronicling America* (http://chroniclingamerica.loc.gov) Historic American Newspapers : accessed online 26 April 2014.

219   Budiansky, *The Bloody Shirt,* 56.

220   Ibid., 53.

221   South Carolina, Freedmen's Bureau Field Office Records, 1865-1872, Aiken (subassistant commissioner—Edgefield district), Roll 39, Letters and endorsements sent, Feb-Sept 1866, [Image 9 of 87], images database, *FamilySearch Record Search,* https://familysearch.org/search/collection : accessed 9 October 2014. Transcribed by the author.

222   "The Condition of Edgefield. Report of Col. T. W. Parmele to the Governor," *The News and Courier* (Charleston, South Carolina), 1

March 1875; digital images, *Newspapers.com*, (http://www.newspapers.com).

223 Budiansky, *The Bloody Shirt*, 56-57.

224 How did this region earn the nickname, the "Dark Corner?" *See* Chapman, John Abney. *History of Edgefield County: From the Earliest Settlements to 1897*, (Newberry, S.C., Elbert H. Aull, 1897), 115.

225 Ibid., 114-15.

226 Ibid., 115.

227 "Pic Nic At Rocky Ponds," *Edgefield Advertiser* (Edgefield, South Carolina), 12 August 1857, image 2; digital images, *Chronicling America*, (http://chroniclingamerica.loc.gov) Historic American Newspapers : accessed 17 October 2014.

228 Report and Testimony, Volume 4 (U.S. 42nd Congress, Testimony Taken by the Joint Select Committee to Inquire into the Conditions of Affairs in the Late Insurrectionary States. South Carolina, Volume II), (Washington, Government Printing Office, 1872), 1208; digital images, *Google Books* (https://books.google.com).

229 *Congressional Series of United States Public Documents, Volume 1728* (Jack Picksley-The Election; Columbia, SC, 10 January 1877), 109-110; digital images, *Google Books* (https://books.google.com : accessed 11 October 2014).

230 *Congressional Series of United States Public Documents, Volume 1728* (John Martinborough-Edgefield County (Columbia, SC 10 January 1877), 624-25; digital images, *Google Books* (https://books.google.com : accessed 11 October 2014).

231 "Smalls v. Tillman," *Index to the Miscellaneous Documents of the House of Representatives for the First Session of the Forty-Seventh Congress, 1881-1882* (Washington: Government Printing Office, 1882), 515, 516; digital images, *Google Books* (https://books.google.com : accessed 24 May 2016).

232 "The Democrats of the Dark Corner," *The News and Courier* (Charleston, South Carolina), Tuesday Morning 10 June 1890, p. 4, col. 2; digital images, *Newspapers.com* (http://www.newspapers.com).

233 Carter, Lawrence E., Sr., *Walking Integrity: Benjamin Elijah Mays, Mentor to Martin Luther King, Jr.*, (Mercer University Press, 1998), 75.

234 *Index to the Miscellaneous Documents of the House of Representatives for the First Session of the Forty-Fifth Congress, 1877* by J. H. Acklen, Tillman v. Small. Papers in the case of (vol. 3, no. 11)) 603-04, 606-07; digital images, *Google Books* (https://books.google.com : accessed 22 October 2014).

235 1880 United States Census, Sheldon Township, Beaufort County, South Carolina; p. 44, dwelling 438, family 439, line 32; 24 June 1880; National Archives Microfilm T9, Roll 1221. (Source Information: Ancestry.com and The Church of Jesus Christ of Latter-day Saints. *1880 United States Federal Census* [database on-line]. Provo, UT, USA: Ancestry.com Operations Inc., 2010) accessed 10 October 2014.

236 (a) Age 33, born about 1837, residing in Chestnut Log District, Campbell County, Georgia and (b) Age 12, born about 1858, residing in Subdivision 128, Walker County, Georgia.

237 1880 United States Census, Meriwether Township, Edgefield County, South Carolina; p. 66, dwelling 686, family 697, line 15; 26 June 1880; National Archives Microfilm T9, Roll 1228. (Source Information: Ancestry.com and The Church of Jesus Christ of Latter-day Saints. *1880 United States Federal Census* [database on-line]. Provo, UT, USA: Ancestry.com Operations Inc., 2010) accessed 10 October 2014.

238 1880 United States Census, Moss Township, Edgefield County, South Carolina; p. 18 (no dwelling number or family number assigned), line 34, 10 June 1880; National Archives Microfilm T9, Roll 1228. (Source Information: Ancestry.com and The Church of Jesus Christ of Latter-day Saints. *1880 United States Federal Census* [database on-line]. Provo, UT, USA: Ancestry.com Operations Inc., 2010) accessed 10 October 2014.

239 1880 United States Census, Mobley Township, Edgefield County, South Carolina; p. 51, dwelling 18, family 19, line 30, 2 June 1880; National Archives Microfilm T9, Roll 1228. (Source Information: Ancestry.com and The Church of Jesus Christ of Latter-day Saints. *1880 United States Federal Census* [database on-line]. Provo, UT, USA: Ancestry.com Operations Inc., 2010) accessed 10 October 2014.

240 (a) 1880 United States Census, Sleepy Hollow Township, Aiken County, South Carolina; p. 23, dwelling 228, family 231, line 4, 11 June 1880, National Archives Microfilm T9, Roll 1218. (Source Information: Ancestry.com and The Church of Jesus Christ of Lat-

ter-day Saints. *1880 United States Federal Census* [database on-line]. Provo, UT, USA: Ancestry.com Operations Inc., 2010) accessed 10 October 2014. (Tom Coleman born about 1830).

(b) 1880 United States Census, Sleepy Hollow Township, Aiken County, South Carolina; p. 14, dwelling 153, family 153, line 48, 9 June 1880, National Archives Microfilm T9, Roll 1218. (Source Information: Ancestry.com and The Church of Jesus Christ of Latter-day Saints. *1880 United States Federal Census* [database on-line]. Provo, UT, USA: Ancestry.com Operations Inc., 2010) accessed 10 October 2014 (Tom Coleman born about 1850).

241 (a) 1880 United States Census, Coleman Township, Edgefield County, South Carolina; p. 18, dwelling 142, family 146, line 5, 8 June 1880; National Archives Microfilm T9, Roll 1228. (Source Information: Ancestry.com and The Church of Jesus Christ of Latter-day Saints.*1880 United States Federal Census* [database on-line]. Provo, UT, USA: Ancestry.com Operations Inc., 2010) accessed 10 October 2014 (Tom Coleman born about 1859).

(b) 1880 United States Census, Coleman Township, Edgefield County, South Carolina; p. 29; dwelling 248, family 252, line 13, 15 June 1880; National Archives Microfilm T9, Roll 1228. (Source Information: Ancestry.com and The Church of Jesus Christ of Latter-day Saints. *1880 United States Federal Census* [database on-line]. Provo, UT, USA: Ancestry.com Operations Inc., 2010) accessed 10 October 2014 (Tom Coleman born about 1854).

242 1880 United States Census, Mobley Township, Edgefield County, South Carolina; p. 56, dwelling 20, family 21, line 50, 5 June 1880; National Archives Microfilm T9, Roll 1228. (Source Information: Ancestry.com and The Church of Jesus Christ of Latter-day Saints. *1880 United States Federal Census* [database on-line]. Provo, UT, USA: Ancestry.com Operations Inc., 2010) accessed 10 October 2014.

243 "Aiken County, South Carolina Genealogy," (https://familysearch. org/wiki/en/Aiken_County,_South_Carolina_Genealogy) accessed 22 September 2016.

244 General Assembly, Committee Reports, 1859, #397, p. 41. List of Managers of Elections and Polls for Edgefield District. (Paper copy reproduced from Microfilm in South Carolina Department of Archives and History, Columbia, SC).

245 "Election Notice!" *Edgefield Advertiser* (Edgefield, South Carolina), 17 September 1862, vol. XXVII – no. 37, p. 3; digital images, *Chroni-*

cling America (http://chroniclingamerica.loc.gov) Historic American Newspapers.

246 "Appointments for Edgefield District." *Edgefield Advertiser* (Edgefield, South Carolina), 23 December 1863, image 1; digital images, *Chronicling America* (http://chroniclingamerica.loc.gov) Historic American Newspapers.

"Election Notice. State of South Carolina, Edgefield District." *Edgefield Advertiser* (Edgefield, South Carolina), 30 December 1863, image 2; digital images, *Chronicling America* (http://chroniclingamerica.loc.gov) Historic American Newspapers.

247 "Local Items," *The Daily Phoenix* (Columbia, South Carolina), 15 October 1872, p. 2, col. 6; digital images, *Newspapers.com* (https://www.newspapers.com/image/72088665), (C. L. Blair identified as an additional supervisor of elections appointed for Edgefield for Democrats).

"Election Supervisors," *The Charleston Daily News* (Charleston, South Carolina), 14 October 1872, p. 4, col. 2 digital images, *Newspapers.com* (https://www.newspapers.com/image/76781351) (C. L. Blair identified as an appointed election supervisor for Edgefield County, Democrats for Red Hill).

248 "Managers of Election." *Edgefield Advertiser* (Edgefield, South Carolina), 15 August 1900, vol. LXV – no. 33, p. 2; digital images, *Chronicling America* (http://chroniclingamerica.loc.gov) Historic American Newspapers ("The following is a list of managers appointed by the County Democratic Executive Committee for the Primary election to be held August 28th, 1900, and for the secondary primary to be held two weeks later, if said primary election be necessary").

249 "Notice of Election for State and County Officers. State of South Carolina, County of Edgefield," *Edgefield Advertiser* (Edgefield, South Carolina), 31 October 1900, vol. LXV – no. 44, p. 3; digital images, *Chronicling America* (http://chroniclingamerica.loc.gov) Historic American Newspapers ("The following named persons have been appointed Managers of Election for State and County offices. . . .").

250 "To the Voters of Edgefield District," *Edgefield Advertiser* (Edgefield, South Carolina), 13 April 1864, image 1; digital images, *Chronicling America* (http://chroniclingamerica.loc.gov) Historic American Newspapers.

To the Voters of Edgefield District," *Edgefield Advertiser* (Edgefield, South Carolina), 21 April 1864, image 1; digital images, *Chronicling America* (http://chroniclingamerica.loc.gov) Historic American Newspapers.

251 "School District Trustees," *Edgefield Advertiser* (Edgefield, South Carolina), 9 February 1893, vol. LVIII, no. 2, image 4; digital images, *Chronicling America* (http://chroniclingamerica.loc.gov) Historic American Newspapers, ("28-North Washington: C. L. Blair, Dr. T.E. Jennings, Winchester McDaniel").

252 "To the Public," *Edgefield Advertiser* (Edgefield, South Carolina), 15 February 1865, image 1; digital images, *Chronicling America* (http://chroniclingamerica.loc.gov) Historic American Newspapers ("The undersigned have secured the services of MISS HATTIE L. MORGAN, of this District, to take charge of a School at Liberty Academy this year. Miss M. is a thorough Scholar, having graduated at one of the first Colleges in the State, with the Second Honor. The first session will continue four months—20 days each. The Second session, the same time. Rates of Tuition, the same as charged in other Schools of the same order. Scholars charged from the day they enter to close of Session. JOSEPH PRICE, JOHN DOUGHERTY, WASH. JENNINGS, C. L. BLAIR, GEO. W. MORGAN").

253 "The Greenwood and Augusta Railroad," *The Abbeville Press and Banner*, (Abbeville, South Carolina), 6 December 1871, vol. XIX, no. 33, image 2; digital images, *Chronicling America* (http://chroniclingamerica.loc.gov) Historic American Newspapers.

254 *Reports and Resolutions of the General Assembly of the State of South Carolina at the Regular Session of 1879.* (Columbia, SC: Calvo & Patton, 1879), 885; digital images, *Google Books* (https://books.google.com : accessed 22 October 2014).

255 Ibid., 889-90.

256 *Journal of the Senate of the General Assembly of the State of South Carolina* (Columbia, S.C.: Calvo & Patton, 1880), 113, digital images, *Google Books* (https://books.google.com : accessed 22 October 2014).

257 CHAP. 161. – An ACT to incorporate the Jennings [A]ssociation of the United States of America, *Acts of the General Assembly of the Commonwealth of Virginia During the Session of 1876-77* (Richmond, VA: F. Walker, Superintendent Public Printing, 1877), 147; digital images, *Google Books* (https://books.google.com : accessed 18 October 2014).

258 Notice: South Carolina, Edgefield District. Columbus Blair, Applicant vs. Sarah Blair and others, Defendants. Summons in Partition. *Edgefield Advertiser* (Edgefield, South Carolina), 27 January 1847, vol. XII, no.1, image 4; digital images, *Chronicling America* (http://chroniclingamerica.loc.gov) Historic American Newspapers ("IT appearing to my satisfaction that Christopher Blair, Pulaski L. Blair, Geo[.] W Blair, Robert Jennings and Clement Jennings, heirs and distributes of the estate of Jas. M. Blair, deceased, lives beyond the limits of this State. It is therefore ordered, that they do appear and object to the sale or division of the real estate of said deceased on or before the first Monday in February next, or their consent will be entered of record. Given under my hand, at my office, this 3rd day of November, 1846. John Hill, O[rdinary] [of] E[dgefield] D[istrict]").

259 "Sheriff's Sale: State of South Carolina, Edgefield District. Columbus Blair, Appt. vs. Sarah Blair, & others, d'fts. Summons in Partition." *Edgefield Advertiser* (Edgefield, South Carolina), 31 March 1847, vol. XII, no.10, image 4; digital images, *Chronicling America* (http://chroniclingamerica.loc.gov) Historic American Newspapers.

260 "Land for Sale," *Edgefield Advertiser* (Edgefield, South Carolina), 25 March 1863, vol. XXVIII, no. 12, image 3; digital images, *Chronicling America* (http://chroniclingamerica.loc.gov) Historic American Newspapers ("The Subscriber offers for sale privately the HOMESTEAD PLANTATION of Robert Jennings, dec'd, in Edgefield District, containing **NINE HUNDRED ACRES**").

261 "Sheriff's Sale: Rhoda Ramsay vs. S. Samuel Tompkins and John W. Tompkins, Ex'ors James Tompkins, dec'd." *Edgefield Advertiser* (Edgefield, South Carolina), 26 October 1871, vol. XXXV, no. 44, image 6; digital images, *Chronicling America* (http://chroniclingamerica.loc.gov) Historic American Newspapers.

262 "Master's Sale. State of South Carolina, Edgefield County. Court of Common Pleas. Mrs. Victoria Evans, et al., —vs.—C.G. Matthews, et al." *Edgefield Advertiser* (Edgefield, South Carolina), 2 December 1896, vol. LXI, no. 45, image 3; digital images, *Chronicling America* (http://chroniclingamerica.loc.gov) Historic American Newspapers.

263 *The Railway News*, Volume 33, 695 (22 May 1880), digital images, *Google Books* (https://books.google.com : accessed 27 October 2014).

264 "Augusta and Knoxville Railroad." *The Abbeville Press and Banner* (Abbeville, South Carolina), 16 May 1877, vol. XXIV, no. 49, image 2; digital images, *Chronicling America* (http://chroniclingamerica. com) Historic American Newspapers.

265 E-mail from the author to Sameera Thurmond of 17 January 2014 at 9:49 a.m.

266 E-mail from Sameera Thurmond to the author of 22 January 2014 at 8:42 a.m.

267 Rev. Charles Newman Blackwell – S.C. Genealogy.com (http://www.genealoytreemaker.genealogy.com/forum/surnames/topics/blackwell/2196/) accessed 22 January 2014.

268 Furman University, *"South Carolina and Other Baptist Resources"* (http://library.furman.edu/specialcollections/baptist/baptist_resources.htm) accessed 23 January 2014.

269 *South Carolina Baptists, 1670-1805*, by Leah Townsend, Ph.D., Florence, South Carolina, 1935 (contributed by Dena W. for South Carolina Genealogy Trails) (http://genealogytrails.com/scar/baptist_churches11.htm) (accessed 24 March 2014).

270 The first four paragraphs of this post states,

The name of Samuel Cartledge is not new in our consideration, for we viewed him when he was a young constable in Georgia and arrested the Reverend Daniel Marshall. We recounted that Samuel Cartledge was saved and after serving as a deacon in Kiokee, Georgia, was ordained and pastured faithfully for a number of years.

Cartledge was born July 15, 1750, near Rockingham, North Carolina. Samuel's father had been reared as a Quaker, but he married an Anglican woman, and the family assumed the Anglican faith. In that background young Samuel grew. He was confronted with the gospel by Mrs. Marshall at the arrest of her husband, Daniel, and in 1777 Samuel Cartledge was baptized by her husband. Before long, Cartledge was ordained as a deacon in the Kiokee Baptist Church. After being under the spiritual teaching of Daniel Marshall as a "licentiate" for several years, he was ordained into the gospel ministry by Abraham Marshall, Daniel's son, in 1789. Soon a fruitful ministry began which lasted more than fifty years.

After serving for a short time in Georgia, Cartledge "was recorded as a new minister in the Georgia Association in 1792." [1] He moved to South Carolina and became pastor of the Callahan's Mill Church "where he served...for over fifty years, until his death in 1843." [2] In those days, few rural churches held services every week, and often pastors served multiple churches and trained their deacons to care for the spiritual needs of the flock in their absence. Thus it was that in 1792 Cartledge accepted the oversight also of the Plum Branch Baptist Church and ministered there concurrently, serving there also for over fifty years. During his long ministry, he "served at least three other churches, but it is not clear how many years he remained at these." [3]

Of course, travel was limited to horseback, and the "work" of the ministry consisted of many grimy miles of laborious travel to preach the Word. The man of God is commissioned to "preach the word...in season, out of season," and the Reverend Mr. Cartledge did just that! For years there was little moving of the Holy Spirit's power, but in 1830 revival swept the area. The man of God was now eighty years old, but a "series of meetings, in the day and at night, was held at the Callahan's Church, which continued two weeks...A large number, especially of the young persons, became convicted and converted; and were baptized." [4] From 1827 through the revival of 1830, the membership of the Callahan Church had grown by almost two hundred percent, and that with an eighty-year-old pastor! The lengthy obituary that announced his death claimed that thousands had been won to Christ through the ministry of Samuel Cartledge, and it spoke of his unquestionable zeal and piety.

271   Ibid.

272   *Baptist History Homepage: Georgia Baptist History* (http://baptisthistoryhomepage.com/georgia.histories.index.html) accessed 25 March 2014.

273   *Baptist History Homepage: Georgia Baptist Association* by J. H Campbell, 1874, p. 61-62 (http://baptisthistoryhomepage.com/georgia.bapt.assoc.histry.html)accessed 25 March 2014.

274   Furman University, *"South Carolina and Other Baptist Resource,"* (http://library.furman.edu/specialcollections/baptist/church_records_by_county.htm) accessed 28 March 2014.

275   Parksville Baptist Church, *The History of Calliham's Mill – Parksville Baptist Church 1785-1985 Parksville, South Carolina.* (Parksville, S.C.: Parksville Baptist Church, 1985).

276   Ibid., 2.

277   Ibid., 8.

278   Ibid., 1-2.

279   Ibid., 3.

280   Ibid., 6.

281   Ibid., 5.

282   Parksville Baptist Church (formerly called Callahan's [sic]Mill) (McCormick County, S.C.), Church Minutes, Membership Rolls, 1856-1876, 1883-1907, 1922-25 (scattered), call number BX6480. M226, P374. Baptist Historical Collection, Furman University Library, Greenville, South Carolina.

283   Ibid., Roll 1, Frame 8 (pp. 1-2) (transcribed by the author).

284   Ibid., Frame 9 (p. 1).

285   Ibid.

286   Ibid.

287   Ibid., Frame 11 (p. 1).

288   Ibid., Frame 14 (p. 1).

289   Ibid., Frame 16 (p. 2).

290   Ibid., Frame 20 (p. 2).

291   Ibid., Frame 26 (p. 2).

292   Ibid., Frame 37 (p. 1).

293   Ibid., Frame 51 (p. 2).

294   Ibid., Frame 59 (p. 2) (transcribed by the author).

295   Ibid., Frame 60 (p. 2) (transcribed by the author).

296   Ibid., Frame 3 (p. 2).

297   Census Return for Edgefield County, SC (Population Schedule), 1869, p. 66, line 3. (South Carolina Archives Microcopy Number 17; South Carolina Department of Archives and History, Columbia, SC).

298   In 1870 Columbus Blair was the head of household. Three white females resided with him: his wife, his mother Sarah, and his

daughter. *See* 1870 United States Census, Washington Township, Edgefield County, South Carolina; p. 163A, dwelling 57, family 60, lines 12-15; 2 September 1870; National Archives Microfilm M593, Roll 1494. (Source Information: Ancestry.com. *1870 United States Federal Census* [database on-line]. Provo, UT, USA: Ancestry.com Operations, Inc., 2009) accessed 5 August 2013. The three white females in C. L. Blair's household in 1869 were certainly his wife, his mother, and his daughter.

299 1870 United States Census, Washington Township, Edgefield County, South Carolina; p. 163A, dwelling 58, family 61, lines 16-24, ; 2 September 1870; National Archives Microfilm M593, Roll 1494. (Source Information: Ancestry.com. 1870 United States Federal Census [database on-line]. Provo, UT, USA: Ancestry.com Operations, Inc., 2009) accessed 24 September 2016.

300 1870 United States Census, Washington Township, Edgefield County, South Carolina; p. 163A, dwelling 56, family 59, lines 7-11; 2 September 1870; National Archives Microfilm M593, Roll 1494. (Source Information: Ancestry.com. 1870 United States Federal Census [database on-line]. Provo, UT, USA: Ancestry.com Operations, Inc., 2009) accessed 24 September 2016.

301 Thirteen of those individuals are listed as Blair. Four others, the author's 2nd great-grandparents Nathaniel and Lucy, their daughter Josephine, and Julius, are identified as *Blore* on Ancestry.com and as *Blare* on FamilySearch.org.

302 Ancestry.com transcribed the surname as *Blas*. In reviewing the original document, this author transcribes the surname as *Blar*.

303 1860 United States Census, Edgefield District, South Carolina, slave schedule, p. 162, Sarah Blar, owner or manager, National Archives Microfilm M653. (Source Information: Ancestry.com. *1860 U.S. Federal Census-Slave Schedules* [database on-line]. Provo, UT, USA: Ancestry.com Operations, Inc. 2010) accessed 5 August 2013.

304 1860 United States Census, Edgefield District, South Carolina, slave schedule, p. 163, C.L. Blar, owner or manager, National Archives Microfilm M653. (Source Information: Ancestry.com. *1860 U.S. Federal Census-Slave Schedules* [database on-line]. Provo, UT, USA: Ancestry.com Operations, Inc. 2010) accessed 5 August 2013.

305 The eldest slave owned by C. L. Blair was a 25 year old black female, possibly Rachel, whom Columbus/C. L. Blair purchased

from James M. Blair in 1847. There were four male children in the household. The black males were ages 7, 6, and 1. There was also a 1 year old mulatto male. This author therefore deduces from a review of the slave schedule that her 2nd great-grandfather was not owned by C. L. Blair.

306   1850 US Census, Edgefield District, South Carolina, slave schedule, Sarah Blair, owner or manager, National Archives Microfilm M432. (Source Information: Ancestry.com. *1850 U.S. Federal Census-Slave Schedules* [database on-line]. Provo, UT, USA: Ancestry.com Operations Inc., 2004) accessed 5 August 2013.

307   1840 United States Census, Edgefield, South Carolina, Roll: 511, p. 90, Image: 189, Family History Film: 0022509. (Source Information: Ancestry.com. *1840 United States Federal Census* [database on-line]. Provo, UT, USA: Ancestry.com Operations, Inc., 2010. Images reproduced by FamilySearch) accessed 5 August 2013.

308   1900 United States Census, Militia District 129, Columbia County, Georgia, p. 2B, dwelling 40, family 40, line 86, 2 June 1900, National Archives Microfilm T623, Roll 190. (Source Information: Ancestry.com, *1900 United States Federal Census* [database on-line]. Provo, UT, USA: Ancestry.com Operations Inc., 2004) accessed 15 February 2014.

309   1910 United States Census, Washington Township, Edgefield County, South Carolina, p. 5A, dwelling 83, family 84, line 13, 20 April 1910, National Archives Microfilm T624, Roll 1459. (Source Information: Ancestry.com. *1910 United States Federal Census* [database on-line]. Provo, UT, USA: Ancestry.com Operations Inc., 2006) accessed 15 February 2014.

310   1880 United States Census, Bonham Bear, Wilcox County, Alabama, p. 31, dwelling 195, family 213, line 12, 15 June 1880, National Archives Microfilm T9, Roll 35. (Source Information: Ancestry.com and The Church of Jesus Christ of Latter-day Saints. *1880 United States Federal Census* [database on-line]. Provo, UT, USA: Ancestry.com Operations Inc., 2010) accessed 15 February 2014.

311   1830 United States Census, Edgefield, South Carolina, p.130, National Archives Microfilm M19, Roll 172. (Source Information: Ancestry.com. *1830 United States Federal Census* [database on-line]. Provo, UT, USA: Ancestry.com Operations, Inc. 2010) accessed 15 February 2014.

312 1830 United States Census, Edgefield, South Carolina, p.134, National Archives Microfilm M19, Roll 172. (Source Information: Ancestry.com. *1830 United States Federal Census* [database on-line]. Provo, UT, USA: Ancestry.com Operations, Inc. 2010) accessed 15 February 2014.

313 1820 United States Census, Edgefield, South Carolina, p. 110A, Image 198, National Archives Microfilm M33, Roll 118. (Source Information: Ancestry.com. *1820 United States Federal Census* [database on-line]. Provo, UT, USA: Ancestry.com Operations, Inc., 2010. Images reproduced by FamilySearch) accessed 5 August 2013.

314 1810 United States Census, Edgefield, South Carolina, p. 102, line 16, Christopher Blair, image 0181421; Family History Library Film: 00086. (Source Information: Ancestry.com. *1810 United States Federal Census* [database on-line]. Provo, UT, USA: Ancestry. com Operations, Inc., 2010. Images reproduced by FamilySearch) accessed 5 August 2013.

315 1790 United States Census, Edgefield, South Carolina, p. 513, image: 332, Family History Library Film: 0568151; National Archives Microfilm M637, Roll 11. (Source Information: Ancestry. com. *1790 United States Federal Census* [database on-line]. Provo, UT, USA: Ancestry.com Operations, Inc., 2010. Images reproduced by FamilySearch) accessed 5 August 2013.

316 Jury Lists, 1779 Acts #1123 [at SC Archives], p. 10, Family Number 88 [Blair, George; 1780, Coffee Town and Turkey Creek, Ninety-Six District, South Carolina]. (Source Information: Ancestry.com. *US Census Reconstructed Records, 1660-1820* [database on-line]. Provo, UT, USA: Ancestry.com Operations, Inc., 2011) accessed 5 August 2013.

317 From the Journals of the Council of the Colony of South Carolina. Names and land allotments under the Bounty Act of 1761. Blair, George, p. 57. (Source Information: Ancestry.com. *U.S. and Canada, Passenger and Immigration Lists Index, 1500s-1900s* [database on-line]. Provo, UT, USA: Ancestry.com Operations, Inc., 2010) accessed 5 August 2013.

318 "From 1680 to 1783, the city was known as Charles Town. No "e" on the end. At the end of the American Revolution in 1783, the name was shortened to Charleston, which has been in use ever since." "A History of Charles Town, South Carolina," (http://

www.carolana.com/SC/Towns/Charles_Town_SC.html) accessed 5 August 2013

319 BLAIR, GEORGE, Land Grant for 100 Acres in Granville County. (Royal Grant). Series S213019, Volume 0014, Page 00432, Item 000 (SC Department of Archives and History), Columbia, SC.

320 Ibid.

321 "A History of Londonborough Township, South Carolina" (http://www.carolana.com/SC/Towns/Londonborough_Township_SC.html) accessed 29 May 2016.

322 23andMe (https://you.23andme.com/reports/ancestry_composition/) accessed 9 July 2017.

●•••●

EPILOGUE 1

323 Free (http://chroniclingamerica.loc.gov) or subscription service (GenealogyBank.com or Newspapers.com)

324 98% of all males in the United States were captured by this draft.

325 Caution: remember the death certificate is a *primary* source about the decedent (when and where s/he died) but is a *secondary* source regarding the decedent's parents, and place of birth. Remember the information is only as good as the informant. What is the informant's relationship to the decedent?

326 Caution: because delayed birth records were not issued at the time of birth (or shortly thereafter), these documents may be inaccurate. For instance, there are a number of delayed birth certificates of individuals born in Parksville, South Carolina in the late 1890s to 1910. A number of these delayed birth certificates state the individual was born in *McCormick County*. This is factually incorrect because McCormick County was formed or created in *1916*. Thus those individuals born in Parksville between 1890 and 1910 were born in *Edgefield County*.

327 Edgefield County is fortunate to have the Edgefield Baptist Association.

328 Edgefield County has *both* a historical society and a genealogical society.

●•••●

EPILOGUE 2

329   GEDmatch (https://www.gedmatch.com/login1.php) accessed 14 June 2016.

330   Family Tree DNA Learning Center Beta (https://www.family-treedna.com/learn/autosomal-ancestry/universal-dna-matching/exactly-centimorgan-values-dna-segments-mean/) accessed 16 June 2016.

331   *What are SNPs?* (https://www.23andme.com/gen101/snps/) accessed 16 June 2016).

SNPs are Copying Errors

To make new cells, an existing cell divides in two. But first it copies its DNA so the new cells will each have a complete set of genetic instructions. Cells sometimes make mistakes during the copying process - kind of like typos. These typos lead to variations in the DNA sequence at particular locations, called single nucleotide polymorphisms, or SNPs (pronounced "snips").

SNPs as a Measure of Genetic Similarity

DNA is passed from parent to child, so you inherit your SNPs versions from your parents. You will be a match with your siblings, grandparents, aunts, uncles, and cousins at many of these SNPs. But you will have far fewer matches with people to whom you are only distantly related. The number of SNPs where you match another person can therefore be used to tell how closely related you are.

332   GEDmatch (https://www.gedmatch.com/login1.php) accessed 14 June 2016.

●•••●

EPILOGUE 3

333   Record of Richard Burton, Rootsweb, Ancestry.com, posted 23 June 2009.

334   Ibid.

REFERENCES:

Francis Burton Harrison, *Burtons Chronicles of Colonial Virginia* (San Dimas, CA: Golden West Genealogy, 1933).

The Burton from Coast to Coast: From Colonial Virginia to the 20th Century Oilfields of Bakersfield, CA. (online website, accessed 24 August 2016).

A Diary from Dixie, by Mary Boykin Chestnut, ed. by Isabella D. Martin and Myrta Lockett Avary, (New York, D. Appleton and Company, 1905).

Journal of a Residence on a Georgian Plantation, 1838-9 by Frances Anne Kemble (1809-1893). Frances, "Fanny," eventually divorced her husband Pierce Butler and returned to England. Butler owned 436 enslaved people who were sold at "The Great Slave Auction" in Savannah, Georgia in 1859.

INDEX

All page numbers appearing in *italic* type refer to illustrations. Page numbers followed by "t" refer to tables; page numbers followed by "f" refer to figures.

ABOUT THE AUTHORS

•••••

EDNA GAIL BUSH is a native New Yorker and retired NYS administrator. A prolific writer of short family histories, her work has appeared in the *Quill, Homeplace,* and the *Carolina Herald,* the county and state genealogical newsletters throughout South Carolina. She is a member of the National Genealogical Society (NGS), the Afro-American Historical and Genealogical Society (AAHGS), the Old Edgefield District Genealogical Society (OEDGS) and the South Carolina Genealogical Society.

NATONNE ELAINE KEMP is a family historian, writer and presenter. A native of Washington, D.C., she is a graduate of the National Institute on Genealogical Research (NIGR) now known as the Genealogical Institute on Federal Records (Gen Fed). She was editor of *Homeplace,* the official newsletter of the Old Edgefield District African American Genealogical Society, and serves on the Journal Editorial Board for the Afro-American Historical and Genealogical Society (AAHGS).

CPSIA information can be obtained
at www.ICGtesting.com
Printed in the USA
LVHW041633101218
599930LV00003B/432